Einstein: the first hundred years

Some other Pergamon titles of interest

DUMMER: Electronic Inventions and Discoveries, 2nd Revised and Expanded Edition of Electronic Inventions 1745–1976

DUNCAN & WESTON-SMITH: The Encyclopaedia of Ignorance

ELTON & MESSEL: Time and Man

GEORGE: Machine Takeover – The Growing Threat to Human Freedom in a Computer-Controlled Society

GOLDSMITH: Strategies for Europe

LIVANOVA: Landau – A Great Physicist and Teacher

VELIKHOV *et al.:* Science, Technology and the Future

Related Pergamon journals

ENDEAVOUR
LEONARDO, Art, Science and Technology
STUDIES IN HISTORY AND PHILOSOPHY OF SCIENCE

Free specimen copies available on request

Einstein: the first hundred years

Edited by
Maurice Goldsmith
Alan Mackay
and
James Woudhuysen

PERGAMON PRESS

OXFORD · NEW YORK · TORONTO · SYDNEY · PARIS · FRANKFURT

U.K.	Pergamon Press Ltd., Headington Hill Hall, Oxford OX3 0BW, England
U.S.A.	Pergamon Press Inc., Maxwell House, Fairview Park, Elmsford, New York 10523, U.S.A.
CANADA	Pergamon of Canada, Suite 104, 150 Consumers Road, Willowdale, Ontario M2J 1P9, Canada
AUSTRALIA	Pergamon Press (Aust.) Pty. Ltd., P.O. Box 544, Potts Point, N.S.W. 2011, Australia
FRANCE	Pergamon Press SARL, 24 rue des Ecoles, 75240 Paris, Cedex 05, France
FEDERAL REPUBLIC OF GERMANY	Pergamon Press GmbH, 6242 Kronberg-Taunus, Hammerweg 6, Federal Republic of Germany

First edition 1980

British Library Cataloguing in Publication Data

Einstein: the First Hundred Years
1. Einstein, Albert—Influence
2. Civilization, Modern—20th century
I. Goldsmith, Maurice II. Mackay, Alan
III. Woudhuysen, James

530'.092'4   QC16.E5   79-42781

ISBN 0 08 025019 X

Typset by Express Litho Service (Oxford)
Printed and bound in Great Britain by
William Clowes (Beccles) Limited, Beccles and London

Contents

Acknowledgements

The editors are indebted to the various contributors for providing papers for this volume and, in particular, to those who have for the first time sought to understand Einstein's impact on their own specialty. All have been most sensitive to the comments we have made on their original papers.

We are especially thankful to our publisher, Mr Robert Maxwell, who has taken a particular interest in this volume; to Mr Lewis Woudhuysen and Mr Stuart Earl, who designed it; to Mrs Sally Heap, who helped us considerably by retyping much of the manuscript; and to Mr Neil Jeffares, who saw the project through its final stages at Pergamon Press.

The editors themselves performed different tasks. Maurice Goldsmith had the original idea for the book, and for its particular emphasis; Alan Mackay provided sparkling comment; and James Woudhuysen was responsible for the detailed editing.

Specific acknowledgements are due to the following for their consent to the use of articles and illustrations:

Macmillan, London and Basingstoke, and Curtis Brown, London, for "Einstein" by C. P. Snow. Originally published in *The variety of men,* Readers Union, Macmillan, 1968.

Secker & Warburg, London, for "Brief thoughts on the theory of relativity" by Miroslav Holub. Originally published in *Notes of a clay pigeon,* 1977. Translated by Jarmila and Ian Milner.

Jonathan Cape, London, and Hill and Wang, New York, for "The brain of Einstein" by Roland Barthes. Originally published in English in *Mythologies,* 1972, translated by Annette Lavers. First published in French by Editions du Seuil, 1957.

Dennis Sharp for Erich Mendelsohn's drawings of the Einstein Tower, reproduced on pages 135 and 136.

Radio Times Hulton Picture Library for the photograph of Einstein and Dr Ludendorf on page 140.

Philadelphia Museum of Art, Philadelphia, for "Mont Sainte-Victoire" by Paul Cézanne, 1902–6, George W. Elkins collection; and "Nude descending a staircase, No. 2" by Marcel Duchamp, 1912 (definitive version), Louise and Walter Arensberg collection.

The Tate Gallery, London, for "Mandolin" by Georges Braque, 1909–10; "Seated nude" by Pablo Picasso, 1909–10; and "Unique forms of continuity in space" by Umberto Boccioni, 1913.

Museum of Modern Art, New York, for "Equals infinity" by Paul Klee, 1932. Oil on canvas mounted on wood, 20¼ × 26⅞". Acquired through the Lillie P. Bliss Bequest.

The Science Policy Foundation

By science policy we mean a deliberate and coherent attempt to provide a basis for national or international decisions influencing the size, institutional structure, resources and creativity of scientific and technological research in relation specially to their application and public consequences.

Aims

The purpose of the Science Policy Foundation is to promote in this context the scientific investigation of science and technology as social phenomena.

The Foundation, through the very wide scientific/ technological knowledge and experience of its members and contacts, has established itself as a unique centre for multidisciplinary scrutiny of social and economic problems arising from the impact of science and technology on people and institutions.

Activities and publications

The activities of the Foundation include symposia and seminars on topics connected with the national and international management of science, management and productivity, research and national wealth, etc, attended by members of government and its agencies, industry and universities. The Foundation arranges an annual lecture; issues *Science and Public Policy,* a bi-monthly journal, and *Outlook on Science Policy,* a monthly newsletter; organises a lecture service, and publishes reports and books.

The Foundation is based at Benjamin Franklin House, 36 Craven Street, London WC2N 5NG.

Foreword

Sir Hermann Bondi

Sir Hermann Bondi, FRS, FRAS, was born in Vienna in
1919. He came to Britain in 1937 to study mathematics at
Trinity College, Cambridge and graduated in 1940. After
war work on naval radar, he returned to Cambridge as a
Fellow of Trinity College and as a lecturer at the university,
until in 1954 he became professor of mathematics at
King's College, London. His researches have been in cosmology, gravitation and relativity. Since 1967 he has held
posts in the public service, first as Director General of the
European Space Research Organisation, then as Chief
Scientific Adviser to the Ministry of Defence, now as Chief
Scientist at the Department of Energy. He is President of
the Science Policy Foundation.

Foreword

There have not been many events in science that lend themselves so much to celebration as Einstein's work. It is particularly appropriate that the Science Policy Foundation has been able — through the sterling work of its Director, as always — to put together a volume different in character and aim from the many other works that have appeared on the occasion of his birth.

Einstein was a great scientist, one of the greatest in the history of science, but the magic that attaches to his name is more than the fame of a great scientist. A number of factors contribute to this. Within science itself his own work has a personal stamp which sets it apart from that of almost every other scientist this century. Again, he enjoyed the most tremendous reputation with the wider public on both sides of the Atlantic. Some of this was no doubt due to the very personal character of his work, some to his simple and engaging personality, some to the supposed unintelligibility of his work. Whatever the reason for his popular standing, it was this standing itself which contributed to the growing together of science and public affairs that has been such a notable feature of the last 50 years. His very erudite researches in science may not have had the most marked direct effect on the life of the public. But his existence as a scientist who turned out to be a great public figure changed society's consciousness of science for good.

The tasks of the Science Policy Foundation lie in just the field in which Einstein's personality was so uniquely formative. The Foundation is trying to discharge them in part with this volume.

1. The man

Einstein

C. P. Snow

Lord Snow was born in 1905. He did scientific research under Rutherford at Cambridge. An active supporter of the Labour Party, he was parliamentary secretary at the Ministry of Technology, 1964–6. He was specially known for his novel sequence of 11 volumes, *Strangers and brothers,* written between 1935 and 1970. His Rede Lecture on *The two cultures and the scientific revolution* (1959) made a great impact, as did his inventive title, *The corridors of power.* He was a member of the advisory council of the Science Policy Foundation until his death in July 1980.

From *The variety of men,* Readers Union, Macmillan, 1968.

One day at Fenner's just before the last war, G. H. Hardy and I were talking about Einstein. Hardy had met him several times, and I had recently returned from visiting him. Hardy was saying that in his lifetime there had only been two men in the world, in all the fields of human achievement, science, literature, politics, anything you like, who qualified for the Bradman class. One was Lenin and the other Einstein.

I wasn't quarrelling with that. It was clear, all the theoretical physicists told us so, that if Einstein had not existed, twentieth-century physics would itself have been different: this one could say of no one else, not even Rutherford or Bohr: to make that kind of difference was, incidentally, a necessary condition for entry into the Bradman class. Further, his character was inextricably mixed up with his achievement. Neither Hardy nor I were given to exaggerated estimates of human virtue: but again we took it for granted that, if the word 'noble' had any meaning, this was the noblest man we had met.

Good, gentle and wise. Hardy recalled that some bright journalist had thrown off that description of Einstein: could I think of any three adjectives more exact? Here, for the first time, I began to hedge. Yes, they were true; but they didn't tell the whole truth, or anything like it. If one was talking in that kind of shorthand, one ought to add another adjective. But what should it be, without disturbing the impression? 'Obstinate' was too weak and too carping, 'counter-suggestible' was faintly grotesque, 'independent' or 'non-conformist' did not say anything like enough, 'deliberately impersonal' was a half-truth. There was something in him that I couldn't describe but was stuttering towards. That conversation happened nearly thirty years ago, and, whenever I have thought about Einstein since, I have still found myself stuttering.

To begin with, he was much more unlike 'ordinary' men and women than the others I am writing about. In psychological structure, though not, of course, in gifts, one can find plenty of parallels to Lloyd George, Rutherford, Wells, Hardy: most of us have met people bearing them a family resemblance in the course of our work-a-day lives. Churchill was much stranger. In some ways, I have come to think there were faint likenesses between Churchill and Einstein. I don't mean that they were alike in terms of spirit or intellect: in those respects no one could bear comparison with Einstein. But in some aspects of their psychological nature, in the ways in which their characters formed themselves, I believe one can find some links. If I had thought of this while Hardy was alive, he would have repudiated me for good.

As with Churchill, there were some singular paradoxes in Einstein's career. I suspect that in natures like theirs, where the ego starts abnormally strong – though Einstein, unlike Churchill, learned to subjugate his personal self or forget it – these paradoxes are more likely to occur than with less inflexible men. Anyway, Einstein was universally recognized at 37 as the greatest theoretical physicist of his age, the equal of Newton. That is still his ranking: the work he did between 22 and 37 stands there for ever. But – it isn't that, like Newton, he gave up physics. It remained the prime internal devotion of his life, he worked at it with the ultimate concentration which was one of his supreme qualities until he died at 76: and almost all his colleagues thought, and still think, that he wasted the second half of his life.

There were other paradoxes. He was the voice of liberal science, the prophet of reason and peace, for a generation. At the end, he believed, without bitterness, in the depth of his gentle and tranquil spirit, that it had all been in vain. He was the most complete of internationalists: he broke away from the Jewish community, he hated all separatisms and nationalisms: yet he was compelled to take his place as the most eminent Jew alive, the committed Zionist. He wanted to lose his personality in the world of nature; but that personality became one of the most publicised of the century, and his face – at first glance the face of an inspired and saintly golliwog – as well known as a film star's.

Just to add to the list, he was credited, or blamed, with a paradox that did not exist. It has become a legend that he was responsible for the atomic bomb — that he, the prophet of human brotherhood, had to take on his conscience the slaughter of Hiroshima and Nagasaki, and the possibility of genocides to come. It would have been an irony, but it was not true. In practice, the discovery of nuclear fission owed nothing to his work: and his part in sending the famous letter to Roosevelt in 1939 was not significant. I will try to depersonalise this story a little later.

It was, of course, his moral character which demonstrated itself in those paradoxes of his life. That character was already formed before he was 16. Here we have to rely on the facts (his career is unusually well documented, especially through Swiss sources) and to take his own comments, written when he was an old man, as rationalisations after the event.

'I have never belonged wholeheartedly to a country, a state, nor to a circle of friends, nor even to my own family.'

'My personal external circumstances played only a minor role in my thoughts and my emotions.'

'Perception of this world by thought, leaving out everything subjective, became, partly consciously, partly unconsciously, my supreme aim.' (Of himself, in early adolescence.)

'When I was still a rather precocious young man, I already realised most vividly the futility of the hopes and aspirations that most men pursue throughout their lives.'

'Well-being and happiness never appeared to me as an absolute aim. I am even inclined to compare such moral aims to the ambitions of a pig.'

These statements (which came from the bone of his character, and altogether omit the jolly, laughing flesh) were written in old age. They couldn't have been made by many men — perhaps by Spinoza, whom Einstein so much admired and in spirit resembled. But, even from Spinoza or Einstein, they need a bit of understanding. After all, these men did live on this earth like the rest of us.

Einstein's family were easy-going, free-thinking *petit bourgeois,* whose ancestors had lived in Swabia for generations. They were Jewish by origin, but agnostic and indifferent to religion. It was a tolerant and casual home: uncomfortably casual insomuch as his father, who started a small electrical factory in Munich when Einstein was one year old (in 1880), did not have the drive to make a go of it. But they were never really poor, as the Wellses and the Rutherfords were.

The young Einstein was not a brilliant child. Intellectually, he seemed backward (this was also true of Churchill). He was late in learning to talk. All this is curious, particularly so for a future mathematician. As a rule, mathematical talent shows itself at a very early age. A high proportion of eminent mathematicians have asked questions about large or infinite numbers before they were three: the stories about Hardy and Dirac, for example, are well authenticated. The only really bright juvenile mathematician I have personally watched was in good form at the age of four. Now we are beginning to learn more about this sharp and specific talent, I believe that we shall normally know whether children do or do not possess it before they have learned to read.

Well, Einstein was not a mathematician in the sense Hardy was, but no one would suggest that he was devoid of mathematical ability. Little or none of this was detected in his early childhood. He did begin, at the age of 10, to show precocity: but it was a precocity, not of intellect, but of character.

His parents, who might have been Catholic converts if they had had any religion at all, sent him first to a Catholic primary school. That he didn't mind. At 10 he went to one of the Munich gymnasia. That he hated: and he hated it for just the same reasons as he would have hated it at 70. It was militaristic: at once, and for ever, he detested German militarism. Children marched and drilled: teachers barked: it was a barracks. In later life he became as unqualified a nonconformist as a man can be. He often rationalised his actions, but they deserve some inspection. At 10 he was already certain that this disciplined machine was not for him. He had a horror of constraint, in any shape or form, physical, emotional, intellectual. *Zwang*. Did I know the German word, he asked me, as we talked about English manners. In the Munich high school he made his first strike against *Zwang*.

He did, in fact, both a brave and an odd thing. He became, for a short period, about a year, a religious Jew. It was an attempt, as he saw it later, to 'liberate himself from purely personal links'. It was also an attempt to mark himself out from the conformity which surrounded him. As we shall see, he repeated this pattern at the height of his fame: when, without belief, he once more stamped himself as a Jew, an active Zionist. If he was going to be identified with any group — and that was difficult, so unyielding was his ego — then it must be with the poor and persecuted of the world.

This decision, like each single decision that he took in his life, came from within himself. At 10 he seems to have rested as much certainty in his own thought as he did at 70: his own thought, and that of no one else alive. The religious phase did not last long. Once more he applied his own thought to it: and at 12 he emerged into the kind of cosmic religious non-belief which lasted him a lifetime. He used the word God so often that people were sometimes deceived. From his boyhood he possessed deep religious *feeling*: but when he spoke of God, he did not mean what a religious believer means (although he might perhaps have accepted Bonhoeffer's God). As he said himself in middle age: 'I believe in Spinoza's God who reveals himself in the harmony of all being, not in a God who concerns himself with the fate and actions of men'.

That conclusion he reached in early adolescence, brooding by himself as a pupil — not at all a distinguished one — at the Munich high school. With the same total independence he decided what to work at. He was quite good, no more, at physics and mathematics. Most of the academic drill struck him as intolerable, and he would not play. In this he was quite unlike most clever boys and nearly all future academics. People like Rutherford (who was as original in creative power, though not in temperament) took what they were given and made the best of it. Hardy disliked Winchester, but was a born competitor who wanted the prizes and the Trinity scholarship. To Einstein competition meant nothing: he had no temptation to compromise or please. Here again one can see a ghostly resemblance to the young Churchill, unable or unwilling to make a serious effort at school, except at writing English essays, which he happened to enjoy.

Einstein's father was a peculiarly unsuccessful businessman. The Munich business was a flop, and so, more or less absent-mindedly, he moved on to Milan, where he did slightly worse. This move happened when Einstein was 15: he was left behind in Munich to complete his schooling. Since his mind had been totally independent before, it could not become more so: but he had six months alone and reached three more solitary decisions.

He arrived in Milan and announced them to a family which seems to have been as cheerful about them as he was himself. The first was to leave the Munich school, which he hated, and to abandon the final examination, which he despised. The second was to leave the Jewish community, to which he still formally belonged. The third, and the most dramatic, was to give up his German citizenship. He decided to have no obligations which he did not make himself. His moral confidence was absolute. He was enough, just on his own.

As an anti-climax, he promptly failed his entrance examination to the Zürich polytechnic. He wanted to study there, in order to become an electrical engineer — which sounds quaint, because of the legend of Einstein's unpracticality: in fact he was no more unpractical than

Hardy was absent-minded: these cheap stereotypes are hard to destroy. Although Einstein's father could not find a franc, better-off members of the Einstein family — scattered all over Europe in the Jewish wanderings — thought a Zürich education might not be a bad idea, and were prepared to scrape an allowance for him until he graduated. Not entirely surprisingly, he passed the entrance examination in the subjects he had studied, and failed in those he had not.

So he, already mature to an extent most men never achieve, had to put in a year in a Swiss cantonal school, and, with a trace of cussedness, enjoyed it. From there he duly passed into Zürich, now intending to train as a physics teacher. As usual, he immediately came into opposition with *Zwang*. Not that he didn't like the Swiss, who, in his view, were civilised and democratic. This time *Zwang* cropped up in the shape of examinations. The curriculum could have been better devised, thought Einstein. The examinations so constrained his mind that, when he had graduated, he did not want to think about scientific problems for a year.

Actually, he was quite lucky. He was taught by one man of genius, Minkowski, who later recognised, after Einstein's early publications, that his pupil was a much greater genius (but as a student 'a lazy dog'). The general standard of the Zürich polytechnic was high. He made friends who thought that he was a superior being. He was probably as well off at Zürich as he would have been at Hardy's Cambridge.

The truth was, no university in the 'nineties could have contained or satisfied him — and it is doubtful whether any university could satisfy a young Einstein today. He was beyond the normal limits of independence. He passed his final examinations all right, though not spectacularly. But Zürich did not keep him on as an assistant (ie the lowest grade of post-graduate job). That was a gross error in talent-spotting: it was almost the only misadventure which rankled with him. And yet, at almost exactly the same time, Cambridge failed to keep the much more accommodating Rutherford, who, instead of being given a fellowship, was encouraged to remove himself to Montreal.

So Einstein was a graduate, but unemployed. For a while it looked as though he was unemployable. He took one or two temporary teaching posts. He had no money at all. The Einstein clan had financed his education, but now they expected him to earn a living. He had one old suit, which didn't matter, and little food, which did. He was rescued by a generous and admiring friend, Marcel Grossman, who became himself a good scientist. Grossman persuaded his father, a well-to-do Swiss industrialist, to recommend Einstein for a position.

The position was, of all extraordinary things, that of patent examiner in the Swiss federal patent office. As an even more extraordinary thing, Einstein was appointed. The job was not specially arduous, and Einstein turned out to be good at it. One of his greatest intellectual gifts, in small matters as well as great, was to strip off the irrelevant frills from a problem: that happens to be the prime gift of a good patent examiner. He was also, as I have said, not at all devoid of practical sense. He liked gadgets, understood them, and even tried to invent them himself. Thus he did his patent work at great speed, efficiently, soon got extra pay, and was left, at 23, with time to meditate: which for him meant time to meditate, day after day, night after night, week after week, with the kind of concentration which was like a man gripping an object in his fist, on the nature of the physical universe.

He needed only one resource, which was his own insight. His thinking, of course, carried abstraction very far, but it is important to realise that his insight was first and foremost a *physical* one. At Zürich he had spent most of his time in the physics laboratory. When he did much of his major work his knowledge of mathematics was, by the standard of the top theoretical physicists, thin and patchy: he was much less well equipped than Clerk Maxwell, Born, Heisenberg, Pauli: to an extent, he had to pick up his mathematics as he went along, for the rest of his career. He said himself:

'my intuition in the mathematical field was not strong enough to be able to distinguish with basic conviction the fundamentally important from the rest of the more or less dispensable erudition. Moreover, my interest in acquiring a knowledge of Nature was infinitely stronger, and as a student it was not clear to me that the approach to a deeper knowledge of the principles of physics was bound up with the most intricate mathematical methods. This only dawned on me after years of independent scientific work.'

It only dawned on him, in fact, when his physical insight had already led him to solve some of the great problems: when the special theory of relativity was behind him, and he was brooding on the general one: it was then he saw that the physical insight had to be interwoven with the heavy machinery of the tensor calculus.

It was like him to begin his work — and to achieve more than most mathematical physicists in a lifetime — with the aid of nothing but his own pure, unaided thought. No one else would have started with that suspicion of mathematical techniques. At 23 he was already the man whom the world later wished, and failed, to understand. He had absolute confidence. He had absolute faith in his own insight. He was set on submerging his personality, for good and all, in the marvels of the natural world.

No one has stripped away the claims of self more ruthlessly, not even Niels Bohr, another of the saints of science. But it is wrong to romanticise anyone, even Einstein. It seems to me that a man has to possess a pretty hefty ego to need to subdue it so totally. A more naturally self-forgetful man wouldn't have required such a moral effort to forget himself. He did it: perhaps that was why, when I met him, I felt that he had been shaped by moral experience. It is here that one can pick out the black and white difference from Churchill, a similarly structured personality. Churchill too had a pretty hefty ego: but he didn't submerge it or even try to, he simply let it rip. It was probably only in action that he felt the same impersonality into which, by a moral imperative, Einstein serenely made himself.

But the old-Adam-ego was not quite drowned. I think one ought to be a little wary of his attitude to the conventions. Yes, no one has been less conventional: but his rationalisations were somewhat too masterly. Somehow a man isn't as totally unconventional as that if he is absolutely free. It's easier sometimes to wear socks, even if other people have the habit of wearing socks, than to explain that socks get holes in them. It takes too much effort to question each social action. Free-and-easy people take the conventions more lightly, sometimes dropping them, sometimes drifting along. It's more convenient, I should have thought, to get into a dinner jacket than to hack away at shirt-sleeves with a razor in order to make a kind of under-vest: but Einstein would firmly have thought the opposite. About him, even in Jehovianic old age, there was still a residue — no, not really a residue but a vestigial air — of a non-conformer from a central European café, the sort of character one used to meet between the wars, who made an impact by wearing odd shoes and his coat on backwards.

As a very young man, when he was producing great discoveries, Einstein's only society was in just those cafés. He was the least gregarious of humankind — he spoke of his own 'unconcealed lack of the need to frequent my fellow human beings and human communities'. Yet he enjoyed the desultory easy-going European nights, the cigars, the coffee, the talk; he was both witty and merry, he had a reverberating laugh, he didn't give a damn. When life had sobered him, when he felt responsibility for so much, he missed those nights. He never got used to American parties, where people drank hard and didn't want to argue about ultimates. So far as he was ever at home, at any time in his life, it was in Berne and Zürich before the First World War.

He got married in Berne, as soon as he took on his job at the patent office there. About this marriage, and his first wife, there is a conflict of evidence: much of the biographical material is good (there is a specially attractive account by Antonia Vallentin), but here there is some factual mystery. This first wife was a fellow-student at Zürich, four years older than he was: she was a Serbian called Mileva Maric. Here the certainty stops. She seems to have had a limp. Most of Einstein's Swiss contemporaries thought she was gloomy and incompetent; she may have been a genuine depressive. None of this sounds alluring, but other reports give her a Slav nakedness to life, a defenceless charm.

Was the marriage unhappy from the beginning? This will presumably never be known, though I picked up what may have been a clue. Einstein was utterly reticent about his personal life: a 'puritanical reserve' was necessary, he said, to a scientist seeking truth. Antonia Vallentin, who knew his second wife well, suggests that he was a man of powerful sensuality. When I met him, that was certainly one of the impressions that he gave: but it is entirely possible, and perhaps more probable than possible, that he, like Tolstoy and Gandhi, both of whom he revered, felt that his sensuality was one of the chains of personality that ought to be slipped off. Anyway, in his first marriage he soon had two sons — those two he certainly loved. The older gave him no trouble, and in due course became an excellent engineering professor in California. The younger one seems to have inherited, in an acute form, his mother's melancholia, and brought Einstein in middle age what was perhaps his deepest private grief.

Meanwhile, his first child born, Einstein, 26 years old, only three years away from crude privation, still a patent examiner, published in the *Annalen der Physik* in 1905 five papers on entirely different subjects. Three of them were among the greatest in the history of physics. One, very simple, gave the quantum explanation of the photoelectric effect — it was this work for which, sixteen years later, he was awarded the Nobel Prize. Another dealt with the phenomenon of Brownian motion, the apparently erratic movement of tiny particles suspended in a liquid: Einstein showed that these movements satisfied a clear statistical law. This was like a conjuring trick, easy when explained: before it, decent scientists could still doubt the concrete existence of atoms and molecules: this paper was as near to a direct proof of their concreteness as a theoretician could give. The third paper was the special theory of relativity, which quietly amalgamated space, time and matter into one fundamental unity.

This last paper contains no references and quotes no authority. All of them are written in a style unlike any other theoretical physicist's. They contain very little mathematics. There is a good deal of verbal commentary. The conclusions, the bizarre conclusions, emerge as though with the greatest of ease: the reasoning is unbreakable. It looks as though he had reached the conclusions by pure thought, unaided, without listening to the opinions of others. To a surprisingly large extent, that is precisely what he had done.

It is pretty safe to say that, so long as physics lasts, no one will again hack out three major breakthroughs in one year. People have complained that Einstein was not immediately recognised. That seems mildly unrealistic. Within a few months physicists at Cracow were saying that a new Copernicus had been born. It took about four years for the top German physicists, such as Planck, Nernst, and von Laue, to begin proclaiming that he was a genius. In 1909, before he had any academic job at all, he was given an honorary degree at Geneva. Just afterwards Zürich university (not the polytechnic) offered him a professorship. In 1911 he went to a full chair at the German university in Prague. In 1912 he was recalled to the Zürich polytechnic, which had had, only a dozen years before, no use for him. In 1913 he was elected to the Prussian Academy of Science, at a high salary for those days, to be left free in Berlin for no duties except his research. He was by then 34. He was being treated as handsomely as any scientist alive. I don't think the academic community, in particular the German-speaking academic community, comes out of that story badly.

There was, however, trouble in his home. No one knows how deeply it affected him. By the time he had moved to Prague, his marriage was going wrong. Altogether, the stay in Prague was an unhappy one. Einstein had to become a state official of the Hapsburg empire: in order to do this he had to declare his religion. He had lost all connections with Judaism: but anti-semitism was strong in Austria, and that was enough reason for Einstein to insist on registering himself – Israelite. His wife, Mileva, was sunk in melancholia: it didn't help that she was a Slav, in the midst of racial unrest.

Yet Einstein's laugh was still ringing out, his spirits were not yet damped. He was showing a new ability as an actor – with a touch of ham – on the lecture platform. There are pleasant stories of his playing the violin to a cultivated salon which discussed Kant, Hegel and Fichte and enjoyed chamber music. The party often included Franz Kafka, not yet known to fame. One wonders if they ever talked to each other. They would not have had much in common.

When he went to Berlin in 1914, he left his wife and sons in Zürich. The marriage was over: he must have known it, though it seems that he did not say it. He was overcome by sadness, of a kind rare in him, when he left his sons.

He arrived in Berlin some months before war broke out. He was already famous in the scientific world. He was going to attract fame in the world outside such as no scientist has known before or since. He was a pacifist soon forced to watch what he regarded as German madness among, not only the crowd, but his fellow members of the Academy. He had preserved his Swiss nationality, which was some sort of protection when, with his habitual courage, he became an ally of Romain Rolland. But he soon came to experience the blackest unpopularity. He could shrug it off: 'Even the scientists of various countries behave as though eight months ago [he was writing to Rolland in May 1915] they had had their brains amputated'.

Nevertheless, in the middle of militaristic tumult, he found both personal and creative peace. Perhaps, or probably, the two were connected. Anyway, he went to live in Berlin with one of his uncles: and with this uncle's daughter, who had been unsatisfactorily married, divorced, and had two small daughters, he was happy. Maybe he fell in love: but, once again, this is unknown. Certainly he wanted no one else. When he was himself divorced, some years later, he married her. She protected him from nuisances until he died. She was unexacting, she was high-spirited, she was fun, she was shrewd about people. Unlike his first wife, who was trained as a mathematician, she knew nothing whatever about his work. It was the kind of marriage that some of the greatest scientists have made. It set him free, and left him free. Before he met her, he had been going through a fallow period scientifically. Almost immediately after, he was thinking with a concentration, and reaching a creative ecstasy more intense, than he had known.

In November 1915 he wrote to Arnold Sommerfeld, himself a fine physicist, one of the classical scientific letters:

'This last month I have lived through the most exciting and the most exacting period of my life: and it would be true to say that it has also been the most fruitful. Writing letters has been out of the question. I realise that up till now my field equations of gravitation have been entirely devoid of foundation. When all my confidence in the old theory vanished, I saw clearly that a satisfactory solution could only be reached by linking it with the Riemann variations. The wonderful thing that happened then was that not only did Newton's theory result from it, *as a first approximation,* but also the perihelion motion of Mercury, *as a second approximation.* For the deviation of light by the Sun I obtain twice the former amount.'[1]

Sommerfeld wrote a cautious and sceptical reply. Einstein sent him a postcard: 'You will become convinced of the general theory of relativity as soon as you have studied it. Therefore I shall not utter a word in its defence'.

It did not need defence. It was published in 1916. As soon as it reached England — across the increasing harshness of the war — scientists thought that it was almost certainly right. The greatest revolution in thought since Newton, they were saying. As a consequence of his theory Einstein had made a prediction. It was the prediction of an experimental effect which astronomers could test. In his paper, he asked them to do so. The English astronomers decided that this should be done. In March 1917 — again across the war — they announced that on 29 March 1919 a total eclipse of the sun was taking place. The critical experiment would be set up and Einstein's theory tested.

That is an old story. The test, of course, came out as predicted, and Einstein's theory stood.

It is a strange theory. As with Rutherford, as with most scientists, if Einstein had never lived most of his work would soon have been done by someone else, and in much the same form. He said himself that that was true of the special theory of relativity. But, when he generalised the special theory so as to include the gravitational field, he did something that might not have been done for generations: and, above all, might not have been done in that way. It might, some good theoreticians have suggested, have ultimately been done in a way easier for others to handle. It remains an extraordinary monolith, like a Henry Moore sculpture, which he alone could have constructed — and at which he himself hacked away, hoping to make something grander, for the rest of his scientific life.

I will return in a moment to the second half of his scientific life, which was at the same time extraordinary, unsuccessful, and profoundly characteristic. In the meantime his public life, as soon as the general theory was published (his fame had already mounted *before* the confirmation), was unlike that which any other scientist is likely to experience again. No one knows quite why, but he sprang into the public consciousness, all over the world, as the symbol of science, the master of the twentieth-century intellect, to a large extent the spokes-man for human hope. It seemed that, perhaps as a release from the war, people wanted a human being to revere. It is true that they did not understand what they were revering. Never mind, they believed that here was someone of supreme, if mysterious, excellence.

As a symbol of science, either Rutherford or Niels Bohr might have been chosen. Rutherford left a more direct mark on twentieth-century science (Einstein said: 'I consider Rutherford to be one of the greatest experimental scientists of all time, and in the same class as Faraday. The reason I had no opportunity of mentioning him in my writings is because I concentrated on speculative theories, whereas Rutherford managed to reach profound conclusions on the basis of almost primitive reflection combined with relatively simple experimental methods'). Bohr founded a great Socratic school of theoretical physicists, and influenced others as Einstein never did. Both Rutherford and Bohr were good men, but Rutherford hadn't Einstein's moral independence or resource: Bohr may have had, but could not project it. No, the public instinct was correct. As Hardy used to quote — it's only the highbrows (in the unpleasant sense) who do not admire the real swells.

Throughout the 'twenties he made himself the champion of good causes. He became a Zionist, though his religious thinking was quite un-Judaic: he was on the side of Zion, out of an ultimate loyalty and also, as I have said before, because the Jews were the insulted and injured of this world. He spent a lot of time trying to promote international pacifism. This sounds strange to us now, but the 'twenties was a period of ideals, and even Einstein, the least suggestive of men, shared them. At a later period of his life, some Americans used to call him naïve. This made me angry: he was not in the slightest naïve: what they meant was that he didn't think that the United States was always 100 per cent right, and the Soviet Union 100 per cent wrong.

If they had studied his public attitudes they might — but they couldn't, reason had gone to sleep — have realised that he had always stood above the battles. He could not have become a partisan if he had tried. In one sense, he was totally detached. In another, he felt an absolute duty to his fellow men. Antonia Vallentin says with accuracy that spiritually he was free of all chains, but that morally he was bound by them. He loved his solitude — 'painful when one is young, but delightful when one is more mature': but still, the more so as he became world-famous, he knew his duty. 'The concern for man and his destiny must always be the chief interest of all technical effort. Never forget it among your diagrams and equations'. Later he said: 'Only a life lived for others is worth while'.

In the 'twenties life had still not quite sobered him. He went about the world, sockless, rather like an itinerant musician. Everyone, including himself, complained about the ordeals of publicity. Here, for once, I register a dissenting vote. There was a streak in him, major prophet though he was, which enjoyed the photographers and the crowds. He had an element, as I have indicated before, of the exhibitionist and the ham, coexisting with his spiritual grandeur. If there had not been that element, there would have been no photographers and no crowds. Nothing is easier to avoid than publicity. If one genuinely doesn't want it, one doesn't get it. Einstein was under no compulsion to travel round the world. If he had retired — it would have been perfectly practicable — to his birthplace in Swabia, he could have revelled in obscurity.

But he didn't. Some of his remarks about publicity in the 'twenties sounded, as usual, like the Old Testament. But — much more than we think in our rationalisations — what you want is what happens to you.

That wasn't true, though, on the world scene. He had always been more realistic than most men about German politics: he knew the violence seething underneath the Weimar state. As soon as Hitler took the power, Einstein was quicker than any politician to judge what was going to happen. International pacifism, the world community, intellectual co-operation — all his hopes had to be put aside. He was much more rapid than Churchill in recognising that the Nazi Reich had to be put down by force.

He was himself Hitler's greatest public enemy. He was out of Germany when Hitler became Chancellor: he was a brave man, but he knew that if he returned he would be killed. Through most of 1933 he lived in the little Flemish seaside town of De Haan (Coq-sur-Mer). There he kept a kind of intellectual court for refugees. De Haan was temporarily the capital of the German-speaking scientific world. Incidentally, it is the most agreeable village on the Flanders coast, and they have a pleasant custom of naming streets after great men — Shakespeare laan, Dante laan, Rembrandt laan, and so on. But they haven't yet named a street after their most illustrious resident.

Belgium suited him. He was more comfortable in small cosy countries (Holland was his favourite), but he wasn't safe from the Nazis. Unwillingly he set off on his travels again, went to Princeton, and stayed there until he died.

It was a kind of exile. There is no doubt that he, who had never recognised any place as home, sometimes longed for the sounds and smells of Europe. Nevertheless it was in America that he reached his full wisdom and his full sadness. His wife died soon after he got there. His younger son, back in Switzerland, had gone into a mental home. His merriness had finally been worn away. He was left with his duty to other men.

He was left with something else, too. He could still lose his personality, forget everything else, in speculating about the natural world. That was the deepest root of his existence: it remained strong until the night before he died. He once said in public: 'Whoever finds a thought which enables us to obtain a slightly deeper glimpse into the eternal secrets of nature, has been given great grace'. He continued — this was the grace of his solitariness — to try to find such thoughts. Quite unlike Newton, who gave up physics entirely in order to become Master of the Mint and perform textual researches on the Bible, Einstein stayed working at science long after most theoreticians, even the best, have taken to something easier. But he worked – and this was the final strangeness of his life – in a direction flat opposite to that of his major colleagues. In the public world, against militarism, against Hitler, against cruelty and unreason, nothing had ever made him budge. In the private world of theoretical physics, with the same quiet but total intransigence, he would not budge against the combined forces of the colleagues he loved: Bohr, Born, Dirac, Heisenberg, the major intellects in his own profession.

They believed that the fundamental laws were statistical – that, when it came to quantum phenomena, in Einstein's picturesque phrase, God had to play at dice. He believed in classical determinism – that, in the long run, it should be possible to frame one great field theory in which the traditional concept of causality would re-emerge. Year after year he explained and redefined his position.

To Carl Seelig: 'I differ decisively in my opinions about the fundamentals of physics from nearly all my contemporaries, and therefore I cannot allow myself to act as spokesman for theoretical physicists. In particular I do not believe in the necessity for a statistical formulation of the laws.'

To Max Born: 'I can quite well understand why you take me for an obstinate old sinner, but I feel clearly that you do not understand how I came to travel my lonely way. It would certainly amuse you, although it would be impossible for you to appreciate my attitude. I should also have great pleasure in tearing to pieces your positivistic-philosophical viewpoint.'

To James Franck: 'I can, if the worst comes to the worst, still realise that God may have created a world in which there are no natural laws. In short, a chaos. But that there should be statistical laws with definite solutions, i.e. laws which compel God to throw the dice in each individual case, I find highly disagreeable.'

God does *not* play at dice, he kept saying. But, though he worked at it for nearly 40 years, he never discovered his unified field theory. And it is true that his colleagues, who passionately venerated him, sometimes thought that he was 'an obstinate old sinner'. They believed that he had misspent half the mental lifetime of the most powerful intellect alive. They felt they had lost their natural leader.

The arguments on both sides are most beautiful and subtle. Unfortunately they cannot be followed without some background of physics: otherwise Bohr's *Discussion on epistemological problems* and Einstein's *Reply* ought to be part of everyone's education. No more profound intellectual debate has ever been conducted – and, since they were both men of the loftiest spirit, it was conducted with noble feeling on both sides. If two men are going to disagree, on the subject of most ultimate concern to them both, then that is the way to do it. It is a pity that the debate, because of its nature, can't be common currency.

Perhaps I can, by an analogy, suggest the effect on Einstein's colleagues of his one-man counter-revolution. It was rather as though Picasso, about 1920, at the height of his powers, had announced that some new kind of representational painting alone could be made to contain the visual truth: and had spent the rest of his life industriously but unavailingly trying to find it.

The great debate did not reach its peak until Einstein was old, years after the war. It was never resolved. He and Bohr, with mutual admiration, drew intellectually further apart. In fact, though, when I met Einstein in 1937 he had already separated himself totally, and as it proved finally, from the other theorists.

I had already shaken hands with him once or twice at large gatherings. That summer I happened to be in America, and my friend Leopold Infeld, who was collaborating with Einstein at the time, suggested that I might like to spend a day with him.

It turned out to be an abnormally hot day, even for a New York summer. The seats were hot in the car, as Infeld, a woman friend and I drove out to Long Island. We had a snack by way of lunch, and aimed at arriving at one o'clock. Actually we turned up late. Einstein had taken a house for the summer, since sailing remained one of his continuing pleasures. Infeld had not been there: no one in the neighbourhood knew where Einstein was living, nor apparently had the slightest idea who he was. Infeld, not the most patient of men, was getting distinctly cross. We had no telephone number. Finally we had to ring back to Princeton, track down one of the Institute's secretaries (which wasn't easy, because it was either a Saturday or a Sunday) and get directions. At last we made it, three-quarters of an hour late.

Not that that mattered to Einstein. He was amiable to all visitors, and I was just one of many. He came into the sitting-room a minute or two after we arrived. There was no furniture apart from some garden chairs and a small table. The window looked out on to the water, but the shutters were half closed to keep out the heat. The humidity was very high.

At close quarters Einstein's head was as I had imagined it: magnificent, with a humanising touch of the comic. Great furrowed forehead: aureole of white hair: enormous bulging chocolate-brown eyes. I can't guess what I should have expected from such a face if I hadn't known. A shrewd Swiss once said it had the brightness of a good artisan's countenance, that he looked like a reliable old-fashioned watchmaker in a small town who perhaps collected butterflies on a Sunday.

What did surprise me was his physique. He had come in from sailing and was wearing nothing but a pair of shorts. It was a massive body, very heavily muscled: he was running to fat round the midriff and in the upper arms, rather like a footballer in middle age, but he was still an unusually strong man. All through his life he must have had much greater physical strength than any of the others I am writing about. He was cordial, simple, utterly unshy. The large eyes looked at me, as though he was thinking: what had I come for, what did I want to talk about? Infeld, not only a man of distinguished intellect, but sharp-witted, set to work to find topics, as he went on doing through the afternoon and evening ahead. I was a friend of G. H. Hardy, Infeld began. Einstein smiled with pleasure. Yes, a fine man. Then, quite sharply, he asked me: was Hardy still a pacifist? I replied, as near as made no matter.

'I do not understand,' he said sombrely, 'how such a fine man can be so unrealistic'.

Then he wanted to know if I also was a pacifist. Far from it, I explained. I was by that time certain that war was inevitable. I was not so much apprehensive about war, as about the chance that we might lose it. Einstein nodded. About politics that afternoon, he and I and Infeld were united. About politics in the widest sense, I don't think there has been a world figure in my time who has been wiser than Einstein. He wasn't much interested in political techniques, and brushed them off too lightly: but his major insights into the world situation, and his major prophecies, have proved more truthful than those of anyone else.

The hours went on. I have a hazy memory that several people drifted in and out of the room, but I do not remember who they were. Stifling heat. There appeared to be no set time for meals. He was already, I think, eating very little, but he was still smoking his pipe. Trays of open sandwiches — various kinds of wurst, cheese, cucumber — came in every now and then. It was all casual and Central European. We drank nothing but soda water. What with the heat and the sandwiches I got as thirsty as if I had been dehydrated, and drank more soda water in eight hours than I normally did in eight months.

Mostly we talked of politics, the moral and practical choices in front of us, and what could be saved from the storm to come, not only for Europe but for the human race. All the time he was speaking with a weight of moral experience which was different, not only in quantity but in kind, from anything I had met. By this period he had lost any intrusion from his own ego, as though it had never existed. It was something like talking to the second Isaiah.

It would be easy to give a false impression. In the face of someone so different from the rest of us, it was hard not to get one. In fact, he was neither sentimental nor illusioned. His view of life was not illusioned at all. It was far darker than that of his great friend Paul Langevin. Einstein thought that we should be lucky if the human race was going to stand a chance: but nevertheless, as an absolute moral imperative, we had to do what little we could until we dropped.

Infeld, who knew him better than anyone at this stage, later wrote — and it seems to me precisely true:

'This "conscience of the world" [Einstein] nurses a deep repugnance for all types of boastfulness, terrorising of one's fellow-men and overbearing brutality. One could, therefore, easily have been tempted to portray him as an over-sensitive man, who trembles at the very mention of injustice and violence. This picture would be utterly false. I know no one who leads such a lonely and solitary life as he. His great benevo-lence, his absolute integrity and his social ideas, despite all appearances to the contrary, are thoroughly impersonal and seem to come from another planet. His heart does not bleed, his eyes do not weep.'

And yet, he had suffered much, in a way difficult for more ego-bound men to under-stand. I had heard a lot of his old merriness. That had all disappeared, and for ever. Just once in eight hours I heard the great laugh of his young manhood come rumbling out. It was at a curious turn in the conversation. He had been speaking of the countries he had lived in. He preferred them, he said, in inverse proportion to their size. How did he like England, I asked. Yes, he liked England. It had some of the qualities of his beloved Holland. After all, by world standards, England was becoming a small country. We talked of the people he had met, not only of the scientists but the politicians. Churchill. Einstein admired him. I said that progressives of my kind wanted him in the government as a token of resistance: this was being opposed, not so much by the Labour party, but by Churchill's own Tories. Einstein was brooding. To defeat Nazism, he said, we should need every kind of force, including nationalism, that we could bring together.

Then, because there wasn't much useful to say, I asked why, when he left Germany, he hadn't come to live in England.

'No, no!' said Einstein.

Why not?

'It is your style of life.' Suddenly he had begun to laugh. 'It is a splendid style of life. But it is not for me.'

He was enjoying some gigantic joke. But I was puzzled. What was this mysterious 'style of life'? It appeared that, on his first day in England, he had been taken to a great country house. A butler. Evening dress. Einstein had never worn a dinner jacket in his life. Then Lindemann had taken him in to dinner at Christ Church. More butlers. More evening dress. Einstein chortled. He seemed to have the fixed idea that the English, or certainly the English professional classes, spent much of their time getting in and out of formal clothes. Any protests I made (did he think Hardy lived like that?) were swept aside. It was then that he introduced me to the word *Zwang*. No *Zwang* for him. No butlers. No evening dress.

That was my single glimpse of what he might have been like in Switzerland 30 years before. But he did say something which may have been, though I cannot be sure, more personal. It was much later in the day, and getting dark outside. Einstein was talking about the conditions for a creative existence. He said that, in his experience, the best creative work is never done when one is unhappy. He could scarcely think of any physicist who had done fine work in such a state. Or any composer. Or any writer.

It seemed a strange and unexpected remark.

The only exception he could think of, Einstein went on, was Bohr, who had produced his great paper on the hydrogen spectrum when in deep misery.

Neither Infeld nor I knew that. Einstein was speaking of his famous contemporaries, a generation before our time. I pulled myself together, and suggested Tolstoy when writing *Anna Karenina.* He had been in a state of profound despair. Einstein was interested. Tolstoy was one of his favourite writers. Just as his taste in physics, and his feeling for the nature of the physical laws, was classical, so was his taste in art. He detested romantic art, in particular German romantic art. He didn't like subjectivism. We talked about books. The novel he valued most of all was *The Brothers Karamazov.* Then Einstein came back to his thoughts upon the creative life. His great head was shaking to and fro:

'No, to understand the world one must not be worrying about oneself.'

Back in New York, late that night, I found those remarks of his about happiness jumbling with others. At that time I knew little about his own life: I did not know then, and still don't know, whether what he said had any personal relevance. But if it had, it may have been drawn from memories of his own two major creative periods. The first produced the great papers of 1905: he was not long married, his first son was born. I am inclined to fancy that, despite some accounts of those early years, that marriage began by being happy. About his second major period, nearly all the evidence agrees. Despite the war, he was joyous: his cousin Elsa had lifted a burden from him: almost at once he had the transcendental scientific experience of his life.

It was, I think, in that same Long Island house, two years later, that Einstein signed the well-known letter to Roosevelt about the possibility of an atomic bomb. But this event, as I mentioned before, has been wildly melodramatised. Einstein was a mythopoeic character. Some of the myths are true and significant; this myth, though factually true, is not significant.

Let me try to clear the ground. First, Einstein's work had nothing to do either with the discovery or the potential use of nuclear fission. From the moment of the Meitner–Frisch paper in January 1939 (as Niels Bohr said at the time, everyone ought to have seen the meaning of Hahn's 1938 experiments much earlier – 'we were all fools'), nuclear fission was a known fact to all physicists in the field. Second, the possible use of nuclear energy had been speculated about long before Einstein produced the equation $E = mc^2$. After the fission experiments, it would have been empirically apparent if there had been no theory at all. Every nuclear physicist in the world – and a good many non-nuclear physicists – were talking about the conceivability of a nuclear bomb from early 1939 onwards. Third, all responsible nuclear physicists wanted to bring this news to their governments as effectively as they could. It happened in England months *before* the Einstein letter was signed. Fourth, a group of refugee scientists in America (Szilard, Wigner, Teller, Fermi) had no direct channels of communication with the White House. Very sensibly, they explained the position to Einstein. It was easy for him to understand. A letter drafted by them, signed by him, handed on by Sachs (an economist with an entrée to the President) would get straight to Roosevelt. 'I served as a pillar box,' said Einstein. It was signed on Long Island on 2 July: it did not reach Roosevelt until 11 October. Fifth, if this letter had not been sent, similar messages would have been forced on Roosevelt. For some time *after* the letter, the Americans were much slower off the mark than the English. Peierls's calculations which showed that the bomb was a possibility, were ready by mid 1940. These had, in historical fact, a major effect upon the *American* scientists. Sixth, in July 1939 there was – unless one was an unqualified pacifist, — no moral dilemma. Everyone was afraid that the Nazis would get the bomb first. If so, they would rule the world. It was as simple as that. It was as simple to Einstein as to the crudest of men.

It is a pity that the story of the letter has obscured the genuine moral dilemma of his last years. Which was — now that the bomb exists, what should a man do? He probably knew little or nothing of the actual development of the bomb. He was not one of the Franck group (once again, organised by Leo Szilard) who protested in advance against its military use on Japan. He was not one, simply because he did not know that the bomb was as good as made. When the first bomb was dropped on Hiroshima, he said simply '*O Weh!*' (Oh horrible!). Nothing would convince him that Hiroshima was forgivable, either in moral or practical terms: just as nothing has convinced many of us, with all the information of the twenty subsequent years, and with our knowledge of how the world has gone.

The bomb was made. What should a man do? He couldn't find an answer which people would listen to. He campaigned for a world state: that only made him distrusted both in the Soviet Union and in the United States. He gave an eschatological warning to a mass television audience in 1950:

'And now the public has been advised that the production of the hydrogen bomb is the new goal which will probably be accomplished. An accelerated development towards this end has been solemnly proclaimed by the President. If these efforts should prove successful, radioactive poisoning of the atmosphere, and, hence, annihilation of all life on earth will have been brought within the range of what is technically possible. *A weird aspect of this development lies in its apparently inexorable character. Each step appears as the inevitable consequence of the one that went before.* And at the end, looming ever clearer, lies general annihilation.'

That speech made him more distrusted in America. As for practical results, no one listened. Incidentally, in the view of most contemporary military scientists, it would be more difficult totally to eliminate the human species than Einstein then believed. But the most interesting sentences were the ones I have italicised. They are utterly true. The more one has mixed in these horrors, the truer they seem.

He joined in other warnings, one of them signed in the last week of his life. He did not expect them to bite: he retained the hope of his strong spirit, but intellectually he seems to have had no hope at all.

He was physically the strongest of the men I am discussing. He was also the strongest in spirit. He was used to being solitary. 'It is strange', he wrote, 'to be known so universally and yet to be so lonely'. Never mind. He was isolated in his search for the unified field. And the latter was the great theme of his life. He could endure it all, impregnable, and work stoically on. He said: 'One must divide one's time between politics and equations. But our equations are much more important to me'.

From his late sixties until his death at 76 he was continuously ill — from what appear to have been a variety of causes, an intestinal growth, a disease of the liver, finally a weakening of the aorta wall. He lived on in discomfort, and often in acute pain. He stayed cheerful, serene, detached from his own illness and the approach of death. He worked on. The end of his life was neither miserable nor pathetic. 'Here on earth I have done my job,' he said, without self-pity.

By his bedside, one Sunday night, lay some pages of manuscript. They included more equations leading to the unified field theory, which he had never found. He hoped to be enough out of pain next day to work on them. Early in the morning the aortic blister broke, and he died.

Good, gentle, wise, Hardy called him, that day at Fenner's. At the time I wanted to add another word. If we were having the conversation again, I think I should have chosen a clumsy one. Of all the men I have heard of, this one was — in any sense I can imagine, intellectual, emotional, spiritual — the most unbudgeable.

Note

1. The perihelion motion of Mercury had already been measured, but not explained. The measurement agreed exactly with that which was required by Einstein's theory. Einstein was also predicting another very small optical effect which in 1916 had not yet been measured.

Personal reminiscences

Reinhold Fürth

Dr Reinhold Fürth, FRSE, was born in Prague in 1893. He studied physics and mathematics at the German University of Prague, 1912–16, and graduated as a doctor of philosophy in 1916. He was Dean of the Faculty of Science at the university, 1937–8, but left in 1939 to work with Max Born at Edinburgh, where he was appointed Dewar Research Fellow and lecturer at the university in 1942. From 1947 to 1961 he was reader in theoretical physics at Birkbeck College, London University.

Dr Fürth was interviewed by James Woudhuysen shortly before his death in 1979.

I first came across Einstein in 1912, when I started my studies in physics and mathematics at the former German University in Prague. At that time Einstein had just left Prague to take up his professorship at Zürich. I missed him directly, but everywhere there were traces. For instance, stored in a cupboard was a machine for multiplying electric charges; Einstein had designed it, although he rarely concerned himself with experimental matters. More important, Einstein's successor as professor of theoretical physics, Philipp Frank, was one of the few people who had taken up research on his ideas. He introduced me to relativity theory. Some of my senior colleagues had themselves been pupils of Einstein, so they acquainted me with his methods of teaching and his personality.

Frank also drew my attention to Einstein's fundamental work on statistical mechanics and in particular to his theory of Brownian motion. This field fascinated me so much that I soon started research work in it myself. After a few years I wrote to Einstein to be allowed to edit a collection of his papers on the Brownian movement.

I met him at last in 1920, when I was 27. Before the war, there had been a series of annual international conferences on natural science and physics. Each conference had been held at a German town or spa. The series had been interrupted by the First World War, but resumed with a conference at Bad Nauheim that year. Just before the proceedings began I was introduced to Einstein at a gathering in Berlin.

By 1920, of course, Einstein's investigations had given him a big name everywhere. At the conference, the big question in everybody's mind was whether there would be a fight between Lenard and Einstein. Lenard was professor of physics at Heidelberg, and well known for his dislike both of the theory of relativity and of Jews. He was widely regarded as crazy, and had just founded a discipline that he called 'Deutsche Physik'. All his electrical instruments, for instance, were calibrated in Webers rather than Amperes. As it happened, Planck cooled everything down from the chair. Einstein gave a very clear, calm, and good-natured lecture; it may have been his first and last really major one, because he hated giving speeches. I remember that Pauli, who was still very young, appeared to be one of the very few who understood the general theory of relativity.

The following year, Einstein accepted an invitation to give a popular lecture at Prague. At that time Frank and his wife lived in one of the rooms of the Institute of Theoretical Physics where Einstein used to work. They invited Einstein to stay with them, and he accepted with great pleasure, for it allowed him to avoid publicity, which he hated. Because he was director of the scientific research branch of the Kaiser Wilhelm Institute, I talked to him to obtain some funds for an experiment that I had planned. He was interested and arranged for the assistance I needed. He struck me as a very simple, kind man.

At the university Einstein delivered a very comprehensible lecture, though in all probability not everyone understood it. At a reception afterwards Einstein played a Mozart violin sonata in return for his audience's congratulations. He liked chamber music very much. In general, he played quite well, but not outstandingly. With his hair all over the place, he looked just like a travelling musician, except that he was tall and far from frail.

The day after his lecture Einstein answered questions on it. A German professor of philosophy attacked his theory of relativity, especially in relation to geometry. He said it was illogical. Einstein did not take him very seriously. He remarked that a young student's question was the only good one he had heard that session.

Einstein never returned to Prague again, though I know he was happy during his professorship there. He did, however, dislike lecturing, and hated the work of preparation for lectures months in advance. He only lectured in what he was interested in.

In 1928 I went to Berlin to ask Einstein to come to the Prague Physikalische Gesellschaft's meeting that year. He was often quite shabbily dressed; but on this occasion he appeared absolutely informal – in slippers – in his study. It was situated in a tower attached to his house. Einstein refused my request on health grounds: he had overstrained his heart rowing in Berlin (though perhaps he did not want to go to the conference anyway). As we were talking we were interrupted by his wife, who appeared in an evening gown and announced that guests had arrived. Einstein was embarrassed. He had forgotten the engagement, was wrongly dressed for it, and was forced to end our conversation. He was always quite untroubled by what he looked like, and quite often took to twiddling his hair. His wife was fairly severe with him when he was abstracted.

In my opinion the work Einstein did before he wrote about relativity was not directed towards a single goal. He picked things up as he became interested in them. He was strongly influenced by Mach, who had done a great deal of fundamental research as professor of physics at Prague before he was called to Vienna as professor of philosophy. However, Einstein believed in the existence of atoms and Mach did not.

Einstein's first papers on the Brownian movement were constructed with a fantastically penetrating and convincing logic. He wrote them irrespective of what people thought was self-evident. If he came across something new it would seize his attention. The differences between the fields he covered did not matter to him. It was quite mystical: I think hardly anybody can explain how he packed such a lot of genius into those first papers over such a short space of time. He was very quick to take things up. On the other hand, he tried to do as little guessing or undisciplined speculation as possible. For instance, though he was prepared to accept new ideas, he rejected Max Born's probabilistic quantum theory. He was really a classical physicist, as was Planck.

Pick, professor of mathematics at Prague and a fellow violin player, drew his attention to the Italian, Levi Civita, and his absolute differential calculus; and certainly Einstein's mathematical presentation of the general theory was his most important achievement. But the verifiability of the theory was crucial too.

The theory of relativity was probably nurtured by Einstein's highly cosmopolitan background, but I do not believe that there was any connection between Einstein's unitarian, religious views of the universe and its simplicity and his scientific enquiries. Einstein kept the two fields separate. But it was always my impression that his failure to solve the unified field theory problem led to a certain spiritual pessimism in his later life.

Note

1. R. Fürth, editor, *Investigations on the theory of the Brownian movement,* translated by A. D. Cowper, 1926.

To Albert Einstein on his 75th birthday

Leopold Infeld

Leopold Infeld became Einstein's collaborator at Princeton in 1936. On a visit to his native country, Poland, in 1949, he decided to stay, and was given the task of organising the theoretical section of the Institute of Physics.

From the *Bulletin of the World Federation of Scientific Workers,* July 1954.

I remember my last visit to Einstein's home, just before I returned to Poland. I told him about my plan to go back to my native country. He understood the reasons for my doing so.

I then took leave of the man to whom I owe so much, who showed me great kindness as he does to everyone who comes in contact with him. Indeed, I probably owe him my life. Had he not invited me to come to him in 1936, I would no doubt have been one of Hitler's six million victims.

I heard Einstein's name for the first time as an undergraduate student in Cracow (Poland) during my second year of studies. At the end of his lectures in mechanics my professor devoted the last two hours to the special relativity theory. Later, while studying the relativity theory from the original manuscripts (there were no books on it at that time), I thought much about the genius and imagination of its inventor. With the exception of some specialists, no one knew Einstein's name at that time (1917).

Then suddenly, almost overnight, Einstein's great fame began. At this time I was a school teacher in a small Polish town and I did what hundreds of others did all over the world. I gave a public lecture on the theory of relativity and the crowd that queued up on a cold winter night was so great that it could not be accommodated in the largest hall in the town. Einstein's photograph appeared in many newspapers, and to my astonishment I saw a face more that of an artist and a prophet than that of a scientist.

I saw Einstein for the first time in Berlin in 1921, when I was pacing the streets, trying my best to become a student at the university where Planck, Laue and Einstein lectured. I felt unhappy, because I knew nobody. I was lonely, as one can feel lonely only in a great hostile city. For weeks I waited for appointments with people — only to find how little they cared whether or not I was accepted by the university of Berlin. Yet at that time this seemed to me the decisive question of my life. In desperation I rang up Einstein and, to my great astonishment, was asked to come right over.

Kindness is a difficult thing to take when it comes, suddenly against an icy background of hostility and indifference. Einstein greeted me with a smile and offered me a cigarette, talked to me as an equal and showed a childlike trust in everything I said. My short interview was an important event in my life. Instead of thinking about his genius, about his achievements in physics, I thought then and later about his great kindness, about his loud laughs, about the gentle way he talked, about the brilliance of his eyes, about the clumsiness with which he looked for a piece of paper on a desk full of papers, about the queer mixture of great warmth and great aloofness.

I did not see Einstein for the next 15 years. I had a few letters from him on scientific matters, always full of kindness. To me, as to others, he never refused help when it was needed — always writing with simplicity and grace, never with impatience. Now, while writing these words, I am well aware that I was one of the very many who bothered Einstein with their scientific or personal troubles. I do not feel happy now, that upon my publisher's advice, I asked Einstein to write a few words about my first book — just a sentence or two. Instead I received a full introduction, written with warmth and sympathy.

I went to America upon Einstein's invitation in 1936. For the next two years, I worked with him and saw him almost every day. We talked about physics; we wrote two papers and a popular book; we discussed hundreds of things: the Spanish Civil War, the Jewish problem, idealism versus realism in philosophy, and many others.

There are innumerable stories about Einstein — some of them true, some invented. They show that he is witty or unworldly, or trusting or absent-minded; that he bursts quickly into loud laughter, plays with his hair, or goes without socks or tie. But none of these stories give a clue to Einstein's character. In trying to understand him it is difficult to proceed in an inductive way — that is, from facts or incidents to his personality. As in theoretical physics, so in writing about Einstein, the deductive method seems quicker and simpler; the development from theory to particulars. The 'why' of such an approach is fairly obvious. Material facts matter less in Einstein's life than in anyone else's. The world of his sense impressions, of cold, hunger, pain, is dulled by the great intensity of his internal life. The adventure of Einstein's life is that of his mind.

Once, as Einstein and I walked across the Princeton campus towards his home, discussing questions only loosely connected with physics, I asked Einstein why he thought his fame had become greater than that of any other living scientist, perhaps greater than that of any scientist in the past. I remember vaguely that the question did not seem to interest Einstein, that he did not say anything striking or worth recalling.

When Einstein explains his theories, the thought of impressing anyone is as absent from his mind as water from the moon. He expresses his ideas slowly, thoroughly, repeating essential points, answering questions patiently, never assuming that his listener is either bright or dull. He speaks as though his object were to make the ideas clear to his own mind. The overtone 'I did it, wasn't it clever of me?' is simply not there. Einstein may praise his work but only like a man who by accident has stumbled upon a priceless gem, never like a man who created it by the work of his own hands.

Many times while we worked together, I marvelled at the depth of his thoughts, at the breadth of his vision and, above all, at the tenacity with which he clings to his problems. (Einstein often remarked to me that research ability is essentially a matter of character.) Yet all these things seemed to me the less important the longer I worked with him. As great as Einstein is as a physicist he is equally great as a man.

When one comes in contact with him, one is not overwhelmed by his greatness as a scientist. This greatness is engulfed by the greatness and strangeness of his whole personality. Einstein is unlike anyone else. And perhaps this simple fact is the real clue to his fame. The real clue is not the spectacular discovery of the bending of light rays. If this were so, why should this fame persist in a quickly changing world that forgets today its idols of yesterday? It must rather be his inner greatness, which the people of the world somehow sense and need for their comfort.

It is not difficult to comprehend Einstein's distaste for bullying, for pushing others around, or his readiness to defend any just and decent cause. Yet even this is not as simple as it seems. One would be tempted to think about someone sensitive to the outside world and to wrongs done, someone who suffers when he hears of violence or injustice. Yet such a picture would be entirely misleading. I do not know anyone as lonely and detached as Einstein. His extreme kindness, his decency, his straightforwardness in dealing with men and social ideas is, in spite of all the appearances to the contrary, impersonal and aloof. His heart does not bleed, his eyes do not cry, yet his deeds are those of a man whose heart bleeds and whose eyes cry.

Another limitation created by his aloofness is the lack of knowledge of the real life around him. This makes it unavoidable that sometimes people misrepresent to him causes which are worthy of his support; or making use of his kindness and aloofness they induce him to support causes which should not be his. Yet in the end he almost always speaks in the name of humanity. His own great honesty and intellectual integrity were clearly shown when he advised American intellectuals last June not to testify before McCarthy's committee in these words:

'I can see only the revolutionary way of non-cooperation. Every intellectual who is called before one of the committees ought to refuse to testify — that is he must be prepared for jail and economic ruin, the sacrifice of his personal welfare in the interests of the cultural welfare of his country.'

Brief thoughts on the theory of relativity

Miroslav Holub

Miroslav Holub was born in 1923. In 1942 he was conscripted as a railway-worker for several years. After the war
he studied medicine at Charles University in Prague, taking
his MD in 1953. He is now a research immunologist attached
to the Institute of Clinical and Experimental Medicine at a
leading Prague hospital. His *Selected poems* (translated by
Ian Milner and George Theiner) were published by Penguin
Books in 1967, and *Although* (translated by Jarmila and
Ian Milner) by Cape Editions in 1971. He has read at Poetry
International in the Queen Elizabeth Hall, London, in
1969; at the Rotterdam International Poetry Festival in
1974; and at many other poetry festivals in Europe.

From *Notes of a clay pigeon*, Secker & Warburg, 1977.
Translated by Jarmila and Ian Milner.

Albert Einstein, discussing —
    (knowledge is discovering
    what to say) — discussing
    with Paul Valéry,
    was asked:

    Mr Einstein, what do you do
    with your thoughts? Write them down
    immediately they come to you? Or wait
    till evening? Or morning?

Albert Einstein responded:
    Monsieur Valéry, in our craft
    thoughts are so rare
    that when you have one
    you certainly won't forget it

    Even a year after.

2. The impact on science

Assessing Einstein's impact on today's science by citation analysis

Tony Cawkell and Eugene Garfield

Tony Cawkell is vice-president, research, of the Institute for Scientific Information; he is based in Uxbridge, Middlesex, England. A fellow of the IERE and IEEE, he is actively engaged in various aspects of information science. He is a council member of the Institute of Information Scientists.

For nearly 30 years Dr Eugene Garfield has been concerned with making scientific and technical information accessible on an economic, timely basis. He is founder and president of the Institute for Scientific Information. Inventor of *Current Contents* and the *Science Citation Index,* he graduated in chemistry at Columbia and later returned there for a master's degree in library science. He was awarded his PhD in structural linguistics at the University of Pennsylvania. In recent years he helped establish the Information Industry Association, on which he has served as president and chairman of the board.

Citation analysis

A convenient way of identifying authors or articles which are likely to be of outstanding interest is to take note of those which are being heavily cited as shown in the *Science Citation Index* (*SCI*). An examination of the citing articles will reveal the nature of that interest or 'impact'.[1] After a period to allow for assimilation of the published material it is unlikely that any significant or controversial article will remain uncited. On the other hand, work which contributes substantially to the advancement of science will eventually become part of the fabric and then may be cited only rarely. Nobel prize winners such as Wilhelm Roentgen or Marie Curie are only occasionally cited today, usually in an historical context, but for some work carried out more than 50 years ago there are notable exceptions; for instance, there must be something extraordinary about the heavily cited works listed in Table 1. Of the 11 articles published before 1912, four are by Albert Einstein.

Table 1. The eleven articles,[2] published before 1912, cited most heavily between 1961 and 1975

Bibliographic details	Times cited
G. Mie, 'Beiträge zur Optik trüber Medien, speziell kolloidaler Metallösungen', *Ann. Physik*, vol. 25, 1908, pp. 377–445.	521
W. M. Bayliss, 'On the local reactions of the arterial wall to changes of internal pressure', *J. Physiology*, vol. 28, pp. 220–31.	234
A. Einstein, 'Eine neue Bestimmung der Moleküldimensionen', *Ann. Physik*, vol. 19, 1906, pp. 289–306.	227
A. Einstein, 'Die von der molekularkinetischen Theorie der Wärme geförderte Bewegung von in ruhenden Flüssigkeiten suspendierten Teilchen', *Ann. Physik*, vol. 17, 1905, pp. 549–60.	206
H. H. Dale, 'On some physiological actions of ergot', *J. Physiology*, vol. 34, 1906, pp. 163–206.	181
A. Einstein, 'Berichtigung zu meiner Arbeit: Eine neue Bestimmung der Moleküldimensionen', *Ann. Physik*, vol. 34, 1911, pp. 591–2.	158
E. H. Starling, 'On the absorption of fluids from the connective tissue spaces', *J. Physiology*, vol. 19, 1896, pp. 312–26.	150
T. Purdie, and J. C. Irvine, 'The alkylation of sugars', *J. Chem. Soc.*, vol. 83, 1903, pp. 1021–37.	131
C. S. Hudson, 'The significance of certain numerical relations in the sugar group', *J. Amer. Chem. Soc.*, vol. 31, 1909, pp. 66–86.	105
G. N. Stewart, 'Researches on the circulation time and on the influences which affect it', *J. Physiology*, vol. 22, 1897, pp. 159–83.	105
A. Einstein, 'Theorie der Opaleszenz von homogenen Flüssigkeiten und Flüssigkeitsgemischen in der Nähe des kritischen Zustandes', *Ann. Physik*, vol. 33, 1910, pp. 1275–98.	103

The cited works of Einstein

To investigate the connections between a particular author's works and current scientific articles, select an annual *SCI* edition (or five year cumulation), look up the author, and scan down the chronologically ordered list of his works, stopping at the cited item of interest; beneath that item will be found a list of current citing articles. The most recent five-year cumulation covers 1970–74; under EINSTEIN A., each of his cited works is listed followed by those articles published between 1970 and 1974 which cited it. Einstein's entry is, to say the least of it, unusual,[3] but certain heavily cited papers stand out (see Table 2).

De Broglie[4] considers Einstein's major contributions to be as follows; the special and general theories of relativity; Brownian movement and statistical theories; development of quantum theory (from photo-electric research) for which he received the Nobel Prize in 1921, and developments in wave mechanics (the Bose–Einstein Statistics). De Broglie also describes Einstein's later preoccupation with the unified field theory; at an early point in his career[5] Einstein searched for a 'theory of principle from empirically observed general properties of phenomena'; later he became preoccupied with this theme and in 1935 attacked Heisenberg's uncertainty principle, an accepted doctrine, because he was unhappy about its incompleteness.

Because many of Einstein's papers are available in several versions Table 2 does not present all the information; moreover, today's authors, by patterns of citation to particular papers, group Einstein's ideas somewhat differently to de Broglie's arrangement. To provide a picture of Einstein's impact, as indicated by citations, we have consolidated all the available information into Table 3. Table 4 lists major works with the titles translated into English.

The impact of Einstein's works

To find out more about the nature of current scientific work we may take a consensus from the articles which cite Einstein.[6, 7] For a first approximation we analysed the frequency of the title words of 'high information content' in the citing articles; words, word strings, or word phrases such as BROWNIAN, PHOTO/, and LIGHT SCATTERING are considered to be 'information rich'; words such as EXPERIMENTAL, DISCUSSION, OF, EFFECT and so on are ignored.

Table 2. The works of Einstein most heavily cited between 1970 and 1974

Bibliographic reference	Subject	Times cited
Ann. Phys., vol. 17, 1905, p. 132	Quantum theory	17
Ann. Phys., vol. 17, 1905, p. 549	Brownian movement	103
Ann. Phys,, vol. 17, 1905, p. 891	Special relativity	55
Ann. Phys., vol. 19, 1906, p. 289	Molecular dimensions	120
Ann. Phys., vol. 19, 1906, p. 371	Brownian movement	29
Ann. Phys., vol. 33, 1910, p. 1275	Theory of mixtures	58
Ann. Phys., vol. 34, 1911, p. 591	Molecular dimensions	95
Ann. Phys., vol. 49, 1916, p. 769	General theory relativity	30
Phys. Z., vol. 18, 1917, p. 121	Quantum theory	16
Meaning of relativity, 1950–6		87
Invest. theory Brownian movement, 1956		45

Table 3. The works of Einstein most heavily cited between 1970 and 1974, classified by subject

Subject	Cited works	Times cited
Special theory of relativity	*Ann. Phys.*, vol. 17, 1905, pp. 891–921; English translation, U. Calcutta, 1920. *Ann. Phys.*, vol. 18, 1905, pp. 639–41	56
General theory of relativity	*Ann. Phys.*, vol. 49, 1916, pp. 769–822; on its own, published by Barth, Leipzig, 1916; together with the special theory, pub. Vieweg, Braunschweig, editions for 1917–20. English popular trans., Methuen, editions for 1920–31. *Meaning of relativity*, U. Princeton, editions for 1921–23	175
Quantum theory	*Ann. Phys.*, vol. 17, 1905, pp. 132–48 *Phys. Z.*, vol. 18, 1917, pp. 121–8 *Phys. Rev.* vol. 47, 1935, pp. 777–80	98
Brownian movement; diffusion	*Ann. Phys.*, vol. 17, 1905, pp. 549–60 *Ann. Phys.*, vol. 19, 1906, pp. 371–81 *Ann. Phys.*, vol. 19, 1906, pp. 289–306 *Ann. Phys.*, vol. 34, 1911, pp. 591–2	147
Mixtures; light scattering	*Ann. Phys.*, vol. 33, 1910, pp. 1275–98	58

Table 4. Selected works of Albert Einstein (with translated titles)

1. 'On a heuristic viewpoint concerning the production and transformation of light', *Annalen der Physik*, vol. 17, 1905, pp. 132–48.

2. 'On the motion of small particles suspended in a stationary liquid according to the molecular kinetic theory of heat', *Annalen der Physik*, vol. 17, 1905, pp. 549–60.

3. 'On the electrodynamics of moving bodies', *Annalen der Physik*, vol. 17, 1905, pp. 891–921.

4. 'Does the inertia of a body depend on its energy content?', *Annalen der Physik*, vol. 18, 1905, pp. 639–41.

5. 'A new method of determining molecular dimensions', *Annalen der Physik*, vol. 19, 1906, pp. 289–306.

6. 'On the theory of Brownian movement', *Annalen der Physik*, 1906, vol. 19, pp. 371–81.

7. 'Theory of opalescence of homogeneous liquids and liquid mixtures in the neighbourhood of critical conditions', *Annalen der Physik*, vol. 33, 1910, pp. 1275–98.

8. 'Confirmation of my work; a new determination of molecular dimensions', *Annalen der Physik*, vol. 34, 1911, pp. 591–2.

9. 'Foundation of the general theory of relativity', *Annalen der Physik*, vol. 49, 1916, pp. 769–822.

10. *A popular exposition of the special and general theory of relativity*, Sammlung Vieweg, Braunschweig, 1917.

11. 'On the quantum theory of radiation', *Physikalische Zeitschrift*, vol. 18, 1917, pp. 121–8.

12. 'Can quantum-mechanical description of physical reality be complete?', with B. Podolsky and N. Rosen, *Physical Review*, vol. 47, 1935, pp. 777–80.

The result of analysing word frequencies from a random selection of 1974–77 citing articles is given in Table 5.

These results indicate that there is a definite subject connection between most cited and citing articles. The presence of the string /POLYM/ (as in COPOLYMER or POLYMERISE) is surprising; this seems to be because Einstein's work in this area has had some very 'practical' consequences, as has his work on light scattering which tends also to be cited in a 'practical' context. The earlier work has become the basis for a range of applications.

By contrast, the more esoteric nature of his work on relativity and quantum theory has prompted intense activity at the basic research fronts of physics and cosmology. In some aspects of this research – for instance, in the detection of gravity waves – Einstein's speculations still await verification, although some very recent research seems almost to provide it.[8]

Having used citations as indicators for assessing the degree of interest today in Einstein's work, we will now review the content of a selection of the current citing articles in order to be more specific.

Relativity

The heart of Einstein's four major papers is as follows. The first 1905 paper contained the hypothesis, subsequently confirmed by experiments, that the speed of light as measured by an observer is the same no matter what the speed of the light source with respect to him, provided that the source is moving at a uniform rate. At the same time Einstein disposed of Maxwell's ether. In the second 1905 paper 4 the equation $E = Mc^2$ is developed. In a 1911 paper, 'On the influence of gravitation on the propagation of light', *Ann. Phys.*, vol. 35,

Table 5. Frequencies of 'high information content' words in the titles of 1974–7 articles citing Einstein's works

Subject	Number of titles examined	'High information content' word	Frequency
Special relativity	25	RELATIV/	12
		EINSTEIN	5
General theory of relativity	20	GRAVIT/	8
		SUN; SOLAR	4
		GAUGE	4
Quantum theory	40	RADIA/	11
		PHOT/	9
		QUANT/	9
		STIMULATED EMISSION/; LASER/;	
		MASER/	5
		EINSTEIN	5
		RELATIV/	4
Brownian movement; diffusion	40	PARTICLE/; POWDER/; BEAD/	12
		/POLYM/	9
		SOLUTION/; SUSPENSION/	9
		DIFFUS/	6
		BROWNIAN	5
Mixtures; light scattering	25	LIQUID/; FLUID/; SOLUTION/	10
		LIGHT SCATTERING	8
		/POLYM/	6

1911, pp. 898–900, the 'principle of equivalence' is introduced. Here Einstein argued that the effect of uniform constant acceleration on an observer was indistinguishable from, and so equivalent to, the observer being at rest but acted on by a uniform gravitational field.

In the 1916 paper on general relativity Einstein formulated equations describing the geometry of space-time. The new geometry provides for the geodesic (curved) propagation of light-rays in the presence of gravitational fields; in weak fields Newtonian laws remain very nearly correct, and the Einstein field equations include a 'stress energy tensor' term for dealing with the interaction between matter, space-time, and gravitation. Einstein also predicted the red-shift of starlight in the presence of gravitational fields. Later he added a 'cosmological term' to make his equations conform to the then existing idea of a static universe. Friedmann (1922) found that this term was superfluous for an expanding universe (a theory to be confirmed later by Hubble) and showed that Einstein's original equations had a solution for this situation. The flavour of current work directly based on these discoveries is easily conveyed. In a well-publicised 1972 paper[9] an experiment with round-the-world travelling clocks was said to have resolved the 'clock paradox' introduced by Einstein in the first 1905 paper. In 1978 it was claimed that Einstein had made a mistake, and that the 1972 experiment was inconclusive.[10] This claim in turn has been rebutted,[11] but the rebuttal has been rejected.[12] Another article[13] about space, time, and gravity, based upon the principle of equivalence, cites the 1911 paper in which Einstein discusses this idea; since it contains a lengthy discussion about the possible effects of inertial acceleration upon clocks, and continues with the field equations, it also cites a translated version of the 1916 paper. From a consideration of standard relativity theory, but especially from 'extended principle of equivalence' equations, the authors show that time-keeping by terrestrial clocks should be latitude-dependent because of the earth's rotation. By comparing the difference between the time-keeping of a number of caesium standard clocks at different latitudes to an accuracy of one part in 10^{15} (taking account of residual errors, gravitational red-shift, velocity, and acceleration), they conclude that inertial acceleration does offset ideal clock rates. The implications of this for international time-keeping are discussed.

Articles embodying current applications of Einstein's theories in particle physics,[14] cosmology[15] and mathematical concepts[16, 17] are numerous, of which those cited here are but a few examples; in one unusual article, Einstein's principle of equivalence is cited in the context of a discussion of direction-finding by hornets in search of food.[18] Current progress in the hunt for gravitational waves has also been discussed.[19] Here there is an exposition of Einstein's 1916 predictions; but in many current articles Einstein's contribution is considered to be so well known that the author only inserts a reference *en passant* following phrases like 'In recent years the problem of quantising non-Abelian gauge fields has received much attention'.

Finally, it is interesting to note that an author starting his article with the words 'Black holes are now the subject-matter of at least half the papers in general relativity' supplies only one *en passant* reference to Einstein attached to the phrase ' . . . so that the global hyperbolicity requirement is obeyed'.[20]

Quantum theory

Quantum theory is about the study of h – the position, path and velocity of wave packets or particles within prescribed limits of uncertainty. In the early years of the twentieth century interest was concentrated on black body radiation in the form of energy quanta or electromagnetic fields – according to Wien, Planck and Rayleigh. Einstein's first major paper explained the radiation of energy in terms of independent energy quanta and the release of electrons by the action of light, a much more precise explanation. This is the paper which Einstein called 'very revolutionary'. The apparent relationship of Einstein's equation ($e = hvn$) to Planck's work is misleading since the idea of a gas-particle-like radiation *was* truly revolutionary. In 1917 article, Einstein developed Planck's radiation formula further, introducing the concept of energy level transitions. This laid the foundation for the idea of the wave—particle duality of light,[21] leading to the work done in the late 'twenties by Pauli, Schrödinger, Dirac, Jordan, and Heisenberg, and to the development of modern quantum mechanics.[22,23]

The reason why some of today's articles citing Einstein's quantum theory contain the words STIMULATED EMISSION/, LASER and MASER (Table 5) is that his 1917 article 'enunciated the basic theory and was then largely ignored; the first successful device was operated in 1954'.[24] Precisely the same comment is made by Arthur Schawlow,[25] colleague of C. H. Townes — inventor of the maser, and optical maser (laser) pioneer. Einstein's first paper is considered to be the major step towards the huge amount of work which followed later in the century on photo-emission from metal surfaces.[26]

Controversies in quantum mechanics are still going strong. Einstein's 1935 paper and an article by Freedman[27] were co-cited by 10 papers published in 1977. Freedman took issue with Einstein's ideas about underlying deterministic structures; later authors cite both papers in the course of developing their arguments about the conflicting viewpoints.

Some mention should be made here of the Bose—Einstein Statistics; they are usually considered to be an aspect of quantum theory. S. M. Bose published an article in *Z. Phys.*, 1924 about a way of counting the possible states of light quanta that gave support to Planck's theories. Einstein applied this idea to counting particles of an ideal gas because of his deep conviction about the analogy between light and matter (A. Einstein, *Sitzungsber. Preuss. Akad. Wiss.*, Berlin, vol. 22, 1924, p. 261). Evidently these statistics are important today for understanding the behaviour of certain gases — for instance, in helium mixtures.[28]

Brownian movement; diffusion

Work in this area is usually considered to be part of Einstein's 'statistical theories'; it is often included with quantum theory because it shares the same basic approach. It is more convenient here to separate these areas because of the applied nature of current work based on Brownian movement.

Einstein's first article about this subject (number 2 in Table 4) dealt with the molecular-kinetic theory of heat, the motion of Brownian particles suspended in a liquid composed of molecules which are very small compared with the particles, and the rate of diffusion of the particles due to random collisions with molecules. The equation ('Einstein's diffusion equation') is $D = kt/f$, where D is the diffusion coefficient, k Boltzmann's constant, t absolute temperature, and f resistance to particle mobility; sometimes it is written $D = Kt \times b$, where b is mobility. In his articles 5 and 8 in Table 4, Einstein worked out some more details about elastic constants — in particular the bulk stress of a fluid and the equation $\mu^* = \mu(1 + 5\phi/2)$, where μ^* is the effective viscosity, μ the viscosity of the suspending fluid and ϕ the volume fraction of the particles.

Einstein demonstrated the reality of molecules when knowledge about the structure of matter was in its infancy. His work in this area is often associated with M. V. Smoluchowski;[29] authors co-cite the work of both men.

The repercussions of Einstein's work are evident in a remarkable variety of disciplines. We find citing articles published in journals such as *Tectonophysics, Polymer engineering and science, Rheologica Acta,* and *Industrial and engineering chemistry.* The relationship between article 2 about Brownian motion and diffusion and articles 5 and 8 about molecular dimensions and elastic constants is well described by Batchelor.[30] Current articles citing article 2 are about applications of the diffusion equation. What could be more topical than the mechanics of aerosol particles in their interaction with the atmosphere[31] or more unexpected than the properties of milk and its casein micelles?[32] Einstein's equations play an important part in both subjects. In an article about semiconductors we learn that 'Einstein's work on diffusion about seventy years ago led to a fundamental relation between diffusivity and mobility of charged carriers . . . of great importance in semiconductor physics for device analysis and design'.[33] The wide impact of Einstein's work is equally well demonstrated in an article about black holes. In this case the reference is to the 'density of states of a dissipative system discovered by Einstein in the course of his work on Brownian motion',[34] with no reference to his work on relativity.

Literature citing articles 5 and 8 is often about composite materials and plastics (see Table 5). Here, current work often starts with a modified version of the viscosity equation to take account of the higher volume loading of filled polymer systems. The rheology and strength properties of the set materials depends upon these considerations.[35, 36] In a different field the equation is used in connection with the effects of the shape of suspended particles upon viscosity.[37]

Light scattering

We have several times mentioned the problem of considering one aspect of Einstein's work in isolation from the remainder. Article 7 is perceived as being isolated by a number of today's authors. In this article a fluctuation theory is proposed for explaining critical opalescence in a one-component system. Smoluchowski[29] also made some proposals independently about the problem. This work was developed for studying two-component systems by Debye and others.

In present-day applications light-scattering is used as a sensitive measure of a change of state; for instance, the 'Spinodal' is the point of phase separation — say the appearance of droplets in suspension in a binary solution. Critical light scattering is a method of determining the spinodal of polymer solutions based on the multi-component development of Einstein's work by Zernicke and Stockmayer. Commercial light-scattering apparatus is available for measuring the light scattered at several angles. The technique is used in metallurgy, glass technology and polymers, and may also be used for determining z-average molecular weights[38] and for gas system studies by X-ray scattering.[39]

Conclusion

We noted that four out of the 11 early articles most heavily cited today were by Einstein (Table 1). In 1977, no less than 105 of the articles processed for the *SCI* had the word EINSTEIN in the title from which it may be assumed that the subject-matter was substantially connected with his work. In 1977 EINSTEIN A., received 452 citations in total. Considering the time which has elapsed since Einstein published his most important articles, the direct influence and on-going interest in his work is quite extraordinary. We have examined a sufficiently large sample of the citing articles to note that a high proportion of them stem directly from his research or contain discussions of developments prompted by his various theories. The number of these articles, their interdisciplinary character and the comments made by their authors confirm the outstanding influence and direct impact of Einstein's work on today's science.

Notes

1. E. Garfield, 'Citation indexing for studying science', *Nature,* vol. 227, 1970, pp. 669–71.
2. E. Garfield, 'Highly cited articles. 26. Some classic papers of the late 19th and early 20th centuries', *Current Contents,* no. 21, 1976, pp. 5–9.
3. Although Einstein died in 1955, a large number of his cited works, published between 1901 and 1973, are listed in the *SCI.* Some, exhibiting bibliographic variations, were 'created' idiosyncratically by citing authors, but others are translations or selected works republished after his death. For example, three almost identical works each collect a number of citations: R. Fürth, ed., *Untersuchungen über die Theorie der Brownschen Bewegungen,* 1922; R. Fürth, ed., A. D. Cowper, trans., *Investigations on the theory of Brownian movement,* 1926; and A. Einstein, *Investigations on the theory of Brownian motion,* Dover Publications, 1956. Each of these includes the 1906 *Annalen der Physik* paper and authors cite this paper or one of the republications as convenient. Similarly any of the translations of the 1917 survey of relativity (in German) into Spanish, Italian, Russian, French, Hungarian, Yiddish and Hebrew are cited.
4. L. de Broglie, 'A general survey of the work of Albert Einstein', in P. A. Schilpp, ed., *Albert Einstein: philosopher scientist,* Harper & Row, 1949.
5. M. J. Klein, 'Thermodynamics in Einstein's thought', *Science,* vol. 157 (3788), 1967, pp. 509–16.
6. The *Science Citation Index* commenced publication in 1961; the *SCI* ('SCISEARCH') file is available on-line (from 1974) in Lockheed's DIALOG service, Palo Alto, California, and is accessible in the UK by direct dialling. Lists of citing articles may be printed out by submitting a 'cited reference' question to DIALOG. For instance a list of the articles with titles citing A. EINSTEIN. ANN. PHYS., 17, 549, 1905, will be printed out on request for any particular year. The generation of lists in this manner is quicker than manual look-up followed by writing or typing from the printed *SCI.*

   The citing articles can also provide another kind of consensus; if *n* of them cite an earlier article *A* and also an earlier article *B*, there may be some relationship between the *co-cited* articles *A* and *B* – particularly if the value of *n* is high. For example, out of the 23 1977 articles which cite ANN. PHYS., 19, 289, 1906, and the 16 which cited ANN. PHYS., 34, 591, 1911, eleven articles cite *both* the Einstein papers (n = 11). This is hardly surprising in view of the subject relationship between these two articles (see Table 4). Computer programs have been developed for operating on *SCI* data to identify pairs of co-citing articles for selected values of *n*; this leads to some interesting new ways of citation analysis (see reference 7). As perceived by co-citing authors, the relationship between the work of Einstein and the work of other scientists has been identified by this method, and will be referred to later.

   We may note, in passing, that Einstein's original major articles in *Annalen der Physik* themselves contained very few references – an indication of their originality. His four major articles, published in 1905, contained a total of 12 references, seven of which were in one article. His 1905 article on special relativity contained no references; in the second he needed 750 words to revolutionise physics; he concluded with the classic understatement 'Es ist nicht ausgeschlossen, daß bei Körpern, deren Energieinhalt in hohem Maße veränderlich ist z.B. bei den Radiumsalzen, eine Prüfung der Theorie gelingen wird' ('It is not impossible that with bodies whose energy content is highly variable, for example as with radium salts, the theory will be successfully tested').
7. H. G. Small and B. C. Griffith, 'The structure of scientific literatures. 1. Identifying and graphing specialities', *Science Studies,* vol. 4, 1974, pp. 17–40, and B. C. Griffith, H. G. Small, J. A. Stonehill and S. Dey, 'The structure of scientific literatures. 2. Towards a macro- and micro-structure for science', *Science Studies,* vol. 4, 1974, pp. 339–65.
8. J. H. Taylor, L. A. Fowler, P. M. McCullouch, 'Measurements of general relativistic effects in the binary pulsar PSR 1913+16', *Nature,* vol. 277, 1979, pp. 437–39.
9. J. C. Hafele and R. L. Keating, 'Around-the-world atomic clocks', *Science,* vol. 177 (4044), 1972, pp. 166–8.
10. L. Essen, 'Relativity and time signals', *Wireless World,* vol. 84 (1514), 1978, pp. 44–5.
11. D. Griffiths, 'Relativity and time signals', *Wireless World,* vol. 84 (1516), 1978, pp. 57–8.
12. L. Essen, 'Relativity and time signals', *Wireless World,* vol. 84 (1516), 1978, p. 58.
13. W. H. Cannon and O. G. Jensen, 'Terrestrial timekeeping and general relativity – a discovery', *Science,* vol. 188 (4186), 1975, pp. 317–28.
14. J. Bailey (and 11 others), 'Measurements of relativistic time dilatation for positive and negative muons in a circular orbit', *Nature,* vol. 268 (5618), 1977, pp. 301–4.
15. E. R. Harrison, 'Observational tests in cosmology', *Nature,* vol. 260 (5552), 1976, pp. 591–2.
16. H. A. Atwater, 'Transformation to rotating coordinates', *Nature,* vol. 228 (5268), 1970, pp. 272–3.
17. C. H. McGruder, 'Field energies and principles of equivalence', *Nature,* vol. 272 (5656), 1978, pp. 806–7.

18. J. Ishay and D. Sadeh, 'Direction finding by hornets under gravitational and centrifugal forces', *Science,* vol. 190 (4216), 1975, pp. 802–4.

19. J. Hough and R. Drever, 'Gravitational waves – a tough challenge', *New Scientist,* vol. 79 (116), 1978, pp. 464–7.

20. F. J. Tipler, 'Black holes in closed universes', *Nature,* vol. 270 (5637), 1977, pp. 500–1.

21. See F. Hund, *The history of quantum theory,* Harrap, 1974.

22. Subsequently Einstein, believing quantum mechanics to be incomplete, argued inconclusively with Bohr. In 1935 he published a paper dealing with what is usually known as the 'Einstein–Podolsky–Rosen paradox' – a two particle problem which appeared to be unsolvable in terms of current theory. A supporting paradox was also introduced by Schrödinger ('Schrödinger's cat'). The unified field concept came nearer in 1978 as a result of experiments with the Stanford accelerator.

23. L. E. Ballantine, 'Einstein's interpretation of quantum mechanics', *Amer. J. Phys.,* vol. 40, 1972, pp. 1763–71.

24. W. A. Gambling, 'Lasers and optical electronics', *Radio and electronic engineer,* vol. 45 (10), 1975, pp. 537–42.

25. A. L. Schawlow, 'Masers and lasers', *IEEE Trans. Electron Devices,* vol. ED-23 (7), 1976, pp. 773–9.

26. M. L. Glasser and A. Bagchi, 'Theories of photoemission from metal surfaces', *Progr. Surface Sci.,* vol. 7 (3), 1976, pp. 113–48.

27. S. J. Freedman and J. F. Clauser, 'Experimental test of local hidden-variable theories', *Phys. Rev. Letts.,* vol. 28 (14), 1972, pp. 938–41.

28. E. G. Cohen, 'Quantum statistics and liquid helium-3-helium-4 mixtures', *Science,* vol. 197 (4298), 1977, pp. 11–16.

29. M. V. Smoluchowski, *Ann. Phys.,* vol. 21, 1906, p. 756.

30. G. K. Batchelor, 'The effect of Brownian motion on the bulk stress in a suspension of spherical particles', *J. Fluid Mech.,* vol. 83 (1), 1977, pp. 97–117.

31. Y. I. Yalamov, L. Y. Vasiljeva and E. R. Schukin, 'The study of various mechanisms of in-cloud scavenging of large, moderately large, and small aerosol particles', *J. Colloid and Interface Sci.,* vol. 62 (3), 1977, pp. 503–8.

32. R. K. Dewan and V. A. Bloomfield, 'Molecular weight of bovine milk casein micelles from diffusion and viscosity measurements', *J. Dairy Sci.,* vol. 56 (1), 1973, pp. 66–8.

33. R. K. Jain, 'Calculation of the Fermi level, carrier concentration, effective intrinsic concentration, and Einstein relation in n- and p-type germanium and silicon', *Phys. Stat. Sol.,* vol. (a) 42, 1977, pp. 221–6.

34. P. Candelas and D. W. Sciama, 'Irreversible thermodynamics of black holes', *Phys. Rev. Letts.,* vol. 38 (23), 1977, pp. 1372–5.

35. R. J. Crowson and R. G. C. Arridge, 'The elastic properties in bulk and shear of a glass bead reinforced epoxy resin composite', *J. Materials Sci.,* vol. 12 (1977), 1977, pp. 2154–64.

36. D. M. Bigg, 'Rheology and wire coating of high atomic number low density polyethelene composites', *Polymer Eng. and Sci.,* vol. 17 (10), 1977, pp. 745–50.

37. P. H. Elworthy, 'The structure of Lecithin micelles in benzene solution', *J. Chem. Soc.,* part 2, 1959, p. 1951.

38. J. Goldsbrough, 'Spinodal – its impact on metallurgy, glass technology and polymer science', *Sci. Progr.,* vol. 60 (329), 1972, pp. 281–97.

39. B. Chu and J. S. Lim, 'Small angle scattering of X-rays from carbon dioxide in the vicinity of its critical point', *J. Chem. Phys.,* vol. 53 (12), 1970, p. 4454.

The excellence of Einstein's theory of gravitation

P. A. M. Dirac

Paul Dirac, FRS, was born in 1902. He was Lucasian Professor of Mathematics, Cambridge, between 1932 and 1969. He was co-winner, with Erwin Schrödinger, of the Nobel Prize for Physics 'for the discovery of new productive forms of atomic theory'. He is at present at Florida State University, Tallahassee, USA.

Paper on the impact of modern scientific ideas on society given to a UNESCO symposium, 1978.

Einstein gave us a new theory of gravitation connected with the curvature of space. He started a whole new line of activity for physicists. He set them working with non-Euclidean space. The particular kind of space that Einstein introduced was Riemann space, a space that can be embedded in a flat space of a larger number of dimensions.

Under the stimulus of Einstein various people have considered introducing other kinds of space into physics, but so far without any real success. So far as is known at present, the space introduced by Einstein is the one used by Nature.

Einstein's theory of relativity remained unknown, except to a few specialists, until the end of 1918, when the First World War came to an end. It then came in with a terrific impact. It presented the world with a new style of thinking, a new philosophy.

It came at a time when everyone was sick of the war — those who had won as well as those who had lost. People wanted something new. Relativity provided just what was wanted and was seized upon by the general public and became the central topic of conversation. It allowed people to forget for a time the horrors of the war they had come through.

Innumerable articles about relativity were written in newspapers, magazines and everywhere. Never before or since has a scientific idea aroused so much and such wide-spread interest. Most of what was said or written referred to general philosophical ideas and did not have the precision required for serious scientific discussion. Very little precise information was available. But still people were happy just to expound their views.

I was an engineering student at Bristol university at the time, and of course the students took up this subject and discussed it extensively among themselves. But the students as well as the professors did not have precise information about it and knew nothing of the underlying mathematics. We could only talk about the philosophical implications and accept the universal belief that it was a good theory.

In England we had one man, A. S. Eddington, who really understood relativity and became the leader and the authority on the subject. He was very much concerned with the astronomical consequences of the theory and the possibilities of checking it by observations. There were three possibilities for testing the theory, which everyone soon became familiar with from the publicity given by Eddington.

The first test involved the planet Mercury. It had been known for a long time that there was a discrepancy between the motion of this planet and the Newtonian theory. Its perihelion was observed to be precessing by the amount 42 seconds per century, which could not be explained by the Newtonian theory. The Einstein theory required such a precession and gave the correct amount, 42 seconds per century. It was a wonderful success for the theory. It is said that Einstein himself was not unduly elated when he heard of this success. He was so confident that his theory had to be right.

The Einstein theory of gravitation requires that light passing close by the sun shall be deflected. The Newtonian theory also requires a deflection, but only half the amount of the Einstein theory. So, by observing stars on the far side of the sun whose light has passed close to the sun to reach us, we can test the Einstein theory. This is the second test.

The observations can be carried out only at a time of a total eclipse of the sun, otherwise the sun's light makes it impossible to see the stars. There was a suitable eclipse in 1919. Two expeditions were sent out to observe it; both were organised by Eddington and one was led by him. Both expeditions obtained results supporting the Einstein theory and against the Newtonian theory. The accuracy of the confirmation was only moderate owing to the inherent difficulty of the observations. Since then similar observations have been made at various later total eclipses. Einstein's theory has always been confirmed, although the accuracy has not been as great as one would desire.

The discovery of radio stars provided an alternative way of checking on the second test, using radio waves instead of light waves. One needs a radio source behind the sun. One just has to wait until the sun passes close in front of a radio star and then observe whether the apparent position of the star is deflected. One does not need a total eclipse for such observations, as the sun is not a strong radio source.

The use of radio waves instead of light waves brings in a complication because radio waves are deflected by the sun's corona. But one can make observations for two different wave lengths, for which the deflection caused by the corona is different, so that it can be separated from the Einstein effect. The result is that the Einstein theory is confirmed, with an accuracy much greater than that attainable with light waves.

The third effect which provides a means of testing the Einstein theory is the red-shift of spectral lines caused by a gravitational potential at their point of origin. The obvious place to look for this effect is in light from the surface of the sun. But the effect here is obscured by the Doppler effect coming from motion of the emitting matter. By estimating the Doppler effect one gets rough support for the Einstein theory, but it is too rough to be an effective test.

The discovery of white dwarf stars provides a better way of testing for this effect. In a white dwarf the matter is so highly condensed that the gravitational potential at the surface is very large, and so the Einstein red-shift is large. When one knows enough about the white dwarf to determine its mass and radius one can made a good test of the Einstein theory. One finds that the theory is well confirmed.

This effect can also be checked by terrestrial experiments, as was shown by R. L. Mössbauer. One sets up in the laboratory an emitter of electromagnetic waves and observes them at a place lower than the place of emission, where the gravitational potential is less. It is best to use gamma rays of a definite frequency for this experiment. One finds that the frequency is increased by the change in gravitational potential. The amount of this increase confirms the Einstein theory, with an accuracy greater than any astronomical test for this effect.

Recently a fourth test has been added to the three classical ones. This is concerned with the time taken by light to pass close by the sun. The Einstein theory requires a delay. This can be observed if one projects radar waves to a planet on the far side of the sun, and then observes the time taken for the reflected waves to get back to earth. With the use of radar waves the retardation is affected by the sun's corona and again one has to use two different wave lengths to disentangle the corona effect from the Einstein effect.

The observations have been carried out by I. I. Shapiro who has found good confirmation of the Einstein theory.

One can also get evidence about the Einstein theory from the observation of binary pulsars. A pulsar emits pulses of radio waves which normally have extremely high regularity. However, if the pulsar forms part of a binary system, its rotation around the other star introduces irregularities, coming from the Doppler effect associated with its motion and also from the Einstein precession effect, like the effect in the first test, in the orbit of the pulsar around its companion. This effect is very large, much larger than in the case of Mercury.

The observations give qualitative support to the Einstein theory, but one cannot make a quantitative check because one does not know enough about the parameters of the binary system.

I have enumerated the successes of the Einstein theory of gravitation. It is a long list, quite impressive. In every case the Einstein theory is confirmed, with greater or less accuracy depending on the precision with which the observations can be made and the uncertainties that they involve.

Let us now face the question: suppose a discrepancy had appeared, well confirmed and substantiated, between the theory and observations. How should one react to it? How would Einstein himself have reacted to it? Should one then consider the theory wrong?

I would say that the answer to the last question is emphatically No. The Einstein theory of gravitation has a character of excellence of its own. Anyone who appreciates the fundamental harmony connecting the way Nature runs and general mathematical principles must feel that a theory with the beauty and elegance of Einstein's theory *has* to be substantially correct. If a discrepancy should appear in some application of the theory, it must be caused by some secondary feature relating to this application which has not been adequately taken into account, and not by a failure of the general principles of the theory. One has a great confidence in the theory arising from its great beauty, quite independent of its detailed successes. It must have been such confidence in the essential beauty of the mathematical description of Nature which inspired Einstein in his quest for a theory of gravitation.

When Einstein was working on building up his theory of gravitation he was not trying to account for some results of observations. Far from it. His entire procedure was to search for a beautiful theory, a theory of a type that Nature would choose. Of course it needs real genius to be able to imagine what Nature should be like, just from abstract thinking about it. Einstein was able to do it.

Somehow he got the idea of connecting gravitation with the curvature of space. He was able to develop a mathematical scheme incorporating this idea. He was guided only by consideration of the beauty of the equations. Of course one is free to choose equations as one likes, subject only to the rigours of the mathematics, but these set a strong limitation on one's freedom.

The result of such a procedure is a theory of great simplicity and elegance in its basic ideas. One has an overpowering belief that its foundations must be correct quite independent of its agreement with observation. If a discrepancy should turn up, one cannot let it interfere with one's confidence in the correctness of the general scheme. One must ascribe it to some detail of the nature of an incompleteness rather than a failure.

Any theory that we can construct is probably incomplete. There is so much that is still unknown. So one need not be too much disturbed by a discrepancy. It should not be considered as detracting from the excellence of a theory that has been put forward on the basis of an inspired feeling of what Nature is like.

I can illustrate these remarks by referring to another important physical discovery of recent times, Schrödinger's discovery of the wave equation of quantum mechanics. Schrödinger was working with de Broglie waves. De Broglie had postulated, simply on the grounds of mathematical beauty, that waves were associated with the motion of any material particle. Schrödinger generalised the idea so as to obtain an elegant equation for waves associated with an electron moving in an electromagnetic field. He applied his equation to the electron in a hydrogen atom and worked out the spectrum of hydrogen. The result was not in agreement with observation.

Schrödinger was then very dejected. He lacked faith in the excellence of his basic ideas and assumed his whole line of approach was wrong. He then abandoned it. Only some months later did he recover from his dejection sufficiently to go back to this work. He then noticed that his theory was in agreement with observation in the approximation in which one neglects effects associated with the special theory of relativity, and he published his equation as a non-relativistic theory of the hydrogen atom.

The discrepancy was later on explained as arising from the spin of the electron, which was unknown at the time Schrödinger did his pioneering work. The moral of the story is that one should be dominated by considerations of mathematical beauty and not be too much perturbed by discrepancies with observation. They may very well be caused by secondary effects which get explained later.

A discrepancy with the Einstein theory of gravitation has not yet arisen, but it may arise in the future. It should then be interpreted, not in terms of the basic ideas being wrong, but as a need to supplement the theory with further developments in it.

There are two directions in which such further developments may be needed. They concern, first, the method by which electromagnetic fields are brought into the theory, and, second, cosmological requirements, which, at great distances, affect the conditions for any application of the equations. Einstein himself was well aware of both these problems.

There is an obvious way of applying the standard equations of electromagnetic theory to a Riemann space so that they can be fitted in with Einstein's theory of gravitation. But does the resulting theory really apply to Nature? One has doubts about it because it leaves the electromagnetic field as something detached, which is only added on afterwards. The gravitational field and the electromagnetic field are the only fields with long-range forces and one is led to believe that the connection between them must be very intimate. Maybe one of them cannot be conceived without the other and one needs a more general kind of geometry that handles both together. Einstein himself had ideas of this kind and spent decades looking for an improved field theory that would unify gravitation and electromagnetism. He did not find a satisfactory result and the first problem must be considered as still unsolved.

With regard to the second one can make some progress. One needs a cosmological model for the universe. In applying it one considers local irregularities associated with the existence of stars and galaxies to be smoothed out.

A first model was soon provided by Einstein himself. Einstein's model gave a static universe of uniform density, closed in spatial directions. It required a constant, the cosmological constant, to be brought into the field equations. It was not an acceptable model because of its static character, which conflicted with the observations that the galaxies are receding from us, with velocities that increase as their distance from us increases.

A second model was provided by de Sitter. De Sitter's model does lead to a recession of distant matter, as required by observation. It also involves a cosmological constant in the field equations. However, de Sitter's model gives zero density of matter in the smoothed-out universe, so it is not acceptable.

A third model was proposed jointly by Einstein and de Sitter in 1932. This model involves the line element

$$ds^2 = dt^2 - t^{4/3}\,(dx^2 + dy^2 + dz^2) \tag{1}$$

It requires no cosmological constant. It gives the recession of distant matter correctly, and it gives the correct order of magnitude for the density of matter. It also gives zero for the pressure, which is what one would require with the approximations involved in this kind of a model. It is thus an acceptable model.

Various other models consistent with Einstein's field equations, with or without a cosmological constant, have been worked out by Friedmann, Lemaitre and others. One may use any of these models as a supplement to Einstein's field equations to fix the conditions at infinite distances. The changes that they would give rise to in the applications of Einstein's equations to the solar system would be too small to affect the successes discussed earlier.

There is a development which is a supplement to the Einstein theory. This is the Large Numbers Hypothesis (LNH), which asserts that all the very large numbers that can be constructed from the various 'constants' of physics and astronomy are really not constant, but are connected with the epoch, the time since the creation of the universe, by simple equations with coefficients close to unity. They are thus varying with the epoch, according to a law which is determined by their size.

If one adopts this LNH, one finds that the only permitted cosmological model is the third model mentioned above. One is no longer bothered by having many acceptable alternatives.

The microwave radiation that is observed to be coming from space uniformly in all directions and that is interpreted as the remains of a primordial fireball agrees with the LNH when combined with the third model. It provides strong evidence in favour of both the LNH and the third model.

The LNH leads to the requirement that the *ds* of Einstein's theory, call it ds_E, is not the same as the *ds* measured by atomic clocks, call it ds_A. They are related by

$$ds_E = t_A \, ds_A, \tag{2}$$

where t_A is the epoch as measured by an atomic clock. This is an effect which can be checked by observation. Van Flandern has been searching for this effect for some years, comparing observations of the moon referred to ephemeris time with observations referred to atomic time, but he has not yet got a reliable result.

Some evidence on this question has recently been obtained from lunar laser ranging carried out by Williams, Sinclair and Yoder. Their results provide weak confirmation of equation (2), but the uncertainties are too large for one to be able to draw any definite conclusions.

Equation (2) can also be tested by radar observations of the planets. Here one sends radar waves to one of the nearer planets and observes the waves that are reflected back to earth. The time taken for the journey to and fro is then measured with an atomic clock. Shapiro and Reasenberg have been working on this method. They obtain results agreeing with equation (2), but the confirmation is only a weak one because the probable errors in the results of the observations are about as large as the effects being sought for.

With the Viking expedition to Mars in 1976, some apparatus was landed on Mars which enables the distance of Mars from Earth to be monitored with very great accuracy. This will enable one to get a much better check of equation (2). The results are not yet available, but will probably come soon.

I have discussed a possible way of supplementing the Einstein theory, by adding to it the LNH. There is as yet no direct confirmation of it by observation. But I feel confident in the basic correctness of the idea because of its simplicity and the natural way in which it fills a gap by providing a unique cosmological model.

Einstein and non-locality in the quantum theory

David Bohm and Basil Hiley

David Bohm was born at Wilkes-Barre, Pennsylvania, in 1917. Until 1947 he worked in the Radiation Laboratory at the University of California on plasma theory and the theory of synchrotrons and synchro-cyclotrons. He has been on the staff at Princeton University, at Sao Paulo University, and at the Technion, Haifa. Since 1961 he has been a professor at Birkbeck College, London University, where he works on the fundamentals of quantum theory, relativity and philosophical questions. His books include *Quantum theory* (1951), *Causality and chance in modern physics* (1957) and *The special theory of relativity* (1966).

Basil James Hiley was born in 1935 at Rangoon, Burma. He was educated at King's College, London, where he obtained his PhD in 1962. At present he is a lecturer at Birkbeck College. He has written various papers on co-operative phenomena, the fundamentals of quantum mechanics and nuclear physics.

It is generally well known that Einstein did not accept the fundamental and irreducible indeterminism of the usual interpretation of the quantum theory. His statement 'God does not play dice' is quite famous.[1] However, it is not commonly realised that quantum mechanics contains another fundamental and irreducible feature which Einstein rejected even more strongly: non-locality. Indeed it was implicit in his entire world view that connections between any elements whatsoever had to be local. That is, connections could either take place when such elements were in contact at the same point in space-time, or be propagated continuously across infinitesimal distances by the actions of fields. Einstein regarded the failure of quantum mechanics to fit in with this notion of locality as a serious weakness in the whole theory, a weakness which indicated the need for developing a fundamentally new kind of theory.

As we shall see in this paper, there is significant evidence to show that Einstein was basically right in this regard, so that the attempt thus to understand non-locality may indeed point to radically new concepts which could help us toward a better understanding of the universe.

Einstein's views on locality

Let us begin with a brief discussion of why Einstein's notion of locality is essential to the theory of relativity. The previous non-relativistic theory did not require locality: indeed, one of the basic notions of non-relativistic mechanics was that of the extended rigid body, which would instantly respond as a whole (that is, non-locally) if a force were applied to any part. We illustrate this feature in the space-time diagram below (Figure 1):

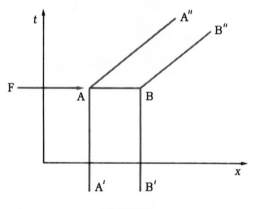

FIGURE 1

The world lines of the boundaries of an object at rest are given by A'A and B'B. A force, F, is applied at A, and the entire object accelerates as a single rigid body, so that the subsequent world lines of its boundaries are AA" and BB". The force, F, is thus transmitted instantaneously from A to B. But, as is well known, relativity theory implied that such an instantaneous transmission of force across a finite distance would be inconsistent with the principle of causality. It follows that the concept of the extended rigid body cannot be used in relativity theory. Nor can we regard such a body as made of smaller objects (atoms, for example) that are rigid, since the same problem of infinite speed of transmission of force would arise with these. Ultimately, we would have to suppose that the particle was a mathematical point, P, of no extension at all (that is, entirely local). Its world line is illustrated in Figure 2:

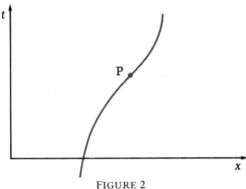

FIGURE 2

However it is necessary in general that particles be considered as sources of field. As soon as we do this we discover that the field at such a point is infinite. This leads to various inconsistencies, such as an infinite mass for the particle. As Dirac has shown in a classical model of the electron,[2] this infinity can be consistently 'subtracted off', but,then this leads to other incorrect features for the motion of the particle, such as instability (that is, self-acceleration). It thus appears that relativity denies the extended rigid body, and yet also must reject the point particle which appears to be a natural alternative to this. (Quantum mechanically, similar infinities arise, and these can also be 'subtracted off' to give what is called a re-normalised theory. But it is not clear what this means, with regard to the local and non-local character of the electron, especially since the very process of renormalisation is, in itself, a non-local transformation of the 'quantum state of the universe'.)

Einstein hoped that a way out of this dilemma could be found through the general theory of relativity. This theory begins with a further extension of the concept of locality. Thus, the principle of the equivalence of inertial and gravitational masses is interpreted through a curvilinear transformation of space-time co-ordinates, which can 'transform away' the gravitational field in a given infinitesimal region, so demonstrating a connection between the properties of inertia and the local gravitational field. Einstein then deduced a set of non-linear differential equations for these fields which were, of course, also local.

It was Einstein's further new idea that he could explain the extended object (a particle, for instance) as a feature of such a field. In particular he supposed that there could exist a singularity of this field, or at least a field function ϕ, which was large only in a small region, as illustrated in Figure 3:

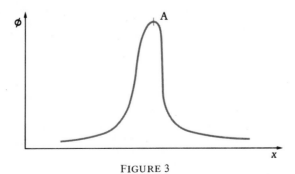

FIGURE 3

The maximum field would be at A, and the field would quickly fall to small values at appreciable distances from A.

If the field equations had been linear, such a field would have been unstable, and indeed would have spread out very quickly. But it was well known that non-linear equations could in principle admit of such pulse-like solutions that were stable and even allowed the field pulse to remain together as it moved as a whole through space, with a certain overall momentum. Einstein took such a pulse as a model of a particle.

In this theory, the basic concept is that of a field, with entirely local properties. A particle is regarded as a non-local form in this field. But this non-local form plays no fundamental part in the theory. It is an abstraction, a shadow, so to speak, which has to move according to the laws of the local fields on which this form lies. Nevertheless it is important to note that highly non-local features of particles may thus be comprehended in terms of local field entities. Consider, for example, the two particles shown in Figure 4:

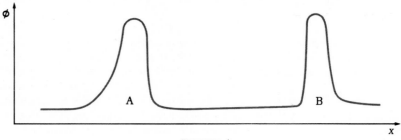

FIGURE 4

Actually, the fields of these bodies never fall to zero, so that in some sense, the two particles merge, in one continuous field which has two maxima. The separate 'particles', A and B, are thus abstractions. They may be generally useful when the pulses are sufficiently separated; but, in a fundamental sense, there is no localisable particle at all. Rather, Einstein describes the universe as an undivided whole. Nevertheless he constructs it as a set of extended forms lying on entirely local field elements, obeying laws based only on local connections of these elements.

It has to be added, however, that Einstein was well aware that the actual stability of matter (for instance, stationary states of atoms) had to be closely related to the laws of quantum theory. Therefore it would be of no use to postulate non-linear equations that gave stable structures whose size and general behaviour were unrelated to these laws. Indeed he hoped that by including some sort of random fluctuations in his field quantities, he could simultaneously comprehend relativistic and quantum laws.

Here one should note that the present quantum theory implies that even in empty space, any field undergoes certain irreducible 'zero-point' fluctuations, which do not directly show up in the movement of matter or light. Current calculations lead to an infinite value for this energy, but one may surmise that some factor not clearly evident in current theories will limit this to a finite but rather large value. Einstein's idea might thus take the form of supposing that empty space contains a random background of fluctuating fields obeying non-linear equations. With the aid of this the statistical features of the quantum theory (as well as other features) could ultimately be explained.

During the latter part of his life, Einstein made a serious and sustained attempt to realise such a programme. In doing this he was hampered by the fact that his non-linear field equations were too difficult to solve by any known methods. On the whole, what he was able to achieve was not very promising, particularly with regard to the ultimate goal of incorporating quantum laws in his non-linear field equations. At best, one can say that his results were inconclusive, but most physicists who work in the field seem to regard his goal itself as unrealisable.

To sum up Einstein's views, then: Einstein took locality as an absolutely inevitable requirement for any reasonable physical theory. Thus, in commenting on the possibility of non-locality in quantum theory, he said: 'Quantum theory cannot be reconciled with the idea that physics should represent a reality in time and space, free from spooky action at a distance'.[3]

This way of thinking was certainly required for consistency with relativity theory. But Einstein did not primarily regard the need for locality as an inference from relativity theory. Rather, he felt that locality was so self-evident that he would regard the feature of non-locality in a theory as evidence that it was either incorrect, or at the very least, a fragmentary abstraction from a more nearly correct theory that would be local in his proposed non-linear field theory; for example, non-local features of extended particles are explained as forms on a deeper local field.

Non-locality as implied by quantum theory

Let us now go on to consider the quantum theory. Here one encounters non-local features even at a very elementary level. Thus, if electrons are diffracted by a pair of slits, one finds that when two slits are open, electrons fail to arrive at certain points where they actually can arrive when only one slit is open. If the electron is thought of as a particle which goes through either one slit or the other, this experiment indicates that its behaviour depends on conditions at the second slit, which is far away. This already is at least some *form* of non-locality. On the other hand, the electron might be thought of as an extended entity that goes through both slits together. But this would be a more extreme form of non-locality, in the sense that it would deny that the electron occupies a definite region of space, even when the region is defined only within microscopic orders of magnitude.

A much more deeply penetrating kind of non-locality in the quantum theory is demonstrated by the well-known experiment of Einstein, Podolsky and Rosen.[4] We shall discuss this experiment briefly in terms of the measurement of spin variables as indicated in Figure 5. Let us begin with a molecule, M, of total spin zero, consisting of two atoms, A and B, each having spin $\frac{1}{2}\hbar$. Let this atom be disintegrated by some means; for example, by purely electrostatic forces, in such a way that its spin variables are not affected significantly. The atoms start to separate, after which they cease to interact. To make the implications clearer, let us imagine that the experiment is done in interstellar space, leaving room to allow the atoms to separate by many miles before they are measured, so that a considerable amount of time (perhaps a minute or an hour) might elapse between the disintegration of the

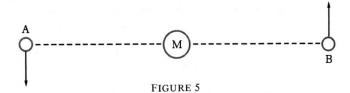

FIGURE 5

molecule and the detection of the atoms. The experiment then consists in measuring the spins of atoms A and B.

Let us begin by measuring the z component of the spin of each atom. The quantum theory predicts that these two results will always come out to be opposite (as indicated by the arrows in Figure 5). We then go on to measure the x component or, indeed, any other component of the spin of each atom. The theory states that these also will come out to be opposite.

It is easy to see that a similar result would be obtained in classical mechanics. Here a molecule of total spin zero would have the respective spin vectors of atom A and atom B oppositely directed. As the atoms flew apart, the spin vectors would remain opposite (since they were not affected by the force that disintegrated the atom). And so, no matter which components were measured, they would evidently have to come out to be opposite. This is explained with the aid of the simple, classical model, which always attributes to each atom a well-defined spin vector opposite to that of the other.

In quantum mechanics, however, this kind of simple model can no longer be used. As is well known, the operators for the spin components in different directions do not commute, from which it follows that they cannot all be determined together in a measurement. Indeed only one component can be measured at a given time, though this may be *any* component.

One may illustrate the meaning of this by considering an atom whose spin is well-defined in the z direction (say, $+\frac{1}{2}\hbar$). It follows then that the x and y directions are not defined. In a rough picture we may imagine that the spin vector lies in a cone, whose axis is in the z direction, as illustrated in Figure 6. Its direction normal to z, however, fluctuates at random so that the x and y components are not determined:

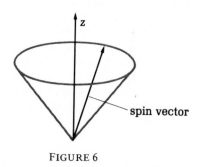

FIGURE 6

If one now measures the spin in the x direction then, after the measurement is over, this cone will point in the x direction, while the y and z components will fluctuate at random. More generally, if the spin is measured in the direction of any unit vector $\hat{n}$, the components perpendicular to $\hat{n}$ will fluctuate at random.

It seems clear from the above description that a measurement of the component of the spin in the direction, $\hat{n}$, must do more than merely establish the value of that component. It must also somehow introduce a random fluctuation into the two perpendicular components. This evidently implies that a measurement *disturbs* or *modifies* the observed system in a certain unpredictable and uncontrollable way. Indeed, the notion of such a disturbance has been long familiar to us, having first been suggested by Heisenberg, in connection with how, in a hypothetical gamma-ray microscope, the particle momentum is unpredictably altered in its interaction with the quantum of electromagnetic energy used to make it visible.

Let us now return to the measurement of spin variables for the two atoms, A and B. It is clear that in measuring the spin of atom A in any direction, $\hat{n}$, we may suppose that the measuring apparatus disturbs the two components of the spin perpendicular to $\hat{n}$ in an unpredictable and uncontrollable way. But what about atom B? Quantum theory predicts not only that the spin component in the direction of n̂ will be opposite to that of B, but that the two perpendicular spin components will also fluctuate at random. But recall that after atoms A and B separate they do not interact in any way at all. How then can a random disturbance of the spin components of atom A normal to n̂ bring about a corresponding random disturbance of these components of the spin of atom B?

To put the difficulty more clearly still: while the atoms are still in flight, the apparatus measuring atom A may be orientated in a different direction, n̂′. Atom B must then respond with an opposite spin in this direction and with a corresponding random fluctuation in the two perpendicular directions. And all of this must happen without any interaction between these two atoms. Surely this would seem to be an example of the 'ghostly' non-local connection of distant events that Einstein regarded as absurd. Certainly, we can at least say that any simple model resembling the classical type which attributes independent spin properties to each of two non-interacting atoms separated in space would not be able to fit in with the implications of the quantum theory (as we shall bring out in more detail later).

As we have already indicated, Einstein regarded such an idea as so unacceptable that he took the analysis of this experiment as a devastating criticism of the quantum theory. In particular, his proposal was that the quantum theory, while probably yielding correct predictions for this experiment, did not provide a complete or even adequate description of the reality which underlies this peculiar connection of distant events. Rather, he considered it to be little more than a fragmentary abstraction — one that was useful for calculations. In doing this he was, of course, going against the views of most physicists, who regarded (and still generally regard) the quantum theory as capable of yielding the most complete description of reality that is in principle possible.

Let us consider experimental tests for whether or not this non-local feature is actually present. One of the earliest such tests[5] was made possible by observations carried out on a pair of gamma ray photons, with mutually perpendicular plane polarisations, arising in the annihilation of positronium. Mathematically, this leads to the same sort of situation as that arising in the example treated in this paper (that is, the molecule of total spin zero). In an analysis of the two-photon experiment,[6] the predictions of the quantum theory were compared with those of a model originally suggested by Furry.[7] In this model it was supposed that, after the two quanta separated, each went into a definite spin state which was opposite to that of the other, but with a random distribution of orientations of this state. The actual experimental results agreed with the quantum theory and clearly did not agree with the predictions arising from Furry's model. Since the essential assumption of this model is that after the two particles separate, their spin states are independent, it is clear that the experiment constitutes a confirmation of quantum mechanical non-locality.

Later, an important refinement of the criteria distinguishing locality and non-locality was developed by Bell,[8] in the form of an inequality which has to be satisfied if the states of two separated particles are to be independent. A considerable number of experiments have been done aimed at testing this inequality,[9] and it may be said that they generally confirm the quantum theory with its feature of non-locality. Other experiments,[10] which are refinements of the test of the Furry model, provide similar confirmation for particle separations as great as five metres.

Stapp has come out with a further mathematical analysis of this problem, which shows unambiguously that if the quantum theory is right, then (in terms of the spin example) the result obtained by any measurement on particle B will, in general, depend on the orientation of the apparatus that measures particle A.[11] Stapp's work thus confirms the conclusion that quantum theory implies non-locality, to which we come in our more intuitive treatment.

A suggested way of understanding non-locality in Einstein's approach

It seems clear both from theoretical analysis and from experiment that non-locality is a fact and that we have, therefore, to understand what it means. If we accept that quantum theory provides the most complete possible description of reality, then non-locality means simply a further extension of the many ways in which this theory defies understanding in terms of any ordinary conception of reality. Thus, we can only agree that to obtain a successful algorithm for computations, correctly predicting the results of experiments, is the only genuine goal of physics. Einstein could not accept this approach. Rather, as we indicated earlier, he felt that the theory must yield an objective description of the universe, whose elements moreover are local, as well as locally connected. As we have already pointed out, experimental proof of the non-locality implied by quantum theory was not contrary to Einstein's expectations. What Einstein insisted on was the need for some new and broader theoretical framework, within which the question of how non-locality of this kind comes about could be discussed on the basis of a more fundamental notion of reality – a reality that is objective and local.

The authors feel that Einstein was right to ask for a concept of a deeper reality that could explain how actual observable events are related and connected. However we do not agree with his insistence that the basic elements of such a theory must be local. We regard this question as open. And, therefore, we feel that it would be worthwhile to explore what can be done in a theory that starts with non-local entities and with non-local connections. We have in fact started to do this in terms of our theory of implicate order.[12] We will not discuss our views in this paper; instead we will indicate a set of ideas that appears to open up the possibility of explaining non-locality on Einsteinian lines – that is, in terms of a local field which has non-local connections and which obeys non-linear equations.

First of all, we call attention to a well-known property of non-linear equations: namely, the existence of stable orbits or limit cycles which are such that small deviations lead either to rapid oscillatory motion around the stable movement, or to motions that die away exponentially. Work on these lines has recently been extended by Thom.[13] He has systematically expressed the conditions in which whole families of orbits bifurcate into two groups, one of which goes towards one stable state of motion while the other goes towards a second such state. This sort of behaviour might well be considered to be a possible model of the transition between quantum states, in which a given atom may jump from any particular state into one of a range of possible states.

If we consider that in Einstein's non-linear field theory the vacuum would contain an intense excitation of field energy, a kind of random background, we can see that even if the basic equations of this field are local, their non-linearity might bring about stable movements involving a co-ordination of fields at separated parts of space and time (just as, for example, separate coupled non-linear oscillators can tend to fall into synchronism). So the universal field may get into a state of motion near a stable set of 'orbits' in which the distant and separate particle-like pulses move together in co-ordination (more like what happens in a ballet dance, rather than what happens in a crowd of people jostling each other at random). We must recall here that this applies not only to the observed system but also to the 'particles' that constitute the observing apparatus. Of course, such co-ordinated sets of movements would correspond only to certain states of movement of the whole (for instance, those containing a molecule of total spin zero) while there would be other states (for example, those containing two atoms, each with well-defined spins) in which there would not be this kind of co-ordination.

Let us now consider the experiment in which positronium decays into a pair of gamma rays with mutually perpendicular plane polarisations (see Figure 7):

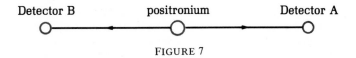

FIGURE 7

We are supposing that, through non-linearity, the movements of the positronium and of the 'particles' constituting the detectors A and B are co-ordinated in a certain way. The nature of the co-ordination is such that a positronium atom decays into two photons with suitably related but well-defined polarisations — when the detectors are in a condition to absorb these photons. Once the photon has started to move toward the detector, it simply 'carries' its own state of polarisation. So there is no direct non-local connection in the movements of the photons. Rather, the non-locality is of a different kind, arising in a new quality of co-ordination of movement. This co-ordination is not the result of 'pre-established harmony' on the lines, for example, of the monads of Leibniz. Nor is it like a 'conspiracy' (any more than the common phase of two coupled synchronous motors would be a conspiracy). Rather, it is a stable form of overall movement, carried in a continuous and local way by the 'vacuum' fields in the background. Small deviations from this stable form of the whole movement either oscillate so rapidly that they produce negligible effects, or else die away exponentially. The results of measurements carried out in any one place may thus come to depend on what measurements are being carried out at another far away place, in the manner required by the experiment of Einstein, Podolsky and Rosen. And yet it may be possible to understand all this by means of an underlying local field.

The above discussion deals with those photons that are actually detected and measured. But one may ask what happens to those that go off in some other direction, and which do not go through any detectors, to be measured? To deal with these, one generalises the idea of co-ordinated movement and says that *any* material system which absorbs a quantum is similarly co-ordinated with the source of that quantum. (Thus, the measuring apparatus now plays no special role in our theory; it is treated as just a special case of the properties of the universal field.) This is essentially an extension of Wheeler and Feynman's absorber theory of radiation,[14] in which no photon is emitted unless there is matter somewhere which will absorb it. As Wheeler and Feynman have shown, this theory can give just as consistent a description of the process of radiation as is given by the current theory, in which an atom radiates independently of whether an absorber is available or not.

More generally, no transitions from one state to another take place unless the rest of the universe, in its co-ordinated movements, is ready to absorb (or emit) the energy which has to be exchanged in this transition.

To return to the experiment with the gamma rays from positronium decay, one sees that it is crucial to understand the question of the relative timing of the operator of detectors A and B. Thus in one of the experiments that has actually been done[11] the detectors are arranged to work simultaneously within 10^{-9} seconds. The distance from source to detector is so large that a light signal would take about 10^{-8} seconds so that there evidently can be no immediate connections of the two events, through the fluctuations of the 'vacuum' field. Nevertheless all the parts of the system have had a long time (many days at least) to come to equilibrium through the forces carried in these vacuum fluctuations. So the positronium will be ready to decay into photons of a certain polarisation only when the detectors are ready to receive these photons. The experiment can therefore still be comprehended within this explanation of quantum-mechanical non-locality.

If we recall that the co-ordinated movements are only the stable limit of fluctuations around them, the idea arises that one might destroy the co-ordination by suddenly disturbing one of the detectors in a way that is not related to what happens to the rest of the system. Thus we might hope to obtain a result in which the predictions of the quantum theory break down. The extreme difficulty of doing this becomes evident, however, when we recall that all matter is constituted of field pulses, on top of the vacuum fluctuations, and that these pulses have generally been in existence for at least some thousands of millions of years. So it seems likely that even the apparatus that is used to 'disturb' the detector will be in 'equilibrium' and will thus simply combine with the rest, to form a larger whole, that is still co-ordinated according to the laws of the quantum theory.

Of course, one cannot say *a priori* how far these co-ordinations will actually go. In principle it is always possible that when the detectors are sufficiently separated, and when they are 'disturbed' in a sufficiently rapid and 'random' way, the co-ordination will break down. Thus, experiments such as those of Aspect,[15] which are designed to test this point, are always worth doing. Yet one must remember that at present there is no known reason to suppose that they will be successful in finding a set of conditions in which quantum theory will yield wrong predictions.

To sum up, then, we say that the non-locality of quantum theory points to the need to develop a new principle of co-ordinated movements, which may well extend over the entire universe. Even though the fields are propagated locally, the forms of matter will have to be understood as an undivided whole, not only because they merge and unite through the background of vacuum fluctuations, but also because through non-linearity they may work together even over long distances. This indicates that though the universe may be immense, the various parts are not basically isolated from each other. Such a universe could perhaps have been contained within Einstein's vision of a fundamental reality, ordered and lawful, and yet rich and subtle enough to comprehend all the complexities of the world as we know it.

Appendix
On the failure of communication between Bohr and Einstein over the meaning
of the quantum theory

The experiment of Einstein, Podolsky and Rosen was actually first suggested as part of a basic criticism of Bohr's views on the quantum theory. As we shall see, the whole issue was never cleared up in a satisfactory way. Indeed, what happened was that Bohr and Einstein failed to communicate, with the result that it eventually became impossible for these two or for anyone else who followed along their lines to develop a common set of concepts that could cover both relativity and quantum theory.[16]

The ideas and attitudes involved in this issue are very subtle and difficult to sum up, but we shall try here to indicate their essential implications. Firstly, it must be emphasised that Bohr's treatment of measurement was very different from the much more generally familiar approach of Heisenberg, in terms of an unpredictable and uncontrollable disturbance of the observed system. In fact, Bohr never used Heisenberg's microscope experiment at all. Rather, he started from the indivisibility of the quantum of action, which is basic to the whole of the quantum theory.[17] From this, he inferred that the usual classical analysis of the world in terms of separate elements (atoms, electrons, and so on) moving continuously and following well-defined causal laws could not actually be carried out at a quantum level of accuracy. Because of this, he regarded the Heisenberg indeterminacy relations as expressing a limit of the domain of applicability of classical concepts (such as position and momentum). He was very deeply concerned with putting this limitation in a *consistent* way, and went to great pains to develop such a coherent formulation of the meaning of the quantum theory. In doing this, he was led to emphasise strongly that the indivisibility of the quantum of action further implies that the classical notion of making a sharp distinction between the observing apparatus and the object that is observed can no longer correctly be applied. Rather the entire experimental set-up, including the form of the experimental conditions and the content (meaning) of the experimental results, has to be regarded as a single whole, which is itself not susceptible to further analysis. Thus it would make no more sense to refer to a separately existing electron which has been observed, for example, through a microscope, than it would to refer to the various items in the pattern of a carpet — such as trees, flowers or people — as separately existent. All of these items are just abstractions, conceptually taken out of a *whole* pattern, and similarly, electron and microscope are also such abstractions, conceptually taken out of the *whole phenomenon*.

If one thinks of the pattern on the carpet, one is led immediately to consider the threads out of which it is woven. It is true that the various items depicted in this pattern are merely abstractions, having no independent reality of their own. But the ground of this whole pattern is the independent reality of the woven structure of the carpet itself. Is there not likewise a deeper non-classical level of independently existent micro-reality, out of which the pattern of the observing apparatus and what is observed are, so to speak, woven? Bohr's answer to this is in the negative. More accurately, he regards it as meaningless even to discuss such a deeper level of micro-reality. All that is meaningful, in Bohr's view, is a description of the *phenomena* and of the relationship between them.

Now we had previously used the algorithms of classical physics (differential equations) to start with one set of phenomena and to predict a later set in a deterministic way — at least in principle. Instead, in quantum theory, we use the quantum algorithm (matrix equations) to make only statistical predictions of similar but later sets of phenomena. But the crucial point is not the statistical character of these predictions: it is that, unlike what happens in classical physics, we cannot find any way at all to obtain a description of a deeper level of micro-reality that could permit us to account for how these phenomena are related.

It seems fairly evident that Bohr's views are closely related to those of Kant. We can know only the phenomena and not 'the thing in itself'. But they are actually much more radical. For example, Kant allowed himself to consider the notion of an atomic theory which went far beyond the phenomena that were available to him at the time. He might have said that ultimately we could not know the 'atoms in themselves' but only their phenomenal manifestations; but unlike Bohr he did not assert that the kinds of phenomena accessible to observation at the time provided an ultimate limit in the concepts that could be used for description and explanation in physics.

What then led Bohr to this radical extension of the Kantian view? In justifying his position, Bohr begins by saying that the description of the experimental conditions and the expression of the content of the experimental results must be capable of being rendered unambiguous in meaning, if the data on which science is based are to be publicly communicable (and without this, science as we know it would evidently be impossible). In his view, one tries at first to achieve this by using the language and concepts that are ready to hand in ordinary common sense. Where greater precision is necessary, one goes on to the language and concepts of classical physics, which he felt were the *only* possible refinements of common sense that could have the sort of freedom from ambiguity that is required. When asked why one might not develop new non-classical language and concepts for this purpose, he simply stated that we are suspended in language, and do not know which way is up and which is down.[18] By this, he seemed to mean that because of the need to use the language and the overall set of general concepts that we actually have, there is no way to get out of these. We are therefore restricted to classical concepts, and since these do not actually apply beyond the limits of the Heisenberg indeterminacy relations, it follows that there can be no way at all to conceive of a deeper and subtler 'woven' structure that underlies the phenomena.

The further development of physics can then only be in finding equations and algorithms that help to describe and correlate the phenomena.

It was on the basis of such notions that Bohr[19] answered the criticisms implied in the experiment of Einstein, Podolsky and Rosen. What he did, in essence, was simply to note that the entire experiment is still a single, whole, unanalysable phenomenon. This is not altered by the fact that some time passes between the disintegration of the molecule, M, and the observation of the spins of atoms A and B. The equations of quantum mechanics simply correlate the phenomena statistically. One sees that there is no inconsistency in the phenomena themselves, as predicted by the quantum theory.

Paradoxes arise only when one insists on going beyond the correlation of phenomena (for example, by supposing that there has to be a 'disturbance' that accounts for the fluctuations of the spin of atom B, which are themselves related to the measurement that has been carried out in particle A).

In this context, it is very significant that Bohr felt that Einstein's theory of relativity was basically similar in spirit to his own approach. Thus, Bohr understood Einstein to be saying that one should give up attempts at a detailed explanation of matter in terms of a deeper level, such as that implied by the assumption of a space-filling ether. It seemed to Bohr that Einstein wanted to discuss only the observable relationships in the movement of matter and to find invariant laws in these relationships. Bohr felt that this was basically similar to what he was doing in the quantum domain.

In this connection, one can note that Einstein, in his early work on relativity, frequently described phenomena belonging to a certain frame of reference in terms of non-relativistic concepts (in particular, whenever these phenomena consisted only of sets of events and structures involving speeds small compared with that of light). In such a case, one could imagine an observer in a co-moving reference frame. If one wished then to see what the phenomena would be like to another observer, one replaced the earlier non-relativistic algorithm (the Galilean transformation) by a new relativistic algorithm (the Lorentz transformation) which is incompatible with the laws of non-relativistic physics. Bohr regarded this as very similar to his own approach, in which he described the phenomena in terms of classical concepts and replaced the classical equations of motion by a new quantum algorithm that is not compatible with classical laws. In view of this and other similarities Bohr was surprised and in fact disappointed to find that Einstein had no sympathy for his approach at all.

Einstein's main comment on Bohr's position can be summed up in his description of it as a 'tranquiliser philosophy'. He felt that it served mainly to allow physicists to remain complacently undisturbed, in the face of a genuine challenge to the generally accepted notion that quantum theory had a fundamental kind of validity, rather than mainly being a broadly useful set of rules of computation.

The whole issue between Einstein and Bohr was never adequately cleared up. Many points of confusion can be detected in the discussion between them. Thus in some respects Bohr's surprise at Einstein's rejection of his views seems well founded. Indeed, it does seem that in his early work Einstein was somewhat influenced by positivist philosophy especially in his emphasis on the role of observers with their frames of reference. As indicated above, this was actually not far from Bohr's views on the subject. However, it seems that Einstein was only superficially influenced by positivism, and not deeply. When asked about this later by Heisenberg,[20] he said that he regarded the emphasis on observers largely as a heuristic device, and not as a fundamental approach to the laws of nature. Indeed, it is clear that in his later views, based on the notion of a universal field, Einstein totally rejected positivism. Thus he regarded his field theory as in essence a kind of revival of the notion of a space-filling ether, which is, however, relativistic rather than non-relativistic. But somehow Bohr could never take such views seriously and probably regarded them as naïve, a return to 'primitive realism'. It is doubtful that he ever understood how superficial was Einstein's commitment to positivism.

Vice versa, Einstein could never take seriously Bohr's primary concern with a consistent description of the wholeness of the quantum process. It is very likely that he took this to be a question of secondary importance, which would probably be cleared up in a simple and natural way when the basic questions had been properly answered. To him, the basic requirement was to obtain a description of the universe as an objective reality (and not merely as a structure of phenomena). And almost equally important was the requirement that the elements of the theory be local and locally connected. Bohr's insistence on the ultimately unanalysable wholeness of the phenomenon was clearly in contradiction with the first requirement of an objective reality. And Bohr's further treatment of an entire process (for example, the disintegration of a molecule and the observation of its constituent atoms), capable of indefinite extension in space and in time, as an unanalysable whole was an even more thoroughgoing denial of all that Einstein felt to be right and true. Thus, merely in stating his position, Bohr was effectively ruling out the very basis of Einstein's thought as irrelevant and indeed meaningless. Likewise, Einstein was doing the same with regard to Bohr's thought. Each was compelled to base his arguments on premises that could not even seriously be considered by the other. And so it was not possible for Bohr and Einstein, so to speak, to 'lay out their differences on the table for inspection'. But since it was never clearly *stated* that this was the case, the whole discussion was pervaded by a certain deep kind of confusion that was very difficult to resolve. Neither was able really to answer what the other deeply meant in his criticisms.

As a result, the two men were never able to meet, and they continued to argue at cross purposes, until gradually they drifted apart with little or no contact or communication. This result was not only unfortunate in itself. It left the whole of physics divided into two parts, relativity and quantum theory, which have never been brought together consistently. Each has its own concepts, which do not cohere with those of the other. (Relativity with its notions of locality, continuity, causality, and quantum theory with its non-locality, non-continuity and non-causality.) Attempts to make a coherent combination of relativity and quantum theory have had a certain limited success as mathematical algorithms, but as yet such attempts have not given the slightest hint of how to bridge the conceptual gap between them. So the failure of communication between Bohr and Einstein has left us with the heritage of a deep cleavage in the whole of physics, which has been sustained and intensified by the fact that those who work in relativity and those who work in quantum theory have generally become progressively more isolated from each other – a development that is almost a reflection of what happened between Bohr and Einstein.

It has been an important part of our intention in this paper to make at least a preliminary step toward ending the state of cleavage between the *concepts* of relativity and those of quantum theory. In doing this, our approach has been to listen carefully and comprehensively to the implications and deeper meanings of what was said both by Bohr and by Einstein.

To begin with, we feel that there is no way to justify Bohr's presupposition that the only suitable concepts for physics are those of common sense, refined where necessary to those of classical physics. To make such a presupposition merely on the basis of the fact that one knows no other will surely prevent us from ever enquiring seriously into this question. Such an approach cannot do other than imprison our minds very firmly in a limited groove which we will be very unlikely to come out of. Our view is that it is perfectly legitimate and indeed quite necessary to explore with the aim of eventually discovering wholly new concepts – concepts capable of describing an underlying reality. This reality should be independent of our particular experimental arrangements, and of what the results of such experiments may mean to physicists, or to others who are studying or observing nature. In terms of these concepts, we can regard what is underlying as primary, while the phenomena (including experimental arrangements and their results) will be secondary, dependent forms (as the forms on the carpet depend on its woven structure). With regard to this point, our view is essentially the same as that of Einstein (except that he gives much more importance to the requirement that the underlying reality be local than we do). But we differ from what Einstein would probably have thought in that we consider the general character of the phenomenal forms, as brought out by Bohr, to be a valuable clue to what the nature of the primary reality has to be. In particular we have used this clue to suggest that the non-linearity of the field equations must be such as to bring about a stable set of motions, co-ordinated over long distances. Of course, the idea of a stable limit cycle has long been familiar in classical mechanics. But such cycles have been regarded as secondary, particular features of specified systems and not part of the primary universal law of all matter and fields. To propose that such limit cycles are primary and universal, and also that they may involve fields in regions distant from each other is, in fact, a new concept. So, by giving more weight to Bohr's ideas that Einstein would have done, we may be able, perhaps, to help define the field concept in new ways that have the possibility of covering both the domain treated by relativity and that treated by quantum theory. Nevertheless, by taking Einstein's ideas more seriously than Bohr did, we have been able to carry over into the relativistic domain what is essential in Bohr's insights into the character of the quantum phenomena. And perhaps in this way we can begin on a new approach that does not continue the rigid grooves of thought that are behind the failure of communication between Bohr and Einstein.

Notes

1. P. A. Schilpp, ed., *Albert Einstein: philosopher scientist,* Harper & Row, New York, 1949.
2. P. Dirac, *Proc. Roy. Soc.,* vol. A. 167, 1938, pp. 148–69; ibid., vol. A. 180, 1942, pp. 1–29.
3. *The Born–Einstein letters,* Macmillan, London, 1971.
4. A. Einstein, B. Podolsky and N. Rosen, *Phys. Rev.,* vol. 47, 1935, pp. 777–80.
5. C. S. Wu and I. Shaknov, *Phys. Rev.,* vol. 77, 1950, p. 136.
6. D. Bohm and Y. Aharanov, *Phys. Rev.,* vol. 108, 1957, pp. 1070–6.
7. W. H. Furry, *Phys. Rev.,* vol. 49, 1936, pp. 393–9.
8. J. S. Bell, *Physics,* vol. 1, 1964, pp. 195–200.
9. J. L. Lopes and M. Paty, *Quantum mechanics, a half-century later,* Reidel, Dordrecht, 1977.
10. A. R. Wilson, J. Lowe and D. K. Butt, *J. Phys.: Nuclear Physics (G),* vol. 9, 1976, pp. 613–23.
11. H. P. Stapp, *Phys. Rev.,* vol. 3D, 1971, pp. 1303–20.
12. D. Bohm, *Foundations of physics,* vol. 1, 1971, pp. 359–81; ibid., vol. 3, 1973, pp. 139–68, and F. A. M. Frescura and B. J. Hiley, ibid., vol. 10, 1980, pp. 7–31.
13. R. Thom, *Structural stability and morphogenesis,* Benjamin, 1975.
14. J. A. Wheeler and R. Feynman, *Rev. Mod. Phys.,* vol. 21, 1949, pp. 425–33.
15. A. Aspect, *Physics Letters,* vol. 54A, 1975, pp. 117–18; and *Phys. Rev.,* vol. 14D, 1976, pp. 1944–51.
16. This question has been discussed in a preliminary way in D. Bohm and D. Schumacher, *On the failure of communication between Bohr and Einstein,* unpublished, 1972.
17. N. Bohr, *Atomic theory and the description of Nature,* Cambridge University Press, 1934.
18. See. A. Petersen, *Quantum physics and the philosophical tradition,* Cambridge, Massachusetts, 1968, p. 188.
19. N. Bohr, *Phys. Rev.,* vol. 48, 1935, p. 696.
20. W. Heisenberg, *Physics and beyond,* Allen & Unwin, 1971.

Einstein as guru? The case of Bose

William Blanpied

Dr William A. Blanpied, an experimental high energy physicist, is head of the US National Science Foundation's
Office of Special Projects. He was formerly editor of the
Harvard University Newsletter on Science, Technology and
Human Values. A serious amateur historian of science, he
became interested in the problems associated with the
transfer of Western science to non-Western cultures while
serving as a member of the US National Science Foundation's
science liaison staff in New Delhi, and has published several
articles on the subject.

Dr Blanpied interviewed Dr Satyendranath Bose in Delhi in
March 1971.

Albert Einstein's contributions to the development of what is now called the 'old' quantum physics may well have been more important than those of any other single physicist. He was the first to take seriously the full implications of the evidence that matter and energy both exhibit discrete, quantum properties at the most fundamental levels. The papers he published on quantum physics between 1905 and 1925 provided insights and interpretations of pivotal significance. Einstein's voluminous correspondence with other physicists during the same period, and the memoirs of many of these same physicists, also reveal the essential role he played as both critic and catalyst to his colleagues. Niels Bohr, who once characterised the history of quantum physics as involving 'a unique cooperation of a whole generation of physicists from many countries', would no doubt have agreed that that co-operation was brought about largely as a result of Einstein's unique efforts.[1]

Despite the encouragement he gave to the members of this generation of physicists, despite the influence many of their own ideas had on his thinking, Einstein never had a real collaborator. Yet, since one of the two consistent quantum mechanical theories that deal with the general, collective behaviour of large numbers of identical atoms or elementary particles is commonly referred to as the Bose—Einstein Statistics, it is sometimes assumed that Einstein at one time must have worked closely with someone named Bose.[2]

In fact, Satyendranath Bose was a rather obscure Indian physicist who met Einstein only briefly, if at all. But the recognition Bose has received by virtue of having his name linked with Einstein's is well deserved. A short paper entitled 'Planck's Law and the Light Quantum Hypothesis'[3] that Bose sent to Einstein on 4 June 1924, from the University of Dacca in East Bengal, solved an important problem in quantum theory, whose solution had eluded Einstein and other physicists for 19 years. More important, it provided Einstein with the essential clue he needed to formulate the first quantum mechanical theory of the ideal gas. It is the mathematical method Einstein employed in deriving that theory, a generalisation of the method introduced by Bose, that has been designated as the Bose—Einstein Statistics.

To Einstein and his European and American colleagues, the Bose—Einstein Statistics represented a significant extension of the power of quantum theory to describe the behaviour of large aggregates of indistinguishable particles. To Bose, they meant that and more, for to him they signified recognition by the one for whom he had the special reverence that an Indian reserves for his *guru*.

Bose in Calcutta

Satyendranath Bose was born on New Year's Day, 1894, in Calcutta, and in 1915 received his MSc degree in Mixed Mathematics from Presidency College in that city.[4] These were the years of the Bengali Renaissance, presided over by the ageing Rabindranath Tagore. One of Tagore's goals was to maintain cultural independence from Great Britain; but to a Bengali, cultural independence has never meant the automatic rejection of all things foreign. On the contrary, as early as 1828 the Bengali reformer, Ram Mohun Roy, had sought to establish a college in Calcutta where his young countrymen could learn Western science, for he regarded that knowledge as vital to them if they were to get on in a world dominated by European ideas.

During the 1870s, the Western-trained Bengali physician, Mahendralal Sircar, had initiated a vigorous and successful campaign among his countrymen for funds to establish an Indian Association for the Cultivation of Science in Calcutta, an institution where Indians could carry out scientific research on their own initiative, with the expectation that this would better equip them to deal with Europeans on their own terms. Sircar's strategy was consistent with that of the Indian National Congress. It held its first national meeting in 1885, and argued that when Indians could demonstrate that they had mastered the forms and substance of Western parliamentary democracy, they would prove to all the world that they were fit for political independence. Thus, when Bose and his class-mates received their college training, they learned to regard recognition by the international scientific community both as a virtue in its own right, and as a means, however indirect, to a political end.

In 1916, Sir Asutosh Mookerjee, a barrister and serious amateur mathematician who had become the first Indian Vice-Chancellor of Calcutta university, obtained funds from several wealthy Bengalis to found the College of Science at the university, the first academic institution in India to offer first-rate post-graduate instruction in science. Among the first lecturers appointed to the college were Bose and Meghnad Saha, who had been one of his class-mates at Presidency College.

These two young scientists and their colleagues were eager to make contributions that would be recognised internationally, and in so doing serve both physics and their country. In 1918, and again in 1920, Bose and Saha co-authored papers on statistical mechanics that were accepted for publication by an international journal.[5] In 1919 they also published a volume of Einstein's papers on relativity in English translation, one of the first such volumes in English to include his first papers on general relativity.

Bose left Calcutta in 1921 to assume the post of Reader in physics at the newly organised university of Dacca. Three years later, he sent off his four-page paper to Einstein for comment. It was to bring him the international recognition he had sought, and perhaps, ultimately, a certain burden of regret as well.

Bose's derivation of the Planck Law

The problem that Bose set out to solve in the paper he sent Einstein was to determine the frequency distribution of the light emitted from an ideal radiator, or *black body,* at a given temperature, without making any reference to the laws of classical electrodynamics.

In 1900, Max Planck had succeeded in obtaining the experimentally correct frequency distribution for black body radiation by imposing an *ad hoc* constraint onto the body of classical electrodynamics. He assumed that the vibrating atoms composing a black body could not emit arbitrarily small amounts of electromagnetic energy, or light, as would be the case in any classical theory. Rather, he constrained them to emit energy in amounts directly proportional to their frequencies. In other words, Planck assumed that vibrating atoms must emit electromagnetic energy in discrete quanta, rather than continuously.

Planck was later to recoil from the full implications of his *ad hoc* quantum assumption. But in a celebrated 1905 paper, Einstein took up the challenge with characteristic vigour. He hypothesised that if light was *emitted* from atoms in quanta, then light should exhibit other quantum properties as well, and proceeded to derive specific, experimentally verifiable conclusions from that hypothesis.[6]

During the next two decades, a growing number of physicists, often aided and abetted by Einstein, extended the quantum idea to the interpretation of additional electromagnetic phenomena, and also to the structure of atoms and molecules. Taken together, these results showed that a good deal of the presumably sacrosanct body of classical physics was suspect. Logical and historical consistency demanded that the Planck Law, which had marked the beginning of quantum theory, should be derivable without reference to classical electrodynamics. But that derivation proved to be elusive.

A quantum theoretical derivation of the Planck Law should have been relatively straightforward. One begins by assuming that the electromagnetic radiation, or light, about to be emitted from a black body is composed of a large number of quanta. This collection of quanta is then regarded as a sort of ideal quantum gas, just as classical physics regarded a container of hydrogen as a collection of atoms, or quanta of matter. To be sure, the 'light' gas is a very special gas, since its 'atoms' all have the same velocity and all have zero rest mass. But, for all that, it is still consistent to regard black-body radiation as a quantum gas. The problem, then, is to find the energy distribution of the 'atoms' of that gas at a given temperature. The Planck proportionality relationship between energy and frequency should then yield the desired frequency distribution.

The problem of finding the energy distribution of the atoms of an ordinary ideal gas had been worked out during the latter part of the nineteenth century, and involved well-known techniques of mathematical statistics.[7] But prior to Bose's 1924 paper, all attempts to derive the Planck Law by applying these methods to a gas consisting of light quanta were unsuccessful. Bose succeeded by noting that since the quanta of such a gas are *indistinguishable,* certain specific permutations of their energies should also be regarded as indistinguishable. If so, then a different statistical method would have to be used to count the number of quanta in each narrow energy range. That is, Bose showed that the Planck Law could be derived without reference to classical electrodynamics, *provided* classical statistical mechanics were modified.

Einstein was impressed with Bose's results. Not only did he translate the paper into German himself and submit it on Bose's behalf to the *Zeitschrift für Physik.* He also added a note to the text stating that: 'In my opinion, Bose's derivation of the Planck formula signifies an important advance. The method used also yields the quantum theory of an ideal gas as I will work out in detail elsewhere.'[8]

The Bose—Einstein Statistics

The paper that impressed Einstein so much did not exhaust Bose's interest in black-body radiation. On 15 June 1924, 11 days after sending his first paper to Einstein, and well before he could have known how it would be received, Bose sent off a second paper dealing with the emission/absorption of electromagnetic radiation by matter. Einstein also had this paper published. But now he added a remark stating that he could not completely agree with the author's conclusions.[9]

In early 1925, Bose tried to respond to these criticisms. But by that time the matter was not of great interest to Einstein. He had recognised almost at once (as he noted in his addendum to Bose's first paper) that the novel statistical method Bose had introduced could also be used to describe the properties of ordinary gases consisting not of identical light quanta, but of identical atoms. If so, then the classical statistical treatment of gases that had been developed during the latter part of the nineteenth century could only yield approximately correct results.

Einstein explored the detailed implications of his generalisation in two papers published, respectively, in July 1924 and January 1925. Taken together, these papers provide the framework for the Bose—Einstein Statistics.[10] They predicted that ideal gases would exhibit certain specific, experimentally verifiable non-classical properties under conditions of high pressure and low temperature; and the second paper placed certain *ad hoc* features of the Bose method on a sounder theoretical footing by appealing to the hypothesis, introduced by Louis de Broglie in 1924, that particles of matter have certain wave-like characteristics. Thus, as Martin Klein has argued, Einstein's generalisation of the Bose statistics was an important step in the transition from the 'old' quantum theory that had been evolving during the previous quarter century, to the full-blown quantum mechanics whose foundations were laid by Werner Heisenberg and Erwin Schrödinger in 1925 and 1926.[11]

Bose and Einstein

Sadly, perhaps, Einstein was ultimately repelled by the implications of that very quantum mechanics whose development he had done so much to foster. He could never reconcile himself to its rejection of classical determinism; nor could he accept its assertion that the fundamental laws of nature had to be formulated in terms of probability rather than strict causality.

Sadly, too, Bose ultimately seemed unable to exploit the recognition Einstein had conferred upon him as fully as he might have hoped. But he did make excellent short-term use of it. At the time he sent his first paper to Einstein his long-standing application for study leave from his university was still being considered. A handwritten postcard from Einstein stating that he regarded the paper as a most important contribution settled the study leave question immediately. Accordingly, in early September, Bose left India for two years in Europe.

The years Bose spent in Europe marked one of the most important periods in the history of modern physics. It would be pleasant to relate that Bose went directly to Einstein in Berlin, was immediately put into contact with a seminal European group, made additional fundamental contributions to quantum physics, and returned to India as its apostle.

Alas, nothing of the sort occurred. Bose went instead to Paris, where he remained for a year before going on to Berlin. Unfortunately, Einstein was in Leiden at that time, and was not to return for several weeks. It is not clear whether or not Bose had an opportunity to meet him when he did return. If so, the meeting must have been unproductive, for Bose later recalled that the only special privilege he ever enjoyed while in Berlin was the right to take books from the university library.

Bose's failure to proceed to Berlin and Einstein immediately after his arrival in Europe may not be as curious as it appears at first sight. As a young Indian who had never before travelled outside Bengal and who spoke English and French but little German, Bose would scarcely have presumed to approach the master without an invitation. Rather than approach Einstein directly, he sought out a circle of his compatriots in Paris and through them obtained an introduction to Paul Langevin, who, he hoped, might provide a route to Einstein.

It is clear that Bose longed for an invitation to work with his chosen master. In a letter written on 26 October 1924, a week after his arrival in Paris, Bose thanked Einstein for 'taking the trouble of translating the paper yourself and publishing it'. The letter concluded: 'I shall be glad if you grant me the permission to work with you, for it will mean for me the realisation of a long-cherished hope'.[12] Since none of Einstein's correspondence with Bose from this period has been preserved, the tenor of the response can only be inferred. But since Einstein never had a real collaborator, it is scarcely conceivable that he would have consented to assume the role of *guru* to a young Indian whom he had never met. Nor could he have been expected to understand either the symbolic meaning that international recognition had for this young Bengali scientist, or the almost mystical reverence that an Indian reserves for his *guru*. Yet, his apparent failure to understand seems to have been a severe disappointment to Bose.

Einstein certainly did send some sort of response to Bose's communication: in a letter dated 27 January 1925, Bose thanked Einstein for a note written in November of the previous year, in which Einstein had explained his objections to Bose's second paper. Bose outlined the way he proposed to deal with those objections. The letter closed with 'I am thinking of going to Berlin at the end of this winter, where I hope to have your inestimable help and guidance', a statement noticeably lacking in his earlier enthusiastic hope that Einstein would consent to let him work with him. Perhaps Bose regarded Einstein's objections to his second paper as a severe setback to his hopes. In any event, he delayed his journey to Berlin for another two months in order to study laboratory techniques in France. When he finally did arrive in Berlin, in October 1925, he discovered that he had lost whatever chance he might have had to work closely with Einstein.

The remainder of Bose's professional career must have been something of a disappointment to him. While he achieved reasonable academic honours, he published little of great significance. A year after his return to Dacca in the summer of 1926 he became professor of physics, and later head of the physics department. He remained at the university until 1945, when he returned to the University of Calcutta, first as professor of physics, then as Dean of the faculty of science from 1952 until his retirement in 1956. He did not publish another scientific paper until 1936, and between 1924 and his retirement published only 19 in all. Only two of the papers written after his return to India were concerned with quantum theory in any way whatsoever. Perhaps, like his *guru*, Bose was repelled with the turn that quantum theory had taken in its rejection of strict classical determinism. But this is only conjecture.

Bose's failure to make additional internationally recognised contributions to physics certainly could not have been due to any lack of interest or support from among his colleagues in India. Meghnad Saha, Bose's Presidency College class-mate, achieved an international reputation as a theoretical astrophysicist, and became one of the most influential scientists in pre-Independence and immediate post-Independence India. From the mid 'thirties until his death in 1956, he was also to play a leading role in the development of science policy in the country. Chandrashekra V. Raman, who was appointed Palit Professor of Physics at Calcutta university in 1918, two years after Bose's appointment as lecturer, was destined to become India's first Nobel laureate in science.

But if Bose's professional career was disappointing in a narrow academic sense, the charisma that attached to his name in the eyes of his countrymen as a result of its association with Einstein's was to endure. He was known throughout his career as a devoted and inspiring teacher. Some of his younger colleagues at the university of Calcutta continue to maintain that Bose made considerable contributions to physics through the work of his students. Perhaps he derived his ability to inspire his young countrymen from the fact that he had once been inspired by the master, no matter at what distance.

On more than one occasion Bose gave evidence that he regarded that charisma as something of a burden. To the end of his life he continued to express disappointment and on rare occasions even some trace of bitterness that he had never been able to work directly with Einstein. Yet Einstein remained his *guru*. In a letter dated 9 December 1945, the first he had written to Einstein in 20 years, Bose addressed him as 'one who owes much to you and your guidance in life'. Bose's last six papers deal with unified field theory, a topic that also absorbed Einstein during his last years, but which was well outside the main currents of conceptual thinking in physics. Indeed, the one extant letter from Einstein to Bose, written on 22 October 1953, deals with comments on a paper on unified field theory that had been sent to him by Bose.

Bose became an increasingly revered figure as he grew older. Special symposia were held at the university of Calcutta to commemorate his seventieth and eightieth birthdays. The second symposium took place a few weeks before his death on 4 February 1974. By that time Einstein was gone. So were Saha, Raman, and the rest of his colleagues who, as young men, had set out to prove that Indians could excel at modern science. Bose was one of the first to succeed in demonstrating the truth of that proposition. And because of that symbolic achievement, his countrymen continued to maintain a special reverence both for him and for his *guru*.

Notes

1. Niels Bohr, *Proc. Phys. Soc.,* vol. 78, 1961, p. 1101.
2. All elementary particles, atoms, and molecules have intrinsic angular momentum, or 'spin', equal either to an integral multiple of Planck's constant or to a one-half odd integral multiple (1/2, 3/2, . . .) of that constant. Identical particles in the first category obey the Bose—Einstein statistics. Those in the latter category obey the Fermi—Dirac statistics, the basic aspects of which were developed independently by Enrico Fermi and Paul Dirac.
3. S. N. Bose, *Z. Phys.,* vol. 26, 1924, p. 178.
4. For biographical details on Bose, see A. K. Datta and Asima Chatterjee, eds., *Satyendranath Bose seventieth birthday Commemorative Volume,* Eka Press, Calcutta, 1964, pp. 6—12.
5. S. N. Bose and M. N. Saha, 'On the influence of the finite volume of molecules on the equation of state', *Phil. Mag.,* vol. 36, 1918, p. 199; and 'On the Equation of State', *Phil. Mag.,* vol. 39, 1920, p. 169.
6. A. Einstein, *Ann. Phys.,* vol. 17, 1905, p. 132.
7. The basic structure of classical statistical mechanics, the Maxwell—Boltzmann statistics, was developed in the latter part of the nineteenth century by James Clerk Maxwell and later refined and generalised by Ludwig Boltzmann.
8. Einstein, in S. N. Bose, *Z. Phys., op. cit.*
9. S. N. Bose, *Z. Phys.,* vol. 27, 1924, p. 384.
10. A. Einstein, *Berl. Ber.,* 1924, p. 261; and *Berl. Ber.,* 1925, p. 3.
11. Martin Klein, *The natural philosopher,* vol. 3, 1964, pp. 38—46.
12. Six letters from Bose to Einstein and one from Einstein to Bose are included among the Einstein papers at the Institute for Advanced Study in Princeton, New Jersey. Five of the former were written between 4 June 1924 and 25 October 1925. These address Einstein variously as 'Respected Sir', 'Respected Master', 'Dear Master', and 'Revered Master'. The sixth letter from Bose is dated 9 December 1945. The single extant letter from Einstein to Bose is dated 22 October 1953. I am grateful to Miss Helen Dukas, custodian of the Einstein papers at Princeton, for providing me with copies of these letters.

3. The impact on society

The theory of relativity and our world view

A. R. Peacocke

Dr A. R. Peacocke is Dean of Clare College, Cambridge, England. Most of his career has been spent in research and teaching in physical biochemistry at the universities of Birmingham and Oxford; at the latter he was a Fellow of St. Peter's College. In 1971 he published *Science and the Christian experiment*, which was awarded the 1973 Lecomte du Nouy international prize, and in 1978 he delivered the Bampton Lectures at Oxford on 'Creation and the world of science'. In 1971 he took Anglican orders and since 1973 he has lectured at Cambridge on the relation of science and theology and on theoretical aspects of physical biochemistry. He has degrees in both science and theology.

What the theory of relativity is not — and what it is

In a much admired and widely used textbook of modern physics, based on lectures given to his classes at the California Institute of Technology, Richard Feynman turns aside in his exposition of relativity in physics to the views of what he calls 'cocktail-party philosophers'.[1] He describes these, while slyly hinting that the category may well include some professionals, as those who say, 'Oh, it is very simple: Einstein's theory says all is relative!' or 'That all is relative is a consequence of Einstein, and it has profound influence on our ideas', or 'It has been demonstrated in physics that phenomena depend upon your frame of reference'. As he rightly goes on to point out, if these remarks genuinely indicate all there is to Einstein's theory of relativity then one can legitimately wonder why so simple an idea underwent such a long period of gestation and needed the intellectual acumen and power of an Einstein to uncover it. The 'cocktail-party philosophers' have, of course, failed to perceive the depth of the theory and how it allows us to make definite predictions about the physical world. It is consistency with experiment that led, rather rapidly, to acceptance of the strange ideas contained in the special theory of relativity; and it was indeed as a result of reflection on certain experimental phenomena that Einstein first proposed the special theory.

The 'cocktail-party philosophers' have too readily and superficially transferred the scientific awareness of the relativity of different frames of reference from physical observations (of signals, length and times) to the cultural relativities which are to be discerned in ethics, social judgements, and political and religious attitudes — relativities based on quite other evidence and considerations. Einstein's theory of relativity is strictly restricted to the cognition and interpretation of physical phenomena and any analogies to other kinds of 'relativism' are superficial and can be highly misleading. Einstein's theory, in itself, warrants no such *general* relativising in these areas of human concern.

Indeed, those who make such extensions may have been misled by the word 'relativity', the usual shorthand title for Einstein's great intellectual creation. For the theory, far from saying that everything is relative, is concerned above all to exclude what is relative in the results of observations made from different moving systems, and to arrive at statements of laws which are the same whether the phenomena are described by one observer or another. In brief, the theory's aim is to arrive at what is *invariant* in the physical situation, and what is independent of a particular observer. We shall discuss this more fully below.[2]

Nevertheless, setting aside the observations of the 'cocktail-party philosophers', it remains true that Einstein's theory of relativity has profound consequences, as Bertrand Russell said, for 'our habits of thought'[3] and for our conception of the world in which we live — and also for the relation of our perceptions to it. That the theory has not already had these repercussions, now a hundred years since Einstein's birth, is testimony to how little education in scientific ideas there is even now among both intellectuals and the generality of the population as a whole. Here our intention is to describe some of the implications of Einstein's theory for the thinking of anyone concerned with the world and man's relation to it — implications relevant to any philosophical or theological interpretation of the world.

The principal features of Einstein's theory of relativity may, following Wenzl,[4] be identified as follows:

(1) For all systems moving uniformly in straight lines, the equal validity of not only Newtonian laws of mechanics, but also Maxwell's equations for the electromagnetic field; and the constancy of the velocity of light (c) with respect to *all* moving systems. Hence, by means of the Lorentz transformations, there follows the relativising of spatial and temporal measurements, and furthermore their co-ordination into a four-dimensional space-time continuum.

(2) The equivalence of mass (m) and energy (E), as expressed in Einstein's equation $E = mc^2$, which thereby connects those previously differentiated concepts of classical physics.

(3) The curvature of the space-time continuum by mass and energy in such a way that the *metric* (that is, its mathematical characteristics purely as space-time) becomes the expression for what appears to us as matter-energy and as gravitational fields.

(4) The world is a spatially limited, finite continuum, conforming to a non-Euclidean geometry and of increasing radius (though not necessarily existing for an 'infinite time').

Some negative consequences of Einstein's theory

By the 'negative' consequences we mean those effects of the theory of relativity that have, in iconoclastic fashion, demoted the status of certain concepts previously held to be given features of human thought — that is, given through the very nature of the intellect in the manner of Kant's synthetic *a priori*. These negative consequences are such that M. Capek, in his important work on *The philosophical impact of contemporary physics,* asserts:

'The present transformation of physics is far more radical than the famous "Copernican revolution" of the sixteenth century . . . the transition from the closed world to the infinite universe was not excessively difficult for human imagination: the earth merely exchanged its position with that of the sun, while the celestial spheres were swept away. The effort of imagination required for such steps was relatively small . . . the new Newtonian view of the universe was as pictorial as the old Aristotelian one; indeed, it was even more so. After elimination of secondary nonvisual qualities . . . its visual character became even more pronounced. . .

'Today we are in the midst of a far more radical transformation of our view of nature. The most revolutionary aspect of this transformation consists in the fact that the words "picture" and "view" lose entirely their etymological meaning. As the so-called primary qualities of matter now join the secondary qualities in their exit from the objective physical world, it is clear that the future conception of matter ought to be devoid of *all* sensory qualities, including even those which are subtly and implicitly present in seemingly abstract mathematical notions.'[5]

There has been, as Karl Heim has said,[6] a 'twilight of the gods' of classical physics — of absolute space, time, object and determinism. There has been almost a Wagnerian *Götterdämmerung* in which the golden prize of absolute intellectual ascendancy over nature's laws, which these gods had tried to grasp, has been finally sunk in the inscrutable depths of nature's fundamental intrinsic reality from which it had been so roughly alienated. The Valhalla of the world those gods had had constructed was consumed by the fires, first of relativity theory, then of quantum theory. Perhaps one of the first consequences of the theory of relativity is to induce a new scepticism within and towards science itself. For, as Feynman has put it,[7] the first discovery resulting from Einstein's principle of relativity is that 'even those ideas which have been held for a very long time and which have been very accurately verified might be wrong . . . we now have a much more humble point of view of our physical laws — everything *can* be wrong!'

Let us now consider some of the absolute 'gods' of classical, Newtonian physics that Einstein demonstrated to have feet of clay. Firstly, *space* was held to be homogeneous, three-dimensional in character and Euclidean in geometry. It was logically prior to any objects existing 'in' it. It was physically inert, infinite in extent and continuous – that is, infinitely divisible. It had an absoluteness which for Newton seemed to be one of the God-given features of creation: 'Absolute space, in its own nature, without regard to anything external, remains always similar and immovable'.[8] All these premises were overthrown by Einstein (except perhaps its infinity, though not in the sense of limitlessness, and possibly its infinite divisibility). Most important of all, the relation of juxtaposition, which seems so basic to any common sense, Euclidean concept of space, cannot be understood coherently, for the denial of absolute simultaneity – as we shall see, an extremely important feature of Einstein's theory of relativity – removes any possibility of there being absolute juxtapositions.

Time was a second fundamental concept in the classical physical picture of the world – the single dimension in which instants followed each other. Like space it too was homogeneous, independent of any objects or events 'in' it, inert, infinite, continuous. As Newton put it: 'Absolute true and mathematical time, of itself and from its own nature, flows equably without relation to anything external, and by another name is called duration'.[9] In the special theory of relativity this conception is modified but not completely subverted. Although absolute simultaneity is lost, it exists for events taking place at the same location. Further, the succession of events at such isotropic locations and of events which form causal chains is independent of the choice of the frame of reference. The only type of succession whose order depends on the frame of reference is that of causally unrelated events. Indeed the concept of *causality* is affected by Einstein's theory of relativity only to the extent that we now have to recognise that causal influences can never be transmitted through the universe at a speed greater than *c*.

Although the metrical scale of time intervals (the 'dilatation of time') depends on the frame of reference, this is a distortion only from the perspective of the relative velocity of the observer. Even this could, however, be disturbing to certain affective assessments of the 'progress' of a time regarded as all-embracing and the same for all observers. Thus, according to Bertrand Russell, the second line of the poet's 'One far-off divine event/To which the whole creation moves' needs to be rewritten as 'To which some parts of the creation move, while others move away from it'.[10]

As he says further

> '. . . the question whether, on the whole, there is progress in the universe, may depend upon our choice of a measure of time. If we choose one out of a number of equally good clocks, we may find the universe is progressing as fast as the most optimistic American thinks it is; if we choose another equally good clock, we may find that the universe is going from bad to worse as fast as the most melancholy Slav could imagine.'[10]

In the general theory of relativity, the concept of time is more fundamentally transformed. Here time loses its classical features of homogeneity and uniformity (its dilatation in a gravitational field is not merely related to a particular frame of reference), independence of physical content and causal inertness. Moreover, certain scientific developments, subsequent to Einstein's general theory, lead to the idea that time may have a beginning (for example, the 'hot big bang') and so it may not be infinitely divisible.

Even before the full blossoming of quantum mechanics, Einstein's special theory of relativity had rendered impossible the classical notion of *matter* as something impenetrable that fills space. For the interconvertibility of matter as mass and energy ($E = mc^2$) blurred the distinction between space (the square of whose differential with respect to time was proportional to kinetic energy) and mass (supposedly calculable by summing a property of each component of a material body; actually dependent also on the binding energy of these components).   Likewise the classical idea of *motion* was also profoundly altered. Moreover, if a 'particle' of matter is but a certain local configuration ('curvature') of space-time, as it is according to the general theory of relativity, how can it be said to 'move in' a 'space' that itself constitutes its own nature? 'Motion of a body' is, in the general theory, simply a series of changes in the local curvature of space-time; only the continuity of these changes can provide any grounds for identifying a 'body' that can be said to be 'in motion'. Thus Einstein's theory completely undermines the natural distinction between motion and that which moves — a distinction whose obliteration was completed by the subsequent representation (in quantum mechanics) of particles as waves. For this reason, many scientific authors have a definite preference for regarding 'events' as the basic constituents of physical reality rather than particles.

The triumphal progress of science from the seventeenth to the nineteenth century was founded on the conviction that the human *observer* could impartially make observations and thereby derive an objective account of the external world on which all observers could agree — as in Newton's claim, whatever his practice, that he did not invent hypotheses but deduced them from appearances or phenomena.[11] This corporate inter-subjectivity of its cognitive assertions is still the basis for the intellectual prestige of natural science. However, the status of the classical 'observer' has been profoundly modified by Einstein in respect to all observations made between frames of reference moving relative to each other, in a way which only becomes experimentally manifest when there are involved large velocities (v, such that $v^2/c^2 \ll 1$). Developments in atomic theory, such as the formulation of Werner Heisenberg's Uncertainty Principle, finally transformed the impartial, objective observer of classical, Newtonian physics into what Richard Schlegel has called 'The Impossible Spectator'.[12]

This process of destroying the image of the classical observer clearly began with Einstein's realisation that the apparently objective 'primary' qualities of mass, length, time and velocity, thought to characterise external objects in themselves, were not in fact independent of the knower but were dependent on the relation of the object to the observer, in particular on their relative velocities and accelerations. But the kind of observer-dependence of observations of 'external' objects that Einstein expounded must not be thought to license a widespread and universal exaltation of human subjectivity, as perhaps Feynman's 'cocktail-party philosophers' might be tempted to adduce. For the limitations that Einstein quantified for each human observer are purely *physical* limitations that would be equally applicable to a set of instruments located in the same frame of reference. Moreover the 'dilatation of time' and the 'contraction of space', together with the constancy of c, are themselves inter-subjectively formulable and quantifiable. So Einstein's ideas provide no support for any general subjectivism in science — let alone in other realms of thought. What they do emphasise is that science arises from the interaction between the world of nature and ourselves; there is no access to any 'objects-in-themselves' apart from the acts of observation. His theories throw into higher relief the limitations of man's own personal experiences.[13] As Sir James Jeans argued, modern physical science does not suggest

'...that we must abandon the intuitive concepts of space and time which we derive from individual experience. These may mean nothing to nature, but they still mean a good deal to us. Whatever conclusion the mathematicians may reach, it is certain that our newspapers, our historians and story-tellers will still place their truths and fictions in a framework of space and time; they will continue to say — this event happened at such an instant in the course of the ever-flowing stream of time, this other event at another instance lower down on the stream, and so on.

'Such a scheme is perfectly satisfactory for any single individual, or for any group of individuals whose experiences keep them fairly close together in space and time – and, compared with the vast ranges of nature, all the inhabitants of the earth form such a group. The theory of relativity merely suggests that such a scheme is private to single individuals or to small colonies of individuals; it is a parochial method of measuring, and so is not suited for nature as a whole. It can represent all the facts and phenomena of nature, but only by attaching a subjective taint to them all; it does not represent nature so much as what the inhabitants of one rocket, or one planet, or better still an individual pair of human eyes, see of nature. Nothing in our experiences or experiments justifies us in extending either this or any other parochial scheme to the whole of nature, on the supposition that it represents any sort of objective reality.[14]

Though Jeans fails to emphasise the impetus of the search for invariance in Einstein's thought in this passage, he does show how far we have come from the view of the scientist as the objective spectator of classical physics – or rather *should* have come, for the latter image still prevails in the popular image of the scientist. This is another example of how, a century after his birth, Einstein's ideas have yet to make a truly general impact.

The negative consequences of Einstein's theories are well summarised by Bertrand Russell's curt remark 'one thing which emerges is that physics tells us much less about the physical world than we thought it did'.[15] Indeed many of what were taken to be true statements about the world turn out, in the theory of relativity, merely to be definitions.[16] This is the logical significance of the theory[16] and this is what gives it an iconoclastic aura. But the absolute gods of classical physics were not just dethroned by Einstein; something positive was put in their place. To this we now turn.

The implications: what we know – our picture of the world

In the theory of relativity the relations of positions and times as measured in one frame of reference (co-ordinate system) and another are not what we would have intuitively expected from our ordinary ideas about *space and time*. Take the positions and times (x, y, z, t) of an event as measured by one observer with respect to his frame of references (which we will, for purposes of exposition, call 'stationary'). Now take the positions and times (x', y', z', t') of the same event measured by another observer, whose frame of reference is moving at a velocity u relative to our first frame of reference along the positive direction of the x axis. For our present purposes, we assume that this x is in the same direction as the x' axis and that the events under consideration are localised upon it. Then the relations between positions and times as measured in the two co-ordinate systems is given by

$$x' = \gamma\,(x - ut)$$

and

$$t' = \gamma\,(t - \frac{ux}{c^2}),$$

where $\gamma = (1 - u^2/c^2)^{-\frac{1}{2}}$ (and $y' \equiv y$, and $z' \equiv z$ if the events are on the x axis).

It is noticeable in the first of these Lorentz transformations that a difference between a space (*x*) and a time measurement (*t*), with appropriate multiplying factors, produces a new space measurement (*x'*); similarly, in the second such transformation this difference, again with the appropriate factors, produces a new time measurement (*t'*). So in the *space* measurements as seen by one observer there is mixed in not only the space but also the *time* measurements of the other. For this reason the separation between events is measured in terms of an interval (*s*) such that

$$s^2 = c^2 t^2 - x^2 - y^2 - z^2 = c^2 t'^2 - x'^2 - y'^2 - z'^2.$$

This quantity (*s²*) is invariant under the Lorentz transformation. The intervals (*s*) are said to be 'space-like' when *s²* is negative and 'time-like' when it is positive. An event is a given point (*x, y, z, t*) in this four-co-ordinate ('space-time') system.

Because of the loss of absolute simultaneity in Einstein's relativity theory the concept of a great three-dimensional 'now', of world-wide instants, loses all physical significance. It is no longer possible, as in classical physics, to take any 'instantaneous' three-dimensional cuts across the four-dimensional process of the world. They do not correspond to anything objective in nature and can be only conventional. Through its incorporation of space into time, the theory of relativity leads to the *dynamisation of space*. This is Capek's view.[17] Capek argues against the more static interpretation of relativity denoted by the phrase 'the spatialisation of time' on the grounds that causal links ('world-lines' in a four-dimensional representation) remain 'incurably *successive,* thus conferring the *dynamic* character upon the world they constitute'.[18] While there are no absolute juxtapositions in the world, there are absolute successions; and the dynamisation of space is an inherent feature of the general theory of relativity in which space-time (or time-space, as he prefers to call it) is merged with its changing physical content.

Thus the theory of relativity

'... shows that space and time are neither ideal objects nor forms of order necessary for the human mind. They constitute a relational system expressing certain general features of physical objects and thus are descriptive of the physical world. . . . These conceptual systems [of space and time in the theory of relativity] describe relations holding between physical objects, namely, solid bodies, light-rays, and watches. In addition, these relations formulate physical laws of great generality, determining some fundamental features of the physical world. Space and time have as much reality as, say, the relation "father" or the Newtonian forces of attraction.'[19]

One danger of 'spatialising time', as distinct from 'dynamising space', is that it is tempting to make deceptive analogies between movement in space and the progression of time, so that time has a direction, which can change, just as direction of motion in space may change. This generates the so-called problem of the 'direction of time' which some authors, such as Capek,[20] regard as largely illusory, being (he would urge) based on 'false kinematic analogies', but which others, such as Reichenbach,[21] still regard as an unsolved real problem. Both agree that time is an asymmetrical relation, for it establishes a genuine serial order, that of causal chains — a concept which, as Reichenbach puts it,

'... can be shown to be the basic concept in terms of which the structure of space and time is built up. The spatio-temporal order thus must be regarded as the expression of the causal order of the physical world. . . . Time order, the order of *earlier* and *later,* is reducible to causal order; the cause is always earlier than the effect, a relation which cannot be reversed. . . .'[22]

But, he goes on to argue:

> 'For the theory of relativity, time is certainly an asymmetrical relation, since otherwise the time relation would not establish a serial order; but it is not unidirectional. In other words, the irreversibility of time does not find an expression in the theory of relativity.'[23]

The directionality of time has to be based on much debated considerations, related to thermodynamics and even to the indeterminacy principle. On these grounds, other than the theory of relativity, it might well be claimed, with Capek, that there has been 'a reinstatement of *becoming* into the physical world'[24] – a conclusion consonant with what the cosmologist and biologist observe concerning the emergence of new forms of complexity of inorganic and living matter, respectively, as time 'proceeds'. The notion of the universality of this evolutionary process has, according to the physicist H. K. Schilling, given time a new meaning as 'that of the carrier or locus of innovative change'.[25] Indeed, we live in an 'inventive universe'.[26] Strictly speaking, such inferences go beyond what may be deduced from Einstein's ideas, but who can doubt that his ideas have not only initiated a profound reconsideration of the whole concept of time in relation to kinematic, gravitational and electromagnetic phenomena, but also made us more open to rethinking the nature of time in the light of the cosmic and evolutionary processes we observe?

The implications: how we know – epistemology

Science is the mode of human enquiry that attempts *par excellence* to attain objectivity. It tries to make formulations that give a view of reality independent of the observer, a view that is impartial and capable of universal agreement (the requirement of inter-subjectivity). This never meant that anyone's sense perception of that reality should be the same for all, but at least Newton's space and time seemed to be objective because everyone thought they could order their sense data satisfactorily by means of these categories of interpretation. But when different spaces and times came to be seen as mathematically possible, a cleavage appeared to have been made between the subjective time and space of each particular observer and possible public, formalised spaces and times. For a theory to be valid in prediction, it came to be realised,[27] it must also have a criterion of objectivity that resides within some formal property of the theoretical scheme purporting to correspond to reality. Einstein looked for patterns or operations in which the fundamental laws are not changed; that is, for laws of mechanics that, unlike Newton's, would remain unchanged by the Lorentz transformation – a transformation which, together with the constancy of c, was already required if the immutability of Maxwell's laws of electrodynamics was to be maintained. For Einstein's theory of relativity, objectivity becomes equivalent to the *invariance* of physical laws in the form of differential equations; it resides in the basic forms of theoretical statements rather than in observations and perception. The significance of this approach has been well expressed by Margenau:

> 'The idea of invariance is the nucleus of the theory of relativity. To the layman, and sometimes to the philosopher, this theory represents quite the contrary, a set of laws which allow for variability from one observer to another. This one-sided conception is linguistically implied by the word relativity which does not characterize the theory as centrally as it should. The true state of affairs can be seen when attention is directed to the aforementioned postulate of objectivity, which requires that the basic

laws (the differential equations of highest order used in the description of reality) shall be invariant with respect to certain transformations. From this the variability, or relativity, of detailed observation may be shown to follow as a logical consequence. To give a simple example: the basic laws of electrodynamics involve the speed of light, c. If these laws are to be invariant, c must be constant. But the constancy of c in different inertial systems requires that moving objects contract, that moving clocks be retarded, that there can be no universal simultaneity, and so forth. To achieve *objectivity* of basic description, the theory must confer *relativity* upon the domain of immediate observations. In philosophic discussions, too much emphasis has been placed upon the incidental consequence, doubtless because the spectacular tests of the theory involve this consequence.'[28]

Thus the theory of relativity appeals to an important general principle, more powerful than anybody might have supposed, namely, that the laws of phenomena should be the same regardless of the relative motion of the frames of reference of the observers of the phenomena. Ever since the sixteenth century, physics had allowed for the individual spectator's point of view, but before Einstein it had never so radically or so profoundly built this awareness into its fundamental intellectual methodology and so into its epistemology. So, in making invariance of the laws its aim, Einstein's theory of relativity at the same time gave an incisive answer to the problem of objectivity.[29] The theologian T. F. Torrance attributes an even wider significance to Einstein's effect on the concept of objectivity:

'... both observational objectivity and methodological objectivity fall away and are superseded in the face of the new conception of the real world. The causal absoluteness of space and time erected by modern [classical] science is now seen to be essentially an artificial device designed to cope with the relativity of appearance, but that kind of corrective is no longer relevant. Instead, there emerges a new and profounder conception of objectivity grounded in the invariant relatedness inherent in the universe, ... in which many fields of relations and forces cohere together through the natural correlation of their different levels ... in such a way that ordinary experience and even so-called appearances figure as real on their own level in correlation with other levels of reality, and are thus treated as relative aspects of the totality of existence.'[30]

No doubt Einstein's drive towards the discovery of invariance in the multiplicity of observations available from different frames of reference was motivated by his conviction that *simplicity* of theories is vital to the theoretical physicist's enquiry:

'The aim of science is, on the one hand, a comprehension, as *complete* as possible, of the connection between the sense experiences in their totality, and, on the other hand, the accomplishment of this aim *by the use of a minimum of primary concepts and relations*. (Seeking, as far as possible, logical unity in the world picture, i.e., paucity in logical elements.)'[31]

and

'Our experience ... justifies us in believing that nature is the realisation of the simplest conceivable mathematical ideas.'[32]

Here 'simplicity' can scarcely mean lack of sophistication; Einstein is upholding an intuition held by physical scientists since Copernicus. This was the root of his refusal to accept the Copenhagen interpretation of the uncertainty principle of quantum mechanics which accepted that there *could* be a basic indeterminism in physical events. So he began a search for 'hidden variables' not previously discerned in atomic physics. He could not believe, as he remarked in a famous letter to Max Born, in 'the dice-playing god' but only in 'the perfect rule of law in a world of something objectively existing'.[33]

Einstein's quest for invariance and simplicity in the mathematical interpretation of physical reality was not simply a deduction from observation — in the way that it was for Newton. As Lenzen says in his comprehensive study of Einstein's theory of knowledge, for Einstein 'experience may guide us in our choice of mathematical concepts; experience also remains the sole criterion of the serviceability of a mathematical construction for physics; but it cannot possibly be the source from which a theory is derived'.[34] For Einstein, as later for Polanyi,[35] mathematical theories of physical reality are the free creations of imaginative and integrative human thought. It may well be surmised[36] that Einstein's own emphasis on the creative role of the theoretician, together with his success in putting into practice, gave twentieth-century scientists a new sense of the personal, creative role of the human mind in developing their concepts and theories. This ability of the human mind never failed to astonish Einstein:

> 'The very fact that the totality of our sense experiences is such that by means of thinking (operations with concepts, and the creation and use of definite functional relations between them, and the coordination of sense experiences to these concepts) it can be put in order, this fact is one which leaves us in awe, but which we shall never understand. One may say "the eternal mystery of the world is its comprehensibility".
> . . . In speaking here concerning "comprehensibility", the expression is used in its most modest sense. It implies: the production of some sort of order among sense impressions, this order being produced by the creation of general concepts, relations between these concepts, and by relations between the concepts and sense experience, these relations being determined in any possible manner. It is in this sense that the world of our sense experiences is comprehensible. The fact that it is comprehensible is a miracle.'[37]

Torrance believes that this distinctive element in Einstein's thought now characterises the whole of science; he regards it as but a rigorous extension of the basic way of organising our ordinary experiences and knowledge, through which we know things in accordance with their nature and what they are in themselves.[36, 38] He goes on to make this the basis of his own 'theological science'.[39] Whether or not we follow him this far, Wenzl's remarks cannot be denied:

> 'The theory of relativity has simultaneously made us freer and richer by showing in the realm of physics, not merely by way of abstract advice but in concrete performance, that our intellectual capacity of knowledge reaches farther than our sensory capacity of perception. It is the same step in the realm of ideas as that in geometry from Euclidean to non-Euclidean geometry. Our perceptual capacity is limited to three dimensions of a homogeneous continuum of the curvature zero. Our thought-capacity reaches farther. We do not feel ourselves imprisoned in the world of appearances and of the workaday world. But neither do we need to resign ourselves so much, as did Kant, who could say nothing aside from his forms of perception and the forms of thought. We do not assert that with the theory of relativity we have reached reality as such; concerning its inner essence we shall never be able to speak otherwise than by analogy and supposition. But we have obviously come closer to objective reality than

by way of our perceptual capacity. Philosophically this means at the same time that we have moved farther away from materialism even through the development of physics. For now we assert of matter only that it is something which is expressed and can be expressed differential-geometrically, by means of differential equations for a many-dimensioned continuum.'[40]

Clearly Russell's assertion[3] that Einstein's work has resulted in 'changes in our habits of thought' and will 'have great importance in the long-run' was something of an understatement.

The implications: whether we know – realism

The quotation above from Wenzl goes beyond methodological and epistemological matters to refer to the question of realism. By reality Einstein meant *physical* reality:

'The belief in an external world independent of the perceiving subject is the basis of all natural science. Since, however, sense perception only gives information of this external world or of "physical reality" indirectly, we can only grasp the latter by speculative means. It follows from this that our notions of physical reality can never be final. We must always be ready to change these notions – that is to say, the axiomatic structure of physics – in order to do justice to perceived facts in the most logically perfect way.'[41]

As Margenau points out,[42] this passage makes a three-fold distinction between an *external world,* the observer's *perception* (said to be 'indirect') of that external world, and our *notions* of it – a hornet's nest of philosophical problems. Subsequent to Einstein, later interpreters of the theory of relativity have come to very different conclusions. Compare that of Russell:

'It throws very little light on time-honoured controversies, such as that between realism and idealism. . . . The "subjectivity" concerned in the theory of relativity is a *physical* subjectivity, which would exist equally if there were no such things as minds or senses in the world.'[3]

to that of Wenzl:

'To the question, what both: matter and energy, are, the general theory of relativity gives us the [following] answer: they are that which creates the metric. The metric of the space-time-continuum is the expression of the intensity of the stresses of their essence. . . . The most noteworthy fact is this: that it is possible to comprehend and represent the physical magnitudes (mass, impulse, force, energy) as producers of geometrical characteristics as they occur in the theory of planes, and to be able to treat the field-forces also [in terms of] differential geometry. For this is by no means self-evident nor simply the invention of a great mathematico-artistic ingenuity; yet *in this possibility lies the decisive objective epistemological value of the general theory of relativity.*'[43]

'What is it possible to say concerning it [reality] today at all? Nothing, except that it is a [type of] reality which effectively confronts us and which is so well mathematically describable that it can be regarded as the realization of mathematical structures and forms. . . . Being effectual for each other and towards us, being the expression and the expressibleness of the orderly relations in mathematically couchable forms: these are today the attributes of "material reality". Is this peculiar? Mathematical expressibility, we already said, is marvellous. But what lies at the base of material appearance is a being-related-to and a becoming-effectual.'[44]

Torrance goes even further:

'For the new [Einsteinian] science, however, these [Newtonian] notions of "reality" wither away, as soon as the dichotomies (between the apparent and the real, subject and object, form and being, etc.) that lie at their root are eliminated, together with the artificial correctives they forced upon science but which are now seen to be incompatible with the actual world of empirical fact. Here the real world is that which forces itself upon our inquiries in the imperious light of its own intrinsic order, is one in which intelligible structure and material content exist in mutual interaction and interdetermination. This is a world in which relations between bodies are just as real as the bodies themselves, for it is in their interrelations that things are found to be what and as and when they are. Thus, as relativity theory has brought to light, space and time are not only fused with one another but fused with the matter and energy of the universe in such a way as to constitute an unresolvable four-dimensional continuum with rationally and physically objective properties. . . . The real world confronts us, then, as a continuous integrated manifold, in which structure and substance, form and being, are inseparately conjoined in the immanent relatedness of the universe. . . . Since the real world exhibits itself to scientific inquiry in this profound unity of form and being, or structure and substance, it not only gives evidence of its existence as an intelligible system independent of our perceiving and conceiving of it, but thereby discriminates itself perpetually from our scientific constructs about it, and remains in its independence the final judge of their truth or falsity. All this implies a powerful restoration of *ontology,* not only for the philosopher or the theologian, but also for the scientist, who precisely as scientist finds that it is "existence and reality", that he wishes to comprehend.'[45]

These latter two expositions (of Wenzl and Torrance) of the nature of the 'reality' implied by the theory of relativity are more positive and definite than Einstein himself might have supported, for he himself seemed to retain a certain scepticism about the meaning of the term:

'Behind the tireless efforts of the investigator there lurks a stranger, more mysterious drive: it is existence and reality that one wishes to comprehend. But one shrinks from the use of such words, for one soon gets into difficulties when one has to explain what is really meant by "the reality" and by "comprehend" in such a general statement.'[46]

In the light of the intense philosophical debates of the last decade[47] on realism in relation to the concept of 'truth' in science (*inter alia*) and its applicability — for example, to propositions, sentences and statements — we should be wise to share Einstein's scepticism, if for somewhat different reasons, and be cautious in making any inferences from his theories about the nature of reality.

Time in relativistic physics and theology[48]

Theological models of the relation of God to the world and the cosmological models of relativistic physics for the most part use entirely different resources for their construction. Nevertheless each has to face the question of how *time* is incorporated into its models. We shall first turn to an examination of certain aspects of the understanding of time in theology.

The principal stress in the Judeo-Christian doctrine of creation is on the dependence on God of all entities and events: it is about a perennial relationship of all-that-is to God, and not about the beginning of the Earth, or of the whole universe at a point in time. The phrase 'the whole universe' is of course ambiguous, since it seems to imply a boundary or limit 'beyond' or outside which, in some sense, God exists — and this will not do at all, for God would then be in a 'beyond' or 'outside' which would be but an extension of the same framework of reference as that in which the 'whole universe' is conceived to exist. To avoid this conceptual impasse, the principal stress in the doctrine of creation has been an affirmation that any particular event or entity would not happen or would not be at all were it not for the sustaining creative will and activity of God.

One of the most influential attempts to understand the relation of God, time and creation was that made by St Augustine in the eleventh chapter of his *Confessions,* in which he addresses himself to those who ask 'What was God doing before he made heaven and earth?'. He outlines the paradox as follows:

' "If he was at rest," they say, "and doing nothing, why did he not continue to do nothing for ever more, just as he had always done in the past? If the will to create something which he had never created before was new in him . . . how can we say that his is true eternity, when a new will, which had never been there before, could arise in it? . . . The will of God, then, is part of his substance. Yet if something began to be in God's substance, something which had not existed beforehand, we could not rightly say that his substance was eternal. But if God's will that there should be a creation was there from all eternity, why is it that what he has created is not also eternal?" '[49]

This provokes St Augustine to undertake a profound analysis of our experience of time. From it he concludes that the world was created along with and not in time. Time itself is a feature of the created cosmos and therefore no 'act of creation' can be located at a point within created time itself. There is no time without events and God's eternity is not just endless *temporal* duration but a mode of existence which is qualitatively different from that of successive temporal experience. Augustine addresses God thus:

'How could those countless ages have elapsed when you, the Creator, in whom all ages have their origin, had not yet created them? What time could there have been that was not created by you? How could time elapse if it never was? You are the Maker of all time. If, then, there was any time before you made heaven and earth, how can anyone say that you were idle? You must have made that time, for time could not elapse before you made it. But if there was no time before heaven and earth were created, how can anyone ask what you were doing "then"? If there was no time, there was no "then".'[50]

'It is therefore true to say that when you had not made anything there was no time, because time itself was of your making. And no time is co-eternal with you, because you never change; whereas, if time never changed, it would not be time.'[51]

'Grant them [those who ask the questions "what was God doing before he made heaven and earth?" or "How did it occur to God to create something, when he had never created anything before?"], O Lord, to think well what they say and to recognise that "never" has no meaning when there is no time. If a man is said never to have made anything, it can only mean that he made nothing at any time. Let them see, then, that there cannot possibly be time without creation. . . . Let them understand that before all time began you are the eternal Creator of all time, and that no time and no created thing is co-eternal with you, even if any created thing is outside time.'[52]

These questions formed part of the later famous debate between St Thomas Aquinas and St Bonaventure.[53] Although both accepted that the world had a beginning in time, on the basis of the revelation in the Scriptures, the former thought that the world could have existed from eternity (that is, for an infinite time) — though, in fact, the biblical revelation shows it does not so exist — whereas the latter argued that, if the world is created, then time necessarily had a beginning. On this latter view, it is more accurate to say the world was created *with* time, which seems to be Augustine's position in the *Confessions.*

The bringing together of time and 'things' in such close connection, so that both are part of the created order, is entirely in accord with the outlook to which Einstein has accustomed us. For, unlike Newton, we can no longer regard time as a flowing river of endless duration, as a mode of extension into which events are inserted as if time had an entirely discrete and unrelated kind of existence from the events themselves and from the matter participating in them. For it is certain distinctive metric features of space and time, or rather space-time, which Einstein has shown us constitute the gravitational forces of matter, which is now known to be interchangeable with energy, a concept which itself involves an intimate relation to the concept of time. Time, in post-Einsteinian physics, is an integral and basic constituent of nature, an aspect of space-time. Hence on any theistic view, it has to be regarded, like the rest of the created world, as owing its existence to God, as St Augustine perceived. It is this 'owing its existence to God' which is the essential core of the Judeo-Christian doctrine of creation.

In investigating and making theoretical deductions about the remote history of our universe, scientific cosmology cannot, in principle, be doing anything which can contradict such a concept of creation. Aided by radio-telescopes and other instruments, we may or may not discover if there was a point in space-time when the universe, as we can observe it, began. But whatever we may be able to infer about what may have happened on the other side of the 'big bang', any grounds for believing that the cosmos has derived and contingent being, and that God alone is Being in himself, would not be perturbed. The doctrine of creation itself would be unaffected, since it concerns the relationship of all the created order, including time itself, to their Creator, their Sustainer and Preserver.

Nevertheless there is an important feature which the scientific perspective inevitably reintroduces into the idea of creation in the form just described. This is the realisation that the cosmos which is sustained and held in being by God is a cosmos which has always been in process of producing new emergent forms of matter. It is a world which is still being made. On the surface of the Earth, for example, man has emerged from prehistoric forms of life and his history is still developing. Any static conception of the way in which God sustains and holds the cosmos in being is therefore precluded, for the cosmos is in a dynamic state and has evolved conscious beings who shape their environment and have the power of choice.

That the world was in flux and change, with all its corollaries for the destiny of the individual man, has been reflected upon since the ancient Greeks. But that the matter of the world developed in a particular direction to more complex and ultimately thinking forms was not established knowledge. The people of Israel, and following them, the Christian church, have always believed in the providential hand of God in human history, with the non-human world usually being regarded simply as the stage for that drama. Science now sees man as part of 'nature' and both together as subject to continuous development. Any static conception of the relation of God and the world is therefore excluded, for if the emergence of new forms of matter in the world is in some way an activity of God, then it must be regarded as his perennial activity and not something already completed. The scientific perspective of a cosmos in development introduces a dynamic element into our understanding of God's relation to the cosmos which was previously only implicit in the Hebrew conception of a 'living God', dynamic in action, and in the formulation of (for example) the Nicene Creed.[54]

A musical epilogue

This new awareness of 'becoming' in the natural processes of the world represents a convergence of many strands of scientific thought, including the biological and cosmological, as well as those stemming from Einstein's theory of relativity. But that theory, especially in its general form, has formulated a conception of space-time which goes far beyond the power of our imagination to picture. However, our experience of time as being characterised by succession and the varying 'metrics' of the passage of conscious time which we observe according to our state of mind do give some clues to how we might now model conceptually the dynamic nature of physical reality by means of *imageless dynamical patterns.*[55]

That reality is characterised[56] by: the incompleteness of becoming and its pulsational character; the compatibility of the emergence of novelty with the causal influence of the past; the individuality of events within the continuity of the flux; the fictitious character of instantaneous acts and, consequently, the impossibility of instantaneous space, and the replacement of the relation of juxtaposition or co-instantaneity of points by that of co-becoming (or contemporaneity of the 'causal tubes'). As Capek says, 'All these features defy any attempt at visualisation'.[56] A source of models of, or analogies for, such imageless, dynamic patterns that Capek and a number of authors have discovered is to be found in the musical experience. A. N. Whitehead long ago noted that in his organic theory (of the nature of the physical world),

'a pattern need not endure in undifferentiated sameness through time. The pattern may be essentially one of aesthetic [that is, qualitative] contrasts requiring a lapse of time for its unfolding. *A tune is an example of such a pattern.* Thus the endurance of the pattern now means the reiteration of its successions of contrasts'.[57]

More recently Capek has developed this idea — a little cautiously, afraid that he may be misunderstood to be attempting to reinstate auditory, or other secondary qualities into the physical world. What he hopes to offer is a 'key to the understanding of the nature of the type of "extensive becoming" that seems to constitute the nature of physical reality'.[58] He wants to find in the auditory experiences of music an imageless, dynamic pattern for time, the 'locus of innovative change'.[25] Let Capek speak for himself:

'Let us consider a piece of music — for instance, a melody or, better, a polyphonic musical phrase. It is hardly necessary to underscore its successive character. As long as its movement is going on, it remains incomplete and in its successive unfolding we grasp in the most vivid and concrete way the incompleteness of every becoming. At each particular moment a new tone is added to the previous ones; more accurately, each new moment is constituted by the addition of a new musical quality.... The relation of ... arithmetical units to their sum total is the same as the relation of *the parts to the whole in space.*

'In the musical experience of melody or polyphony the situation is considerably different. The quality of a new tone, in spite of its irreducible individuality, is tinged by the whole antecedent musical context which, in turn, is retroactively changed by the emergence of a new musical quality. The individual tones are not externally related units of which the melody is additively built; neither is their individuality absorbed or dissolved in the undifferentiated unity of the musical whole. The musical phrase is a *successive differentiated whole* which remains a whole in spite of its successive character and which remains differentiated in spite of its dynamic wholeness. Like every dynamic whole it exhibits a synthesis of unity and multiplicity, of continuity and discontinuity; . . . it is neither continuity in the mathematical sense of infinite divisibility nor is it the discontinuity of rigid atomic blocs.'[59]

'Every musical structure is by its own nature unfolding and incomplete; so is cosmic becoming, the time-space of modern physics. The musical structures, in virtue of their essentially temporal nature, cannot be subdivided *ad infinitum* without being destroyed. . . . As Whitehead says, "a note of music is nothing at an instant, but also requires its whole period to manifest itself". . . . For this reason musical wholes — like physical processes — are not infinitely divisible; in either case durationally instants are mere ideal limits, arbitrary cuts in the dynamic continuity of becoming.
'. . . in concrete temporal experience the emergence of novelty is possible, so to speak, only on the contrasting background of its immediate past; in a similar way a new musical quality of the (provisionally) last tone acquires its individuality in contrast to, as well as in connection with, its antecedent musical context.'[60]

Capek even finds in his 'auditory model' a way of understanding the new meaning of spatiality with which Einstein has replaced the concept of static Newtonian space, even though nothing in a bare succession of tunes corresponds to anything even remotely analogous to the relation of space. However:

'The situation . . . is different when we turn our attention to the dynamic structure of polyphony. The dynamic pattern in this case is more complex. In a contrapuntal composition two or several melodically independent movements, whether harmonious or dissonant, are going on. The component melodic movements, besides each being unfolded successively, are also in a certain sense *beside* or *alongside* each other, and this relation "beside" is analogous to the relation "beside" in space.'[61]

Music, it has often been noted, is the only means of human communication that cuts across all barriers of language, race, class and creed and unites in an experience of reality at once both personal and corporate. So it is not surprising that Whitehead and, more extensively, Capek have resorted to an art form independent of the visual (and so Euclidean) imagery to which even language ties us. To take a quite different context: the search for a 'model' which would represent how God might be conceived as involved in a dynamic creation that continually manifests new potentialities, has led the author to musical resources for expression. I have suggested[62] that we could regard God as somewhat like a bellringer, ringing all the possible changes, all the possible permutations and combinations he can out of a given set of harmonious bells — though it is God who creates the pattern of the 'bells' too. Or, perhaps better, He is more like a composer who, beginning with an arrangement of notes in an apparently simple tune, elaborates and expands it into a fugue by a variety of devices of fragmentation and reassociation; by turning it upside down and back to front; by overlapping these and other variations of it in a range of tonalities; by a profusion of time-sequence patterns, in which the interplay of sounds flows in an orderly fashion from the chosen initiating ploy. Thus does a J. S. Bach create a complex and harmonious fusion of his seminal material, both through time and at any particular instant; beautiful in its elaboration, it only reaches its consummation in the last few bars, when all the threads have been drawn into the return to the home key — the key of the initial melody whose potential elaboration was conceived from the moment it was first expounded. In this kind of way might the Creator be imagined to unfold the potentialities of the universe which he himself has given it. He appears to do this, I have argued, by a process in which the creative possibilities inherent in the fundamental entities of the universe and in their interrelations become actualised within a temporal development which is itself shaped and determined by those selfsame inherent potentialities that he conceived from the very first note.

Such recourse to music for an image of the temporal dynamic process that the theory of relativity opened up would not, I suspect, have been repudiated by Einstein himself. For, so his eldest son has recalled, 'Whenever he felt that he had come to the end of the road or into a difficult situation in his work, he would take refuge in music, and that would usually resolve all his difficulties'.[63]

Notes

1. R. P. Feynman, R. B. Leighton and M. Sands, *The Feynman lectures on physics,* Addison–Wesley, Reading, Massachusetts and London, 1963, p. 16–1.
2. See 'The implications: how we know – epistemology', below.
3. B. Russell, *ABC of relativity,* 3rd rev. edn., F. Pirani, ed., Allen & Unwin, 1969, p. 133.
4. A. Wenzl, 'Einstein's theory of relativity viewed from the standpoint of critical realism, and its significance for philosophy', in P. A. Schilpp, ed., *Albert Einstein: philosopher–scientist,* Open Court, La Salle, Illinois, 1969, pp. 581–606.
5. M. Capek, *The philosophical impact of contemporary physics,* van Nostrand, Princeton, 1961, pp. 378–9.
6. K. Heim, *The transformation of the scientific world view,* SCM Press, London, 1953, p. 24.
7. Feynman et al., op. cit., pp. 16–2, 16–3.
8. Isaac Newton, *Principia,* A. Motte, translator, revised by F. Cajori, University of California Press, Berkeley, 1934, Scholium II to Definition VIII, p. 6.
9. Ibid., Scholium I to Definition VIII, p. 6.
10. Russell, op. cit., p. 136.
11. Newton, op. cit., General Scholium, p. 547.
12. R. Schlegel, 'The Impossible Spectator', Sixth centennial review lecture at Michigan State University, 12 May 1975, *The centennial review,* pp. 218, 230.
13. R. W. Clark, *Einstein: the life and times,* Hodder & Stoughton, London, 1973, p. 111.
14. Sir James Jeans, *The new background of science,* Cambridge University Press, Cambridge, 1933, pp. 95–6.
15. Russell, op. cit., p. 134.
16. See H. Reichenbach, 'The philosophical significance of the theory of relativity', in Schilpp, op. cit.
17. Capek, op. cit., p. 383 ff.
18. Ibid., p. 385, our emphasis.
19. Reichenbach, op. cit., p. 302.
20. Capek, op. cit., pp. 366–7.
21. Reichenbach, op. cit., pp. 303–7.
22. Ibid., p. 303.
23. Ibid., p. 305.
24. Capek, op. cit., p. 395, our emphasis.
25. H. K. Schilling, *The new consciousness in science and religion,* SCM Press, London, 1973, p. 126.
26. K. Denbigh, *An inventive universe,* Hutchinson, London, 1975.
27. H. Margenau, 'Einstein's conception of reality', in Schilpp, op. cit., p. 253.
28. Ibid., p. 254.
29. Ibid., p. 252.
30. T. F. Torrance, 'The integration of form in natural and in theological science', in *Science, medicine and man,* vol. 1, 1973, p. 152.
31. A. Einstein, *Out of my later years,* Thames & Hudson, London, 1950, p. 63.
32. A. Einstein, 'On the method of theoretical physics', in *The world as I see it,* Covici–Friede, New York, 1934, p. 36.
33. Quoted in Max Born, *Natural philosophy of cause and chance,* Clarendon Press, Oxford, 1949, p. 122.
34. V. F. Lenzen, 'Einstein's theory of knowledge', in Schilpp, op. cit., pp. 361–2.
35. M. Polanyi, *The tacit dimension,* Routledge & Kegan Paul, London, 1967; *Personal knowledge,* Routledge & Kegan Paul, London, 1958.
36. Torrance, op. cit., p. 154.
37. Einstein, *Out of my later years,* loc. cit., p. 61.
38. T. F. Torrance, Address to the Templeton Foundation, 1978.
39. T. F. Torrance, *Theological science,* Oxford University Press, London, 1969.
40. Wenzl, op. cit., pp. 605–6.
41. Einstein, 'On the method of theoretical physics', in *The world as I see it,* loc. cit., p. 60.
42. Margenau, op. cit., p. 249.
43. Wenzl, op. cit., pp. 592–3.
44. Ibid., pp. 603–4.
45. Torrance, op. cit., pp. 150–1.
46. Einstein, address at Columbia University, in *The world as I see it,* loc. cit., pp. 137 f.
47. See, for example, H. W. Putnam, *Philosophical papers,* vols. 1 and 2, Cambridge University Press, Cambridge, 1975; 'What is realism?', *Proc. Arist. Soc.* vol. 76, 1975–6, pp. 177–94; *Meaning and the*

moral sciences, Routledge & Kegan Paul, London, 1978; M. Dummett, 'Can truth be defined?', in *Frege: philosophy of language,* Duckworth, London, 1973, chapter 13; 'Truth', *Proc. Arist. Soc.,* vol. 59, 1978–9, pp. 141–67; G. Evans and J. McDowell, eds., *Truth and meaning,* Oxford University Press, Oxford, 1975.

48. This section incorporates material from the author's article 'Cosmos and Creation', in *Cosmology, history and theology,* W. Yourgrau and A. D. Breck, eds., Plenum Press, New York and London, 1977, pp. 365–81.

49. St Augustine, *Confessions,* xi. 10, Penguin Classics edn., R. S. Pine-Coffin, translator, p. 261.

50. Ibid., paragraph 13, pp. 262–3.

51. Ibid., paragraph 14, p. 263.

52. Ibid., paragraph 30, p. 279.

53. For an account of this, see F. Coplestone, *A history of philosophy,* vol. ii, Burns & Oates, London, pp. 262–5, and pp. 363 ff.

54. God the Holy Spirit as 'The Lord and giver of life'.

55. Capek, op. cit., p. 379.

56. Following Capek, op. cit., p. 378.

57. A. N. Whitehead, *Science and the modern world,* Macmillan, New York, 1926, p. 193, our emphasis.

58. Capek, op. cit., p. 399.

59. Ibid., pp. 371–2.

60. Ibid., pp. 372–3. The quotation from Whitehead is from *Science and the modern world,* op. cit.

61. Ibid., p. 377.

62. A. R. Peacocke, 3rd 1978 Bampton Lecture in *Creation and the world of science,* Clarendon Press, Oxford, 1979.

63. Quoted by R. W. Clark, op. cit., p. 115.

The brain of Einstein

Roland Barthes

Roland Barthes was born in 1915 and studied French literature and Classics at Paris University. He taught French at
universities in Rumania and Egypt before he joined the
Centre National de la Recherche Scientifique, where he did
research in sociology and lexicology. Before his death in an
accident in March 1980 he was engaged in teaching a course
on the sociology of signs and symbols. His books include
Writing degree zero and *Elements of semiology*.

From *Mythologies*, Jonathan Cape, 1972. Translated by
Annette Lavers.

Einstein's brain is a mythical object: paradoxically, the greatest intelligence of all provides an image of the most up-to-date machine, the man who is too powerful is removed from psychology, and introduced into a world of robots; as is well known, the supermen of science-fiction always have something reified about them. So has Einstein: he is commonly signified by his brain, which is like an object for anthologies, a true museum exhibit. Perhaps because of his mathematical specialisation, superman is here divested of every magical character; no diffuse power in him, no mystery other than mechanical: he is a superior, a prodigious organ, but a real, even a physiological one. Mythologically, Einstein is matter, his power does not spontaneously draw one towards the spiritual, it needs the help of an independent morality, a reminder about the scientist's 'conscience' (*science without conscience,* they said).[1]

Einstein himself has to some extent been a party to the legend by bequeathing his brain, for the possession of which two hospitals are still fighting as if it were an unusual piece of machinery which it will at last be possible to dismantle. A photograph shows him lying down, his head bristling with electric wires: the waves of his brain are being recorded, while he is requested to 'think of relativity'. (But for that matter, what does 'to think of' mean, exactly?) What this is meant to convey is probably that the seismograms will be all the more violent since 'relativity' is an arduous subject. Thought itself is thus represented as an energetic material, the measurable product of a complex (quasi-electrical) apparatus which transforms cerebral substance into power. The mythology of Einstein shows him as a genius so lacking in magic that one speaks about his thought as of a functional labour analogous to the mechanical making of sausages, the grinding of corn or the crushing of ore: he used to produce thought, continuously, as a mill makes flour, and death was above all, for him, the cessation of a localised function: *'the most powerful brain of all has stopped thinking'*.

What this machine of genius was supposed to produce was equations. Through the mythology of Einstein, the world blissfully regained the image of knowledge reduced to a formula. Paradoxically, the more the genius of the man was materialised under the guise of his brain, the more the product of his inventiveness came to acquire a magical dimension, and gave a new incarnation to the old esoteric image of a science entirely contained in a few letters. There is a single secret to the world, and this secret is held in one word; the universe is a safe of which humanity seeks the combination: Einstein almost found it, this is the myth of Einstein. In it, we find all the Gnostic themes: the unity of nature, the ideal possibility of a fundamental reduction of the world, the unfastening power of the word, the age-old struggle between a secret and an utterance, the idea that total knowledge can only be discovered all at once, like a lock which suddenly opens after a thousand unsuccessful attempts. The historic equation $E = mc^2$, by its unexpected simplicity, almost embodies the pure idea of the key, bare, linear, made of one metal, opening with a wholly magical ease a door which had resisted the desperate efforts of centuries. Popular imagery faithfully expresses this: *photographs* of Einstein show him standing next to a blackboard covered with mathematical signs of obvious complexity; but *cartoons* of Einstein (the sign that he has become a legend) show him chalk still in hand, and having just written on an empty blackboard, as if without preparation, the magic formula of the world. In this way mythology shows an awareness of the nature of the various tasks: research proper brings into play clockwork-like mechanisms and has its seat in a wholly material organ which is monstrous only by its cybernetic complication; discovery, on the contrary, has a magical essence, it is simple like a basic element, a principal substance, like the philosophers' stone of hermetists, tar-water for Berkeley, or oxygen for Schelling.

But since the world is still going on, since research is proliferating, and on the other hand since God's share must be preserved, some failure on the part of Einstein is necessary: Einstein died, it is said, without having been able to verify *'the equation in which the secret of the world was enclosed'.* So in the end the world resisted; hardly opened, the secret closed again, the code was incomplete. In this way Einstein fulfils all the conditions of myth, which could not care less about contradictions so long as it establishes a euphoric security: at once magician and machine, eternal researcher and unfulfilled discoverer, unleashing the best and the worst, brain and conscience, Einstein embodies the most contradictory dreams, and mythically reconciles the infinite power of man over nature with the 'fatality' of the sacrosanct, which man cannot yet do without.

Note

1.   'Science without conscience is but the ruin of the Soul'. Rabelais, *Pantagruel,* vol. ii, chapter 8.

4. The impact on world affairs

Einstein the pacifist warrior

Joseph Rotblat

Joseph Rotblat is Emeritus Professor of Physics at the University of London. He started his scientific career in Poland as a nuclear physicist. During the war he participated in atom bomb work in Los Alamos. As a result of this he turned to medical physics, the treatment of cancer, and research on the biological effects of radiation, at St Bartholomew's Hospital Medical College, London.

For the same reason he became active in scientists' movements for peace. He co-founded the Atomic Scientists Association in Great Britain, of which he was executive vice-president. He is one of the 11 signatories of the Russell—Einstein Manifesto, and a founder of the Pugwash Movement, of which he was secretary-general for 17 years. He is now a member of its executive committee.

Preamble

Einstein's accomplishments in science were so dazzling that they were bound to extinguish anything else he did, even though by the standards of ordinary mortals his attainments in several other fields would have been considered truly remarkable. Among these, the most outstanding were his political activities, and in particular his ceaseless struggle for peace. Einstein considered himself a socialist and a pacifist, but he never joined an established political party. Although he lent his name to many a peace movement, he never followed a rigid pacifist line; indeed, for a time he was regarded as a traitor to the cause of pacifism. In his political activities, as in his scientific work, he was an individualist. He called himself 'an incorrigible non-conformist'. Since he did not follow any established line he was often criticised from both left and right. But throughout his life, he was motivated by love for humanity, reverence for life, esteem for culture, and respect for the intellect. Next to science, it was to these ideals that he devoted most of his time and energy.

The sanctity of life was the main reason for his abhorrence of war and the military machine. This comes through clearly in several of his statements:

> 'My pacifism is an instinctive feeling, a feeling that possesses me; the thought of murdering another human being is abhorrent to me. My attitude is not the result of an intellectual theory but is caused by a deep antipathy to every kind of cruelty and hatred . . .'[1]

> 'To me the killing of any human being is murder; it is also murder when it takes place on a large scale as an instrument of state policy.'[2]

> '. . . This brings me to the worst outgrowth of herd life, the military system which I abhor. I feel only contempt for those who can take pleasure marching in rank and file to the strains of a band. Surely, such men were given their great brain by mistake; the spinal cord would have amply sufficed. This shameful stain on civilization should be wiped out as soon as possible. Heroism on command, senseless violence and all the loathsome nonsense that goes by the name of patriotism — how passionately I despise them! How vile and contemptible war seems to me! I would rather be torn limb from limb than take part in such an ugly business.'[3]

Apart from the destruction of life, war's debasing effect on culture was another reason for his pacifism:

> 'War constitutes the most formidable obstacle to the growth of international co-operation, especially in its effect upon culture. War destroys all those conditions which are indispensable to the intellectual if he is to work creatively. . . . Hence, he who cherishes the values of culture cannot fail to be a pacifist.'[4]

This was not mere rhetoric:

> 'I am not only a pacifist but a militant pacifist. I am willing to fight for peace.'[5]

The whole history of Einstein's life bears witness to his struggles to save mankind from self-destruction, to eliminate cruelty and vulgarity and replace them by kindness and the enjoyment of intellectual achievements. The latter was a natural to Einstein, who received exquisite joy from scientific work.

The First World War: 1914–18

Einstein's pacifist activities began at about the start of the First World War. Much earlier he had shown his dislike of the authoritarianism and militarism which had characterised pre-war Germany by renouncing German citizenship at the age of 16 and becoming a Swiss citizen. (He claimed that he never became a German citizen again, although membership of the Prussian Academy of Sciences, which was conferred on him in 1913, automatically made him a Prussian citizen.) Apart from this manifestation of youthful defiance, he does not appear to have taken part in any political action. But the outbreak of the war, and the destruction and barbarity that followed, shook him to the core, and he expressed his shock in letters to a physicist friend.

The act which provoked him to come out into the open with his opposition to the war was a declaration issued in October 1914 by 93 major German intellectuals. Under the title 'Manifesto to the Civilised World', the document attempted to whitewash the atrocities by the military, and in particular the violation of Belgium's neutrality. But the declaration went further than this; it stated that if it were not for German militarism, German culture would have been wiped off the face of the earth. Within a few days of the publication of the Manifesto, a reply was issued under the title 'Manifesto to Europe'. Its main author was Georg Friedrich Nicolai, a professor of physiology of the university of Berlin; Einstein was its co-author, as well as one of only four signatories. In the highly charged nationalist atmosphere in Germany at the period it required great courage to advocate opposition to war, a call for peace was equivalent to treason. It is evidence of Einstein's profound feelings that he should make such an audacious statement only shortly after accepting a professorship in the university of Berlin and directorship of the Kaiser Wilhelm Institute for physics. Apart from being a retort to the Manifesto of the 93, this first public statement of Einstein's is noteworthy because it contained the foundations for his future political objectives: world government and peace based on international co-operation. In the achievement of these goals there lay an important role for intellectuals too:

'Never before has any war so completely disrupted cultural co-operation. It has done so at the very time when progress in technology and communications clearly suggest that we recognize the need for international relations which will necessarily move in the direction of a universal, world-wide civilization. . . . Technology has shrunk the world. . . . Travel is so widespread, international supply and demand are so interwoven, that Europe — one could almost say the whole world — is even now a single unit. . . . The struggle raging today can scarcely yield a "victor"; all nations that participate in it will, in all likelihood, pay an exceedingly high price. Hence it appears not only wise but imperative for men of education in all countries to exert their influence for the kind of peace treaty that will not carry the seeds of future wars, whatever the outcome of the present conflict may be.'[6]

Forty years later, in his last public statement, Einstein was to echo many of these sentiments, again calling on scientists to help mankind to avert destruction in another war in which there could be no victor.

Hard on the 'Manifesto to Europe' Einstein co-founded a peace movement, the 'Bund Neues Vaterland' (League of the New Fatherland). Its direct aim was to bring about an early and just peace, but it also had a long-term objective: the establishment of an international organisation which would make future wars impossible. The Bund issued pamphlets, made public statements, distributed literature from British pacifists and held meetings at which Einstein spoke. Naturally, the group was harassed from the beginning, and in 1916 its further activities were banned. In spite of this, it continued a clandestine existence until it was able to come out into the open again, a few months before the end of the war. It was formally re-founded on 14 November 1918 with Einstein as a member of its working committee.

While rejoicing in the overthrow of the monarchy and in the new power of the people, he was anxious that the democratic ideals should prevail. At the university of Berlin, in a speech to a student's council which had deposed the Rector and locked up the staff, he said:

> '. . . all true democrats must stand guard lest the old class tyranny of the right be replaced by a new class tyranny of the left. Do not be lured by feelings of vengeance to the fateful view that violence must be fought with violence, that a dictatorship of the proletariat is temporarily needed in order to hammer the concept of freedom into the heads of our fellow countrymen. Force breeds only bitterness, hatred and reaction.'[7]

The League of Nations: 1919–32

Einstein's conviction that the abolition of war required, as a first step, the setting up of a supranational organisation, made him a natural and keen supporter of the League of Nations. Born in 1920, the League of Nations enjoyed Einstein's support for many years, although he was often angered and saddened by its ineffectiveness. Einstein's link with the League of Nations was maintained through his membership of its Committee of Intellectual Co-operation, which might be considered as the precursor of UNESCO. Together with Marie Curie and other eminent scholars, Einstein was invited to the Committee in 1922; but his membership was not without difficulties. Although he was invited as an individual, and not as an official representative of Germany, the French gave expression to the strong anti-German feeling prevalent at the time by objecting to a 'German' as a member. Some Germans objected to a 'Swiss Jew' representing them.

After serving on the Committee for several months, Einstein resigned from it. The reason was characteristic: he resented the exclusion of German scientists from an international scientific congress which was to be held in Brussels. To him science was always international, and he could not tolerate the attitude of French and Belgian scientists who refused to sit down at a table with their erstwhile enemies. In a paper on the internationalism of science, he protested against this narrow-mindedness, asserting that great men among scientists had always known that 'science is and always will be international':

> 'These more enlightened men can make an important contribution to the great task of reviving international societies by keeping in close touch with like-minded men and women the world over, as well as by steadfastly championing the cause of internationalism in their own spheres of influence. . . . I am extremely hopeful for the progress of a general international organization. My feelings are based not so much on confidence in the intelligence and high-mindedness of scientists as on the inevitable pressure of economic developments. Since these developments are so largely dependent upon the work of even reactionary scientists, they too will have no choice but to assist in the establishment of an international organization.'[8]

Einstein's belief in the necessity of the international organisation of science made him rejoin the Committee of Intellectual Co-operation a year later. Recognising what an asset his membership would be, the Committee welcomed him warmly 'both as an old and as a new colleague'. The minutes of the first meeting which he attended state:

'The Committee was happy and proud to count among its members a savant of world-wide reputation. . . . Even during the war, and even before the war, his conception of the relations between peoples might not have been far away from the ideal of the League of Nations. If by his presence on a Committee of the League of Nations he succeeded in attracting to this ideal all those who had been interested in his lofty speculations, he would have rendered a new and very great service to humanity.'[9]

During the next few years, Einstein was very active on the Committee of Intellectual Co-operation and attended most of its sessions. Although his objective was to bring into closer communication national cultures previously separated by language and tradition, he realised that a start could only be made with modest projects. These included the international organisation of scientific reporting, the exchange of publications, the protection of literary property and the exchange of professors and students among various countries. A more ambitious project was the establishment of an international university for the education of statesmen, diplomats, political writers and professors of political science. Einstein was particularly conscious that history was often taught in a narrow way and that many text-books contained offensive passages. As the Committee recorded his views:

'Historians are not sufficiently free of prejudice and it seemed impossible to attain impartiality. It was necessary to establish some kind of institution which should be entirely free and to appoint men according to their qualifications and without regard to their opinions.'[10]

However, despite lengthy discussions, few of Einstein's proposals were implemented; other members of the Committee were fearful of the interference with national sovereignty that they entailed.

Einstein's work in the League of Nations had the long-term objective of providing the basis for the peaceful coexistence of nations by creating more opportunities for collaboration and by fostering better understanding. At the same time, however, he was mindful of a short-term objective, which growing nationalist sentiment had made very urgent – namely, resistance to war. In the period 1925–32, Einstein became one of the most active leaders of the international anti-war movement.

Naturally, he sought to emphasise the role of science. Together with other scientists and scholars he attended many conferences and signed statements and appeals such as this:

'Science and technical skills are daily increasing the power of men to inflict injury on one another. By an automatic process, apparently beyond any partial regulation, scientific development has been used from its very beginning to perfect the art of killing. . . . The undersigned consider it their urgent duty emphatically to denounce the frightful danger threatening the whole of humanity, and in particular the more civilized nations, through these preparations for a new scientific warfare.'[11]

He realised, however, that scientists alone would not be really effective in efforts to abolish war, and that these must be supplemented by the direct action of members of the community in refusing to serve in a war. In a letter to the 'No More War Movement' he said:

'Science is a powerful instrument. How it is used, whether it is a blessing or a curse to man, depends on man himself and not on the instrument. . . . As long as human beings are systematically trained to commit crimes against mankind, the mentality thus created can only lead to catastrophe again and again. Our only hope lies in refusing any action that may serve the preparation or the purpose of war.'[12]

He amplified this by a solemn declaration about himself:

'I would unconditionally refuse all war service, direct or indirect, and would seek to persuade my friends to adopt the same position, regardless of how I might feel about the causes of any particular war.'[13]

Having thus committed himself, he felt obliged to defend those who, having followed his appeal, found themselves in trouble by refusing to do military service. This meant that he had to intercede with the authorities of several countries on their behalf. But his main effort was to give active and moral support to the many international organisations for disarmament and against war. These organisations included the War Resisters' International, the Women's International League for Peace and Freedom, the People's Parliament for Disarmament, the World Peace League, the Joint Peace Council, the League of Nations Association, and the International Union for Antimilitarist Clergymen and Ministers. Whenever he could find the time he participated in their meetings; otherwise he sent letters of support and encouragement. But he exercised discretion in the causes he sponsored. Despite his often expressed keenness for unity among the various groups in the pacifist movement, he refused to support organisations which tended to exploit pacifism for ulterior motives. Thus he declined to attend the International Congress against Imperialist Wars held in 1932 in Amsterdam. In refusing to sign the appeal which was to be issued from the congress, he wrote:

'Because of the glorification of Soviet Russia which it includes, I cannot bring myself to sign it.'[14]

Later he explained his attitude to the Soviet Union as follows:

'I am a convinced democrat. It is for this reason that I do not go to Russia although I have received very cordial invitations. . . . I am an adversary of Bolshevism just as much as of Fascism. I am against all dictatorships.'[15]

The Nazi menace: 1933–9

By 1932 Einstein was the acknowledged international champion of pacifism, the outstanding advocate of peaceful methods of settling disputes, and the staunchest opponent of war in all its ramifications. But all this changed radically in 1933. Within a short time Einstein reversed his pacifist stand and began to advocate military preparedness by the democratic countries of Europe.

The cause of this volte-face was the Nazis' seizure of power in Germany in January 1933. This event had momentous repercussions on his personal life: he left Germany for good and moved to the Institute for Advanced Studies in Princeton, United States, where he remained until the end of his life. The change of his political outlook was simply the result of his sober and realistic assessment of the situation. Einstein recognised the shape of things to come long before this had penetrated the minds of other leaders in the pacifist camp. Quite early on he arrived at the conclusion that the Hitler regime was aiming at the military conquest of Europe, that the war preparations were not a bluff, and that Europe's only hope of avoiding fascist tyranny lay in adopting a posture of military strength. Most pacifists failed to appreciate that the danger was real, or else dogmatically refused to deviate from their rigid pacifist principles under any circumstances. To them, Einstein became an apostate, a traitor to the cause of peace.

Even though he still supported people who refused to be conscripted into military service, he began to be attracted to the idea of securing world peace by setting up an international police force. With the advent of the Hitler regime, Einstein became increasingly convinced of the need for an organised military power to counteract the Nazi menace; but he insisted that the military organisation must have an international character. And he was soon to revise his views about refusal of national military service. Thus he wrote in July 1933:

'... I must confess freely that the time seems inauspicious for further advocacy of certain propositions of the radical pacifist movement. For example, is one justified in advising a Frenchman or a Belgian to refuse military service in the face of German rearmament? Ought one to campaign for such a policy? Frankly, I do not believe so. It seems to me that in the present situation we must support a *supranational* organization of force rather than advocate the abolition of all forces. Recent events have taught me a lesson in this respect . . .'[16]

In reply to a request to intervene on behalf of a conscientious objector, he said:

'... Were I a Belgian, I should not, in the present circumstances, refuse military service; rather, I should enter such service cheerfully in the belief that I would thereby be helping to save European civilization.

'This does not mean that I am surrendering the principle for which I have stood heretofore. I have no greater hope than that the time may not be far off when refusal of military service will once again be an effective method of serving the cause of human progress.'[17]

At first these utterances were greeted with disbelief in the pacifist movement, and Einstein had to confirm his new attitude in several letters to them.

'... my views have not changed, but the European situation has. . . . So long as Germany persists in rearming and systematically indoctrinating its citizens in preparation for a war of revenge, the nations of Western Europe depend, unfortunately, on military defense. Indeed I will go so far as to assert that if they are prudent, they will not wait, unarmed, to be attacked. . . . They must be adequately prepared.

'I take little pleasure in saying this, for in my heart I loathe violence and militarism as much as ever; but I cannot shut my eyes to realities.'[18]

In a general statement issued before leaving for the United States, he said:

'My ideal remains the settlement of all international disputes by arbitration. Until a year and a half ago, I considered refusal to do military service one of the most effective steps to the achievement of that goal. At that time, throughout the civilized world there was not a single nation which actually intended to overwhelm any other nation by force. I remain wholeheartedly devoted to the idea that belligerent actions must be avoided and improved relations among nations must be accomplished.

'For that very reason I believe nothing should be done that is likely to weaken the organized power of those European countries which today represent the best hope of realizing that idea.'[19]

These explanations did not satisfy the pacifist leaders, who launched a bitter attack on him:

'...At a very critical moment Einstein takes the part of militarism....He now thinks he can save European civilization by means of fire bombs, poison gas and bacteria....The apostasy of Einstein is a great victory for German National Socialism. ...Einstein's action has done unutterable harm to the fight against militarism.'[20]

Einstein's comment was blunt:

'...The antimilitarists attack me as being an evil renegade. These fellows wear blinders; they refuse to acknowledge their expulsion from "paradise".'[21]

Nevertheless, he felt bound to explain his views at greater length. In September 1933, in a letter to another pacifist, he wrote:

'I assure you that my present attitude toward military service was arrived at with the greatest reluctance and after a difficult inner struggle. The root of all evil lies in the fact that there is no powerful international police force, nor is there a really effective international court of arbitration whose judgements could be enforced. All the same, antimilitarists were justified in refusing military service as long as the majority of the nations of Europe were intent upon peace. This no longer holds true. I am convinced that developments in Germany tend toward belligerent acts similar to those in France after the Revolution. Should this trend meet with success, you may be sure that the last remnants of personal freedom on the continent of Europe will be destroyed.

'While it is quite true that the deterioration of conditions in Germany is partially attributable to the policies of neighbouring countries, there seems little purpose at this juncture in blaming them for these policies. The plain fact is that the gospel of force and repression, currently prevailing in Germany, poses grave threats to the Continent of Europe and the independence of its inhabitants. This threat cannot successfully be combated by moral means; it can be met only by organized might. To prevent the greater evil, it is necessary that the lesser evil — the hated military — be accepted for the time being. Should German armed might prevail, life will not be worth living anywhere in Europe....To summarize: In the present circumstances, realistic pacifists should no longer advocate the destruction of military power; rather, they should strive for its internationalization. Only when such internationalization has been achieved will it be possible to work toward the reduction of military power to the dimensions of an international police force. We do not cause the danger to disappear by merely closing our eyes to it.'[22]

During the following years, Einstein's public interventions became rarer; his gloom deepened as he observed his predictions about the Nazis' designs gradually coming true, with no measures being taken to counteract them. Writing to his friend, the Queen Mother of Belgium, he said that the gloomy and evil events in Europe paralysed him to such an extent that he was unable to communicate feelings of a personal nature in writing. Increasingly, he resented the shortsightedness of his erstwhile fellow campaigners. In 1937 he wrote to the American League against War and Fascism:

'It is, in principle, reassuring that a widespread organization, such as yours, exists to advocate the ideals of democracy and pacifism. On the other hand, it must be said that of late pacifists have harmed rather than helped the cause of democracy. This is especially obvious in England, where the pacifist influence has dangerously delayed the rearmament which has become necessary because of the military preparations in the Fascist countries.

It is quite true that any increase in military strength represents a danger to democracy. But if the democracies remain unarmed and defenceless in the face of the bellicose Fascist countries, the danger to democracy will be far greater.

In my view, this whole dilemma results from the rather shortsighted policies which the pacifist organizations have pursued. The supreme goal of pacifists must be the avoidance of war through establishment of an international organization, and not the temporary avoidance of rearmament or involvement in international conflict. . . . The main goal of pacifist propaganda should be to support the strongest possible supranational authority for the settlement of international conflicts. But no support should be given to the concept of isolationism which today can only be characterized as the most shortsighted kind of selfishness.'[23]

In 1939, in another letter to the Queen Mother of Belgium, he expressed his premonition of impending catastrophe:

'. . . I have been too troubled to write in good cheer. The moral decline we are compelled to witness and the suffering it engenders are so oppressive that one cannot ignore them even for a moment. No matter how deeply one immerses oneself in work, a haunting feeling of inescapable tragedy persists.'[24]

Soon afterwards the tragedy commenced.

The Second World War: 1939—45

Einstein's role in initiating the work on nuclear weapons which eventually brought the war to an end, has been described in numerous publications, but it is still given a false gloss and he is often described as the father of the atom bomb. On the technological side, he has been given the credit for laying the foundations for it through his 1905 formula ($E = mc^2$) of the equivalence of mass and energy. On the political side, he is acknowledged as the person who gave the impetus to the United States Government to start work on the bomb. In reality, his contribution can hardly be described in these terms. Unlike his other pursuits, both in science and in politics, where he usually actively led the field, his role in the atom bomb project was passive. He himself never thought that the equivalence of mass and energy would find any practical application during his lifetime; he was greatly surprised when told of the possibility of a fission chain reaction leading to an unprecedented release of energy: 'That never occurred to me', he is reported to have said. As for the initiative in starting the bomb project, this was a case of his great reputation being blatantly used by others — admittedly in a cause which Einstein willingly supported once the problem was outlined to him.

The prime mover in this affair was Leo Szilard, a Hungarian scientist whom Einstein had known since 1920. As early as 1934, Szilard foresaw that a chain reaction propagated by neutrons could lead to a large release of energy; but he was unable to pursue his hypothesis for lack of funds.[25] He returned to it immediately after the discovery of fission in 1938, but, once again, his research project met with little enthusiasm. Worried that German scientists would go ahead with the research and perhaps even make the bomb, he turned to Einstein for help. Initially, Szilard's intention was to use Einstein's friendship with the Queen Mother of Belgium to try to persuade the Belgian Government to stop the export of uranium from the Congo to Germany. But this was soon dropped in favour of an appeal to President Roosevelt to authorise research work on chain reactions in uranium with a view to its possible military applications. After Szilard and other scientists had prepared several drafts of a letter to Roosevelt, Einstein arranged for an intermediary, Dr Alexander Sachs, to deliver the following plea:

> Albert Einstein
> Old Grove Road
> Nassau Point
> Peconic, Long Island
> August 2, 1939

F. D. Roosevelt
President of the United States
White House
Washington, D.C.

Sir:

Some recent work by E. Fermi and L. Szilard, which has been communicated to me in manuscript, leads me to expect that the element uranium may be turned into a new and important source of energy in the immediate future. Certain aspects of the situation seem to call for watchfulness and, if necessary, quick action on the part of the Administration. I believe, therefore, that it is my duty to bring to your attention the following facts and recommendations.

In the course of the last four months it has been made probable – through the work of Joliot in France as well as Fermi and Szilard in America – that it may become possible to set up nuclear chain reactions in a large mass of uranium, by which vast amounts of power and large quantities of new radium-like elements would be generated. Now it appears almost certain that this could be achieved in the immediate future.

This new phenomenon would also lead to the construction of bombs, and it is conceivable – though much less certain – that extremely powerful bombs of a new type may thus be constructed. A single bomb of this type, carried by boat or exploded in a port, might very well destroy the whole port together with some of the surrounding territory. However, such bombs might very well prove to be too heavy for transportation by air.

The United States has only very poor ores of uranium in moderate quantities. There is some good ore in Canada and the former Czechoslovakia, while the most important source of uranium is the Belgian Congo.

In view of this situation you may think it desirable to have some permanent contact maintained between the Administration and the group of physicists working on chain reactions in America. One possible way of achieving this might be for you to entrust with this task a person who has your confidence and who could perhaps serve in an unofficial capacity. His task might comprise the following:

(a) To approach Government Departments, keep them informed of the further developments and put forward recommendations for Government action, giving particular attention to the problem of securing a supply of uranium ore for the United States.

(b) To speed up the experimental work which is at present being carried on within the limits of the budgets of University laboratories, by providing funds, if such funds be required, through his contacts with private persons who are willing to make contributions for this cause, and perhaps also by obtaining the cooperation of industrial laboratories which have the necessary equipment.

I understand that Germany has actually stopped the sale of uranium from the Czechoslovakian mines which she has taken over. That she should have taken such early action might perhaps be understood on the ground that the son of the German Under-Secretary of State, von Weizsäcker, is attached to the Kaiser Wilhelm Institut in Berlin, where some of the American work on uranium is now being repeated.

Yours very truly,

A. Einstein[26]

The letter did not reach Roosevelt until the middle of October, weeks after the war started in Europe, but the President replied promptly as follows:

The White House
Washington

19 October, 1939

My Dear Professor,

I want to thank you for your recent letter and the most interesting and important enclosure.

I found this data of such import that I have convened a board consisting of the head of the Bureau of Standards and a chosen representative of the Army and Navy to thoroughly investigate the possibilities of your suggestion regarding the element of uranium.

I am glad to say that Dr. Sachs will co-operate and work with this committee and I feel this is the most practical and effective method of dealing with the subject.

Please accept my sincere thanks.

Very sincerely yours,

Franklin D. Roosevelt

Dr. Albert Einstein
Old Grove Pond
Nassau Point, Peconic
Long Island, New York[27]

The committee mentioned in the letter was immediately set up, but it made very slow progress. In March 1940, at Szilard's instigation, Einstein wrote a letter to Sachs intended for the President, drawing attention to the increased interest in uranium in Germany and urging an acceleration of the American effort. As a result, Einstein was invited to become a member of an enlarged Advisory Committee on Uranium. He declined the invitation, for he did not think that he could contribute to the work of the Committee.

This was the end of Einstein's direct involvement with the atom bomb project, an involvement which later he deeply regretted, calling it the one great mistake in his life. In 1950 he explained his intervention as follows:

> 'I have never taken part in work of a military—technical nature and have never done research having any bearing upon the production of the atomic bomb. My sole contribution in this field was that, in 1905, I established the relationship between mass and energy, a truth about the physical world of a very general nature, whose possible connection with the military potential was completely foreign to my thoughts. My only contribution with respect to the atomic bomb was that, in 1939, I signed a letter to President Roosevelt in which I called attention to the existing possibility of producing such a bomb and to the danger that the Germans might make use of that possibility. I considered this my duty because there were definite indications that the Germans were working on such a project.'[28]

How decisive was Einstein's initiative? It is quite possible that without Einstein's letter to Roosevelt the whole project might have been considerably delayed. On the other hand, independent work on the atom bomb had started in the United Kingdom, and it was here, indeed, that the feasibility of a nuclear explosive was established for the first time. It is believed that it was the transmission of this result to the Americans that finally convinced the United States Government to start the project in earnest.[29]

Einstein became involved in the bomb issue once more — again through Szilard — near the end of the war. By then, the military defeat of Germany was practically accomplished, but work on the atom bomb was continuing with the intention of using it against Japan. Szilard was strongly opposed to this. He foresaw the effect such an act would have on post-war relations and the danger of the nuclear arms race that was bound to follow. Officially, Einstein knew nothing about the progress on the bomb project and Szilard could not put him into the picture. Nevertheless, Szilard impressed him enough to make him write a letter to Roosevelt asking for an appointment for Szilard. This letter was written on 25 March 1945; but it never reached Roosevelt, who died a few weeks later. President Truman subsequently arranged an interview between Szilard and James Byrnes but these two never reached a mutual understanding. Despite further efforts by Szilard and other scientists, two atom bombs were detonated over Japanese cities.

The nuclear age: 1945—55

The war over and fascism defeated, Einstein — at the age of 66 — might have retired honourably from active political life. Instead he intensified his efforts, and the post-war years became a period of strenuous endeavours in the public arena. The reason for this was the new danger that arose as an aftermath of the war: the danger of complete annihilation in a nuclear war. The threat of such a war loomed large as the Cold War deepened and the nuclear arms race accelerated. The last ten years of Einstein's life were devoted to an incessant struggle to prevent a nuclear catastrophe. His age and state of health did not allow him to attend the many conferences and mass rallies that were convened on his initiative, but he sent messages of greetings, wrote articles in newspapers and journals, spoke on radio and television, and engaged in an enormous correspondence with many individuals and groups. He continued his public activities right up until his death.

As always he took the long view in assessing the new situation that had arisen from the development of nuclear weapons. The same perspective guided his attitude to the consequences of the growing divergence between the United States and the Soviet Union – a divergence aggravated by America's insistence on maintaining nuclear superiority. He came to the conclusion that no partial disarmament would be adequate, and that the only hope for the survival of mankind was through world government. The idea of a supranational authority, which he had advocated in the First World War, assumed much greater urgency after the Second World War and became the main focus of his activities.

Einstein was well aware that the Soviet Union was opposed to world government. He knew this even before the point was put to him explicitly in 1947 in a letter from four eminent Russian scientists, who maintained that world government would ensure world supremacy of the capitalist monopolies and that the call for it was prejudicial to the cause of peace which Einstein so warmly espoused. Einstein replied to this 'benevolent attack' on him with a long article in which he analysed the world situation and patiently explained why he has arrived at the idea of a world government as the only solution. The last part of his article reads:

'If we hold fast to the concept and practice of unlimited sovereignty of nations it only means that each country reserves the right for itself of pursuing its objectives through warlike means. Under the circumstances, every nation must be prepared for that possibility; this means it must try with all its might to be superior to anyone else. This objective will dominate more and more our entire public life and will poison our youth long before the catastrophe is itself actually upon us. We must not tolerate this, however, as long as we still retain a tiny bit of calm reasoning and human feelings.

This alone is on my mind in supporting the idea of "World Government", without any regard to what other people may have in mind when working for the same objective. I advocate world government because I am convinced that there is no other possible way of eliminating the most terrible danger in which man has ever found himself. The objective of avoiding total destruction must have priority over any other objective.

I am sure you are convinced that this letter is written with all the seriousness and honesty at my command; I trust you will accept it in the same spirit.'[30]

Einstein realised that, in the prevailing climate, his logic would not be heeded – however persuasive it might be. But he considered that if other countries accepted the need for world government and began to take steps to implement it the Soviet Union would come in sooner or later. In the early period after the war such ideas had a sympathetic response in the Western world, and the various organisations which worked towards this goal enjoyed considerable mass support. But political events such as the Korean War and the growing hysteria in the United States about 'un-American' activities dampened enthusiasm and led to a decline in the campaigns for world government. Einstein met this with increasing gloom about the prospects of the survival of mankind.

Einstein was most interested in the role of scientists in tackling these issues and he gave strong support to the scientists' movements which sprung up after the war. In 1946 he became the chairman of the Emergency Committee of Atomic Scientists, a fund-raising and policy-making agency for several organisations of American scientists. The fund-raising campaign was very successful – the magic of Einstein's name always worked – and assisted the activities of the Federation of American Scientists and the publication of the *Bulletin of the Atomic Scientists,* a journal devoted to the ideals for which Einstein fought. The policy of the Emergency Committee was summarised in the following statement issued at its first conference in 1946:

'These facts are accepted by all scientists:

1. Atomic bombs can now be made cheaply and in large number. They will become more destructive.

2. There is no military defence against the atomic bomb and none is to be expected.

3. Other nations can rediscover our secret processes by themselves.

4. Preparedness against atomic war is futile, and if attempted will ruin the structure of our social order.

5. If war breaks out, atomic bombs will be used and they will surely destroy our civilization.

6. There is no solution to this problem except international control of atomic energy and, ultimately, the elimination of war.

The program of the committee is to see that these truths become known to the public. The democratic determination of this nation's policy on atomic energy must ultimately rest on the understanding of its citizens.'[31]

The Emergency Committee endorsed Einstein's view about world government. Later, however, it lost its impetus and was disbanded in 1951.

From time to time pacifist organisations advocated a kind of Hippocratic Oath for scientists, based upon a refusal to do any work of a military nature. Though he was always opposed to the use of science for military purposes, Einstein thought such ideas unrealistic. In a reply to a call from scientists to support such a cause he said:

'. . . we must first ask ourselves: Would any action by a group as small as the group recently assembled in Princeton have any decisive influence? Would the physicists and engineers necessarily follow our course of action? And assuming they would want to, would they be *free* to do so? To these questions my answer is "no", for the following reasons:

1. Almost all scientists are economically completely dependent.

2. The number of scientists who possess a sense of social responsibility is so small that their "non-participation" would have virtually no effect on the production of armaments.

For these reasons I do not believe that your proposal is, in any sense, practicable; indeed, it is doubtful whether anything of value could be achieved by forcing its adoption.'[32]

However, he was strongly in favour of scientists becoming actively involved in helping the community and governments to lessen the dangers arising from scientific progress. Almost the last act of his life was to endorse an appeal in this spirit.

The initiative came from Bertrand Russell. Alarmed by the development of the H-bomb and the intensifying arms race, Russell conceived the idea that scientists ought to do something dramatic to bring home to the public and governments the magnitude of the disaster that might occur. In February 1955, he wrote to Einstein with the suggestion that a few eminent scientists, headed by Einstein, should issue a public statement to this effect. Russell felt that the signatories of the statement should be so diverse in their politics that any statement signed by all of them would be obviously free from pro-communist or anti-communist bias. In an immediate reply, Einstein fully agreed with the proposal and suggested that Russell should draft the statement and assume leadership of the project. Russell prepared the draft and sent it to Einstein together with a suggested list of signatories. The letter was dated 5 April. Russell recollects[33] that as he flew from Rome to Paris the pilot announced the news of Einstein's death. Russell felt shattered, not only for the obvious reasons, but because he saw the plan falling through without Einstein's support. But, on arrival at his Paris hotel, he found a letter from Einstein with his signature to the statement and agreement to the choice of proposed signatories. This was the last letter that Einstein signed.

The statement was issued at a large press conference in London on 9 July 1955. It reads as follows:

The Russell–Einstein Manifesto

In the tragic situation which confronts humanity, we feel that scientists should assemble in conference to appraise the perils that have arisen as a result of the development of weapons of mass destruction, and to discuss a resolution in the spirit of the appended draft.

We are speaking on this occasion, not as members of this or that nation, continent, or creed, but as human beings, members of the species Man, whose continued existence is in doubt. The world is full of conflicts; and, overshadowing all minor conflicts, the titanic struggle between Communism and anti-Communism.

Almost everybody who is politically conscious has strong feelings about one or more of these issues; but we want you, if you can, to set aside such feelings and consider yourselves only as members of a biological species which has had a remarkable history, and whose disappearance none of us can desire.

We shall try to say no single word which should appeal to one group rather than to another. All, equally, are in peril, and, if the peril is understood, there is hope that they may collectively avert it.

We have to learn to think in a new way. We have to learn to ask ourselves, not what steps can be taken to give military victory to whatever group we prefer, for there no longer are such steps; the question we have to ask ourselves is: what steps can be taken to prevent a military contest of which the issue must be disastrous to all parties?

The general public, and even many men in position of authority, have not realized what would be involved in a war with nuclear bombs. The general public still thinks in terms of the obliteration of cities. It is understood that the new bombs are more powerful than the old, and that, while one A-bomb could obliterate Hiroshima, one H-bomb could obliterate the largest cities, such as London, New York and Moscow.

No doubt in an H-bomb war great cities would be obliterated. But this is one of the minor disasters that would have to be faced. If everybody in London, New York and Moscow were exterminated, the world might, in the course of a few centuries, recover from the blow. But we now know, especially since the Bikini test, that nuclear bombs can gradually spread destruction over a very much wider area than had been supposed.

It is stated on very good authority that a bomb can now be manufactured which will be 2,500 times as powerful as that which destroyed Hiroshima. Such a bomb, if exploded near the ground or under water, sends radioactive particles into the upper air. They sink gradually and reach the surface of the earth in the form of a deadly dust or rain. It was this dust which infected the Japanese fishermen and their catch of fish.

No one knows how widely such lethal radioactive particles might be diffused, but the best authorities are unanimous in saying that a war with H-bombs might quite possibly put an end to the human race. It is feared that if many H-bombs are used there will be universal death — sudden only for a minority, but for the majority a slow torture of disease and disintegration.

Many warnings have been uttered by eminent men of science and by authorities in military strategy. None of them will say that the worst results are certain. What they do say is that these results are possible, and no one can be sure that they will not be realized. We have not yet found that the views of experts on this question depend in any degree upon their politics or prejudices. They depend only, so far as our researches have revealed, upon the extent of the particular expert's knowledge. We have found that the men who know most are the most gloomy.

Here, then, is the problem which we present to you, stark and dreadful and inescapable: Shall we put an end to the human race; or shall mankind renounce war? People will not face this alternative because it is so difficult to abolish war.

The abolition of war will demand distasteful limitations of national sovereignty. But what perhaps impedes understanding of the situation more than anything else is that the term "mankind" feels vague and abstract. People scarcely realize in imagination that the danger is to themselves and their children and their grandchildren, and not only to a dimly apprehended humanity. They can scarcely bring themselves to grasp that they, individually, and those whom they love are in imminent danger of perishing agonizingly. And so they hope that perhaps war may be allowed to continue provided modern weapons are prohibited.

This hope is illusory. Whatever agreements not to use H-bombs had been reached in time of peace, they would no longer be considered binding in time of war, and both sides would set to work to manufacture H-bombs as soon as war broke out, for, if one side manufactured the bombs and the other did not, the side that manufactured them would inevitably be victorious.

Although an agreement to renounce nuclear weapons as part of a general reduction of armaments would not afford an ultimate solution, it would serve certain important purposes. First: any agreement between East and West is to the good insofar as it tends to diminish tension. Second: the abolition of thermo-nuclear weapons, if each side believed that the other had carried it out sincerely, would lessen the fear of a sudden attack in the style of Pearl Harbour, which at present keeps both sides in a state of nervous apprehension. We should, therefore, welcome such an agreement, though only as a first step.

Most of us are not neutral in feeling, but as human beings, we have to remember that, if the issues between East and West are to be decided in any manner that can give any possible satisfaction to anybody, whether Communist or anti-Communist, whether Asian or European or American, whether White or Black, then these issues must not be decided by war. We should wish this to be understood, both in the East and in the West.

There lies before us, if we choose, continual progress in happiness, knowledge, and wisdom. Shall we, instead, choose death, because we cannot forget our quarrels? We appeal, as human beings, to human beings: remember your humanity, and forget the rest. If you can do so, the way lies open to a new Paradise; if you cannot, there lies before you the risk of universal death.

Resolution

We invite this Congress, and through it the scientists of the world and the general public, to subscribe to the following resolution:

"In view of the fact that in any future world war nuclear weapons will certainly be employed, and that such weapons threaten the continued existence of mankind, we urge the Governments of the world to realize, and to acknowledge publicly, that their purpose cannot be furthered by a world war, and we urge them, consequently, to find peaceful means for the settlement of all matters of dispute between them".

Professor Max Born (Professor of Theoretical Physics at Berlin, Frankfurt, and Göttingen, and of Natural Philosophy, Edinburgh; Nobel Prize in physics).

Professor P. W. Bridgman (Professor of Physics, Harvard University; Nobel Prize in physics).

Professor Albert Einstein.

Professor L. Infeld (Professor of Theoretical Physics, University of Warsaw).

Professor J. F. Joliot-Curie (Professor of Physics at the Collège de France; Nobel Prize in chemistry).

Professor H. J. Muller (Professor of Zoology at University of Indiana; Nobel Prize in physiology and medicine).

Professor Linus Pauling (Professor of Chemistry, California Institute of Technology; Nobel Prize in chemistry).

Professor C. F. Powell (Professor of Physics, Bristol University; Nobel Prize in physics).

Professor J. Rotblat (Professor of Physics, University of London; Medical College of St. Bartholomew's Hospital).

Bertrand Russell.

Professor Hideki Yukawa (Professor of Theoretical Physics, Kyoto University; Nobel Prize in physics).'[34]

This statement, which became known as the Russell—Einstein Manifesto, was subsequently endorsed by thousands of scientists from many countries. It became the credo of the Pugwash conferences on science and world affairs. The Pugwash Movement, which is the direct outcome of the Russell—Einstein Manifesto, carries out its activities in the spirit of the Manifesto to this day.

Thus, a quarter of a century after Einstein's death, the ideals for which he strove throughout his life are being cherished, promoted and gradually implemented by an ever-increasing number of scientists.

Notes

1. O. Nathan and H. Norden, *Einstein on peace,* Simon & Schuster, 1960, p. 98.
2. Ibid., p. 93.
3. Ibid., p. 111.
4. Ibid., p. 54.
5. Ibid., p. 25.
6. Ibid., p. 4.
7. Ibid., p. 25.
8. Ibid., p. 60.
9. Ibid., p. 69.
10. Ibid., p. 76.
11. Ibid., p. 94.
12. Ibid., p. 104.
13. Ibid., p. 95.
14. Ibid., p. 78.
15. Ibid., p. 234.
16. Ibid., p. 226.
17. Ibid., p. 229.
18. Ibid., p. 230.
19. Ibid., p. 234.
20. Ibid., p. 232.
21. Ibid., p. 235.
22. Ibid., p. 235.
23. Ibid., p. 276.
24. Ibid., p. 282.
25. B. T. Field and Gertrud Weiss Szilard, eds., *The collected works of Leo Szilard,* MIT Press, 1972.
26. Nathan and Norden, op. cit., p. 294.
27. Ibid., p. 297.
28. Ibid., p. 519.
29. Margaret Gowing, *Britain and atomic energy,* Macmillan, 1964.
30. *Bulletin of the Atomic Scientists,* vol. 4, no. 2, 1947, p. 35.
31. Nathan and Norden, op. cit., p. 395.
32. Ibid., p. 456.
33. *The autobiography of Bertrand Russell,* vol. 3, Allen & Unwin, 1969.
34. J. Rotblat, *Scientists in the quest for peace,* MIT Press, 1972.

Einstein's political struggle

Brian Easlea

Dr Brian Easlea took his BSc and PhD degrees in physics at University College, London. He then worked in nuclear structure theory at the Niels Bohr Institute, Copenhagen, and afterwards taught theoretical physics in the USA, in England, and in Brazil. In 1972 he was appointed a lecturer in history and social studies of science at Sussex University. He is at present investigating the influence of the 'male–female relation' on the development and application of modern science.

From *Liberation and the aims of science,* Sussex University Press, 1973.

In this paper a few extracts are given from Einstein's writings in the crucial period from the end of the Second World War to his death in 1955. They reveal and summarise the thoughts and anguish of an outstanding scientist and revolutionary thinker as he watches the physics he has loved and to which he had contributed so greatly being used not only in a way over which he had no control but in a way which represented the negation of all he had been striving to achieve in life.

It was not only with respect to quantum mechanics that Einstein pursued a lonely path. Time and again he tried to warn his fellow scientists and American citizens that the path they were following would lead to catastrophic consequences. At the end of his life Einstein felt himself forced to acknowledge failure. Although he had been able to keep his independence of judgement, as incessant propaganda took its toll of so many other men whose avowed intention it was to retain the ability to criticise, to judge and to choose, nevertheless Einstein had been unable to change the programme to disaster which he saw so clearly American policy would invite.

Given in chronological order, without comment, the following extracts from Einstein's letters, articles and talks tell their own story. (We begin the series of extracts with a letter written *to* Einstein; all remaining extracts are from Einstein's writings or talks.)

21 October 1945. From a letter written to Einstein by a physicist from the Radiation Laboratory of the Massachusetts Institute of Technology:

> 'The scientists of Cambridge, as well as those throughout the world, need help urgently in these days of turmoil and unprecedented tension. What makes the present atomic power situation so full of anguish for all of us is the cruel irony wherein one of the greatest and most joyful triumphs of scientific intellect may bring frustration and death rather than spiritual uplifting and more audacious life. The final total confirmation of your principle $E = mc^2$ should mark the beginning of an era of light; but we stand perturbed and seem to see ahead an impenetrable night. . . .'[1]

10 December 1945. From an address to a Nobel Anniversary dinner in New York:

> 'Alfred Nobel invented an explosive more powerful than any then known — an exceedingly effective means of destruction. To atone for this "accomplishment" and to relieve his conscience, he instituted his awards for the promotion of peace. Today, the physicists who participated in producing the most formidable weapon of all time are harassed by a similar feeling of responsibility, not to say guilt. As scientists, we must never cease to warn against the danger created by these weapons; we dare not slacken in our efforts to make the peoples of the world, and especially their governments, aware of the unspeakable disaster they are certain to provoke unless they change their attitude toward one another and recognize their responsibility in shaping a safe future. . . . The war is won, but the peace is not. The great powers, united in war, have become divided over the peace settlements. The peoples of the world were promised freedom from fear; but the fact is that fear among nations has increased enormously since the end of war. The world was promised freedom from want; but vast areas of the world face starvation, while elsewhere people live in abundance. The nations of the world were promised liberty and justice; but even now we are witnessing the sad spectacle of armies of "liberation" firing on peoples who demand political independence and social equality, and supporting by force of arms, those individuals and political parties which they consider best suited to represent their own vested interests. Territorial conflicts and power politics, obsolete as these purposes of national policy may be, still prevail over the essential requirements of human welfare and justice. . . .'[2]

29 May 1946. From a radio address to a Chicago rally of the Students for Federal World Government:

'Many people say that, in the present circumstances, fundamental agreement between the United States and the Soviet Union is impossible. Such an assertion might be justified had America made a really serious effort in that direction since the end of the war. It seems to me that America has done just the opposite: It was not wise to admit Fascist Argentina into the United Nations over Russia's protest. Further, there was no need to keep on producing more and more atomic bombs and to spend twelve billion dollars in a single year on armaments, when there was no military threat in sight. Nor was there any sense in denying Trieste to Yugoslavia, a former ally who was in real need of this port that has, in fact, little economic significance to Italy, a former enemy country. There is no further point in further enumerating all the details which indicate that nothing was done by the United Nations to mollify Russia's distrust. In fact, we have done much toward fostering this distrust which the events of the last several decades make only too understandable.'[3]

20 January 1947. In reply to a question from the Overseas News Agency with respect to Professor Wiener's withdrawal from a symposium on computers organised by Harvard University and the United States Navy:

'I greatly admire and approve the attitude of Professor Wiener; I believe that a similar attitude on the part of all the prominent scientists in this country would contribute much toward solving the urgent problem of international security.

'Non-cooperation in military matters should be an essential moral principle for all true scientists, i.e., for all who are engaged in basic research. It is true that it is more difficult for scientists in non-democratic countries to adopt such an attitude; but the fact is that, at present, the non-democratic countries constitute less of a threat to healthy international developments than the democratic nations which, enjoying economic and military superiority, have subjected scholars to military mobilization.'[4]

21 February 1947. In a message broadcast over a New York station in support of the nomination of Lilienthal as head of the United States Atomic Energy Commission:

'You all know that the policies of the United States since the end of the war have caused anxiety and distrust throughout the world. The destruction of large Japanese cities without adequate previous warning, the unceasing production of atomic bombs, the Bikini tests, the expenditures of many billions of dollars for military purposes despite the absence of any external threat, the attempt to militarize science — all this has impeded the development of mutual trust among nations which is indispensable to the establishment of a secure peace.'[5]

17 July 1947. In a broadcast on 'The immediate need for world law':

'The Soviet experiences with the outer world have never been too good. We must remember the support of the West by anti-Soviet generals during the [Russian] Civil War, the long political and economic boycott against the Soviet Union, the constant propaganda campaign of the foreign press against Soviet Russia. Later on the Russians joined the League of Nations, but then they saw how the Fascist aggressions in Manchuria, in Spain, in Abyssinia, in Austria, were accepted and condoned, how agreements were made with the aggressors. And eventually, when they found themselves excluded from the most crucial European settlements in the first period of the Hitler regime, then, understandably enough, they changed their attitude.'[6]

November 1947. In an article entitled 'Atomic war or peace' published in the *Atlantic Monthly:*

'At present, the Russians have no reason to believe that the American people are not actually supporting a policy of military preparedness, which they regard as a policy of deliberate intimidation. . . . Not until a genuine, convincing offer is made by the United States to the Soviet Union, supported by an aroused American public, will one be entitled to be hopeful about a possible response by Russia.'[7]

28 January 1948. From a letter to an army officer who had challenged Einstein's opposition to conscription:

'I believe the danger lies at present in the possibility that America may totally succumb to that fearful militarization which engulfed Germany half a century ago. . . . We should never forget that it is totally unlikely that any country will attack America in the near future, least of all Russia, which is devastated, impoverished and politically isolated. . . .'[8]

27 April 1948. From a message to the One World Award Committee:

'The proposed militarization of the nation not only immediately threatens us with war; it will also slowly but surely undermine the democratic spirit and the dignity of the individual in our land. The assertion that events abroad are forcing us to arm is incorrect; we must combat this false assumption with all our strength. Actually, our own rearmament, because of its effect upon other nations, will bring about the very state of affairs upon which the advocates of armaments seek to base their proposals.'[9]

17 June 1948. From a message to a public meeting organised by Professor Harlow Shapley:

'The United States emerged from the war as the strongest military and economic power and, temporarily, is the only country to possess the powerful atomic bomb. Such power imposes a heavy obligation. To a large extent, the United States is responsible for the ominous competitive arms race which has taken place since the end of the war and which has virtually destroyed the postwar prospects for an effective supranational solution of the security problem.'[10]

May 1949. From an article by Einstein entitled 'Why socialism' which appeared in the first issue of *Monthly Review:*

'The economic anarchy of capitalist society as it exists today is, in my opinion, the real source of the evil. We see before us a huge community of producers the members of which are unceasingly striving to deprive each other of the fruits of their collective labour — not by force, but on the whole in faithful compliance with legally established rules. . . . The result of these developments is an oligarchy of private capital the enormous power of which cannot be effectively checked even by a democratically organized political society. This is true since the members of legislative bodies are selected by political parties, largely financed or otherwise influenced by private capitalists who, for all practical purposes, separate the electorate from the legislature. . . . Moreover, under existing conditions, private capitalists inevitably control, directly or indirectly, the main sources of information (press, radio, education). It is thus extremely difficult, and indeed in most cases quite impossible, for the individual citizen to come to objective conclusions and to make intelligent use of his political rights. . . . This crippling of individuals I consider the worst evil of capitalism. Our whole educational system suffers from this evil. An exaggerated competitive attitude is inculcated into the student, who is trained to worship acquisitive success as a preparation for his future career.

'I am convinced there is only *one* way to eliminate these grave evils, namely through the establishment of a socialist economy, accompanied by an educational system which would be oriented towards social goals. In such an economy, the means of production are owned by society itself and are utilized in a planned fashion. A planned economy, which adjusts production to the needs of the community, would distribute the work to be done among all those able to work and would guarantee a livelihood to every man, woman, and child. The education of the individual, in addition to promoting his own innate abilities, would attempt to develop in him a sense of responsibility for his fellow men in place of the glorification of power and success in our present society.

'Nevertheless, it is necessary to remember that a planned economy is not yet socialism. A planned economy as such may be accompanied by the complete enslavement of the individual. The achievement of socialism requires the solution of some extremely difficult socio-political problems: how is it possible, in view of the far-reaching centralization of political and economic power, to prevent bureaucracy from becoming all-powerful and overweening? How can the rights of the individual be protected and therewith a democratic counterweight to the power of bureaucracy be assured?'

13 February 1950. From a television programme conducted by Mrs Eleanor Roosevelt, which also included Lilienthal and Oppenheimer:

'Outside the United States we . . . establish military bases at every possible, strategically important point of the globe as well as arm and strengthen economically our potential allies. And inside the United States, tremendous financial power is being concentrated in the hands of the military; youth is being militarized; and the loyalty of citizens, particularly civil servants, is carefully supervised by a police force growing more powerful every day. People of independent political thought are harassed. The public is subtly indoctrinated by the radio, the press, the schools. Under the pressure of military secrecy, the range of public information is increasingly restricted.'[11]

16 March 1950. From a letter to Professor Sidney Hook:

'I have endeavoured to understand why the Russian Revolution became a necessity. Under the circumstances prevailing in Russia at the time, I believe that the revolution could have been successfully undertaken only by a resolute minority. A Russian who had the welfare of the people at heart would, under the then existing conditions, naturally cooperate with, and submit to, this minority since the immediate goals of the revolution could otherwise not have been achieved. To an independent person, this must surely have entailed *temporary*, painful renunciation of his personal liberty. But I believe that I myself would have deemed it my duty, and would have considered it the lesser evil, to make this temporary sacrifice. This, however, should not be taken to mean that I approve of the Soviet Government's policy of intervention, both direct and indirect, in intellectual and artistic matters. I view such interference as objectionable, harmful and even ridiculous. I also believe that centralization of political power and limitation of individual freedoms should not exceed the limits determined by such considerations as external security, domestic stability and the requirements of a planned economy. An outsider is hardly in a position to appraise adequately the existing conditions and needs of another country. In any case, there is no doubt that the achievements of the Soviet regime in the fields of education, public health, social wefare and economics are considerable and that the people as a whole have greatly benefited from those achievements.'[12]

October 1950. From a message 'On the moral obligation of the scientist' sent to the forty-third meeting of the Italian Society for the Progress of Science:

'Thus the man of science, as we can observe with our own eyes, suffers a truly tragic fate. In his sincere attempt to achieve clarity and inner independence, he has succeeded, by his sheer super-human efforts, in fashioning the tools which will not only enslave him but also destroy him from within. He cannot escape being silenced by those who wield political power. . . . He also realizes that mankind can be saved only if a supranational system, based on law, is created to eliminate the methods of brute force. However, the man of science has retrogressed to such an extent that he accepts as inevitable the slavery inflicted upon him by national states. He even degrades himself to such an extent that he obediently lends his talents to help perfect the means destined for the general destruction of mankind. . . . If today's man of science could find the time and the courage to reflect honestly and critically about himself and the tasks before him, and if he would then act accordingly, the possibilities for a sane and satisfactory solution of the present dangerous international situation would be considerably improved.'[13]

8 October 1950. From a letter to a professor of English literature who had asked Einstein to sign a statement opposing German rearmament:

'I have not signed the statement you have sent me although I am in full agreement with its content. The reason is simply that I wish to avoid any impression of disagreeing only with the rearmament of Germany. In reality such rearmament is but a link in the chain of measures our government has followed since Roosevelt's death; such measures may, in my opinion, lead to disastrous consequences in the future.'[14]

5 November 1950. From a letter to a physician whose son had been inducted into the army and who had written to Einstein urging him to redouble his efforts on behalf of peace:

'You are very right in assuming that I am badly in need of encouragement. I have indeed the impression that our nation has gone mad and is no longer receptive to reasonable suggestions. Its whole development reminds me of the events in Germany since the time of Emperor William II: through many victories to final disaster.'[15]

5 January 1951. From a letter to the editor of the *Bulletin of the Atomic Scientists:*

'I will say, however, that in my opinion the present policy of the United States constitutes a more serious obstacle to peace in the world than that of Russia. The current fighting is in Korea, not Alaska. Russia is exposed to a vastly greater threat than the United States, and everyone knows it. I find it hard to understand why people here accept the fable that we are in peril. I can only assume that it is because of their lack of political experience. While the government policy is apparently directed toward preventive war, there is, at the same time, a concerted attempt to make it appear as though the Soviet Union is the aggressor.'[16]

6 January 1951. From a letter to the Queen Mother of Belgium:

'While it proved eventually possible, at an exceedingly heavy cost, to defeat the Germans, the dear Americans have vigorously assumed their place. Who shall bring them back to their senses? The German calamity of years ago repeats itself: people acquiesce without resistance and align themselves with the forces for evil. And one stands by, powerless.'[17]

9 October 1952. From a letter to a correspondent in England:

'I am a lonely man, as you are, much older than you but probably not much wiser. What we have in common is a deep skepticism about everything we are told by the press, radio, etc., which are considerably worse in the United States than in Old England. . . .

'The reports we receive about Russia are, of course, one-sided and too black. Yet, it seems certain that in spite of her social and economic achievements, her political organization is still considerably more brutal and barbarous than ours. However, it is clear to me that the postwar change in power relations among the nations of the world has resulted in the West's being much more aggressive than the Communist world.'[18]

18 November 1954. In a statement published in *The Reporter:*

'You have asked me what I thought about your articles concerning the situation of scientists in America. Instead of trying to analyze the problem, I should like to express my feeling in a short remark: If I were a young man again and had to decide how to make a living, I would not try to become a scientist or scholar or teacher. I would rather choose to be a plumber or a peddler, in the hope of finding that modest degree of independence still available under present circumstances.'[19]

17 January 1955. From a letter to Max Born:

'The hired hacks of an accommodating press have tried to tone down the impact of this statement, either by making it appear as if I regretted having been engaged in scientific endeavour, or by trying to give the impression that I attached little value to the practical occupations I mentioned.

'What I wanted to say was just this: In the present circumstances, the only profession I would choose would be one where earning a living had nothing to do with the search for knowledge.'[20]

2 January 1955. From a letter to the Queen Mother of Belgium:

'Yesterday the Nuremberg trials, today the all-out effort to rearm Germany. In seeking for some kind of explanation, I cannot rid myself of the thought that this, the last of my fatherlands, has invented for its own use a new kind of colonialism, one that is less conspicuous than the colonialism of old Europe. It achieves domination of other countries by investing American capital abroad, which makes those countries firmly dependent on the United States. Anyone who opposes this policy or its implications is treated as an enemy of the United States. It is within this general context that I try to understand the present-day policies of Europe, including England.'[21]

19 March 1955. From a letter to the German physicist von Laue:

'My action concerning the atomic bomb and Roosevelt consisted merely in the fact that, because of the danger that Hitler might be the first to have the bomb, I signed a letter to the President which had been drafted by Szilard. Had I known that that fear was not justified, I, no more than Szilard, would have participated in opening this Pandora's box. For my distrust of governments was not limited to Germany.

'Unfortunately, I had no share in the warning made against using the bomb against Japan. Credit for this must go to James Franck. If they had only listened to him!'[22]

2 March 1955. From a letter to Niels Bohr seeking his participation in Bertrand Russell's plan to produce a statement calling on governments to renounce the use of war:

'Dear Niels Bohr,

Don't frown like that! This has nothing to do with our old controversy on physics, but rather concerns a matter on which we are in complete agreement. . . .

'My own participation may exert some favourable influence abroad, but not here at home, where I am known as a black sheep (and not merely in scientific matters). . . .'[23]

On 17 April 1955 Einstein died. In a speech given at the California Institute of Technology in 1931, he had offered the following advice to his fellow scientists:

'Concern for man himself and his fate must always form the chief interest for all technical endeavours, concern for the great unsolved problems of the organization of labour and the distribution of goods – in order that the creations of our mind shall be a blessing and not a curse for mankind. Never forget this in the midst of your diagrams and equations.'

Notes

1. O. Nathan and H. Norden, *Einstein on peace,* Schocken Books, 1968, pp. 341–2.
2. Ibid., p. 355.
3. Ibid., p. 380.
4. Ibid., p. 401.
5. Ibid., p. 403.
6. Ibid., p. 416.
7. Ibid., p. 436.
8. Ibid., pp. 465–6.
9. Ibid., pp. 475–6.
10. Ibid., p. 487.
11. Ibid., p. 521.
12. Ibid., pp. 532–3.
13. Ibid., p. 536.
14. Ibid., p. 537.
15. Ibid., pp. 538–9.
16. Ibid., p. 553.
17. Ibid., p. 554.
18. Ibid., p. 570.
19. Ibid., p. 613.
20. *The Born–Einstein letters,* Macmillan, 1971, pp. 231–2.
21. Nathan and Norden, op. cit., p. 616.
22. Ibid., p. 621.
23. Ibid., pp. 629–30.

Einstein on civil liberties

Interview with Einstein conducted by the Emergency Civil Liberties Committee of the American Association of Scientific Workers. From the *Bulletin of the World Federation of Scientific Workers*, February 1955.

Question: What is the essential nature of academic freedom and why is it necessary for the pursuit of truth?

Answer: By academic freedom I understand the right to search for truth and to publish and teach what one holds to be true. This right implies also a duty: one must not conceal any part of what one has recognised to be true. It is evident that any restriction of academic freedom acts in such a way as to hamper the dissemination of knowledge among the people and thereby impedes rational judgement and action.

Question: What threats to academic freedom do you see at this time?

Answer: The threat to academic freedom in our time must be seen in the fact that, because of the alleged external danger to our country, freedom of teaching, mutual exchange of opinions, and freedom of press and other media of communication are encroached upon or obstructed. This is done by creating a situation in which people feel their economic positions endangered. Consequently, more and more people avoid expressing their opinions freely, even in their private social life. This is a state of affairs which a democratic government cannot survive in the long run.

Question: What in your view are the particular responsibilities of a citizen at this time in the defence of our traditional freedom as expressed in our Bill of Rights?

Answer: The strength of the constitution lies entirely in the determination of each citizen to defend it. Only if every single citizen feels duty bound to do his share in this defence are the constitutional rights secure. Thus, a duty is imposed on everyone which no one must evade, notwithstanding the risks and dangers for him and his family.

Question: What, in your opinion, are the special obligations of an intellectual in a democratic society?

Answer: In principle, everybody is equally involved in defending the constitutional rights. The 'intellectuals' in the widest sense of the word are, however, in a special position since they have, thanks to their special training, a particularly strong influence on the formation of public opinion. This is the reason why those who are about to lead us towards an authoritarian government are particularly concerned with intimidating and muzzling that group. It is therefore in the present situation especially important for the intellectuals to do their duty. I see this duty in refusing to co-operate in any undertaking that violates the constitutional rights of the individual. This holds in particular for all inquisitions that are concerned with the private life and the political affiliations of the citizens. Whoever co-operates in such a case becomes an accessory to acts of violation or invalidation of the Constitution.

Question: What in your opinion is the best way to help the victims of political inquisitions?

Answer: It is important for the defence of civil rights that assistance be given to the victims of this defence who, in the above mentioned inquisitions, have refused to testify, and beyond that to all those who through these inquisitions have suffered material loss in any way. In particular, it will be necessary to provide legal counsel and to find work for them. This requires money, the collection and use of which should be put into the hands of a small organisation under the supervision of persons known to be trustworthy. This organisation should be in contact with all groups concerned with the preservation of civil rights. In this way it should be possible to solve this important problem without setting up another expensive fund-raising machinery.

5. The impact on the arts

Einstein and architecture

Bill Chaitkin

Bill Chaitkin was born 38 years ago in the USA. He was educated at Washington University, St. Louis, where he obtained degrees in science and architecture, and an MA in art history. He has taught widely in the United States and Britain, and is at present a lecturer in art history at the Central School of Art and Design, London. His articles have been published widely in architectural journals.

Exterior of the Einstein Tower, Potsdam, designed by Erich Mendelsohn in 1919

Einstein's Tower

One of the first and most famous landmarks of modern architecture could not be more closely connected with Albert Einstein. Designed by Erich Mendelsohn in 1919, it has always been simply called the Einstein Tower, a working laboratory and a palpable monument to relativity theory. Although a purpose-built facility of the Potsdam Astrophysical Institute, unusual circumstances of creation resulted in a building of interest to students both of architecture and of Einstein.

Chiefly responsible for its inception was the Scottish-German astronomer Erwin Findlay Freundlich, a friend of Einstein since 1911, and of the architect Mendelsohn since 1914. Freundlich also had contacts with a director of I. G. Farben, one Dr Bosch, whom he persuaded, along with other industrialists, to finance an Einstein Institute at Potsdam. This was later amalgamated with the observatory there, and Freundlich was put in charge of the Tower itself.[1] Construction, initiated in late 1919, continued through 1921; apparently Bosch could not raise the funds required until autumn of the latter year.[2] Furthermore, in the midst of post-war Germany's runaway inflation, cement was rationed, which necessitated revised blueprints specifying brick instead of the reinforced concrete in which it was originally conceived. It was not until 1924 that the building was formally inaugurated.

One of the reasons was that the Tower's equipment had to be made to exacting requirements. It included a long-focus telescope specially designed by Freundlich and mounted in the cupola or turret. This reflected rays received from celestial sources (*'kosmische Lichtquellen'*) perpendicularly down the Tower's hollow, 20-metre shaft, to a mirror. There they were bent through a right angle and directed along a 12-metre chamber, which was itself half-buried for constancy of temperature and acoustic insulation. Finally, the beam arrived at a spectrograph for analysis. This combination of telescope and spectrograph had a limited and specific purpose: the verification of the theory of relativity through a demonstration of the so-called 'Einstein Shift'.

Einstein had suggested that light-waves reaching earth ought to be 'shifted' towards the red end of the spectrum of electromagnetic frequencies by the gravitational fields through which they passed, because the atoms emitting them would vibrate more slowly in a strong field than in a weak one. Freundlich had been eager to test the theory of relativity ever since Einstein had discussed the Shift as the 'more esoteric' of the two easily verifiable consequences of his 1911 paper.[3] Einstein's own hopes and fears were enunciated in a letter to Arthur Eddington in 1919: 'If it were proved that this effect does not exist in nature, then the whole theory would have to be abandoned'.[4] That the Potsdam Institute was unable to supply decisive proof in the 'twenties may even have been responsible for Einstein's later estrangement from Freundlich.[5] To outsiders, however, the Tower's function was simple enough: bizarre-looking, its task was to 'prove' the bizarre-sounding Theory of Relativity.

Almost as construction was begun, news came that Eddington had found, during the solar eclipse of 1919, that the apparent position of a star had been altered by the sun's gravitational field acting upon the light emitted by it. In effect this proved the other, less esoteric prediction made by Einstein's 1911 paper — that of spatial rather than temporal warp. So considerable was the impact of Eddington's findings that the Tower and what it stood for were rendered much less controversial and Einstein — by virtue of an eclipse — a luminary figure in science.

At the time Einstein had yet to appear the sage and secular saint he did in later years. The years 1919–24, corresponding to the Einstein Tower's gestation, were for him extremely active. He had only turned 40, and personally believed the missing pieces of the cosmological puzzle to be nearly within grasp. He received the Nobel Prize for Physics. In 1921 he embarked on what amounted to a triumphal tour, visiting Holland, the United

States and England, where 'he was treated as a veritable hero of the mind'.[6] In the following year he went to Japan, Palestine, Madrid, Zürich and Paris.

In the wake of the First World War, many scientists hoped, through Einstein's goodwill trips, to remove the legacy of bitterness between Germany and its former enemies – indeed, to re-establish normal contacts within the international scientific community. At the same time the post-war Weimar Republic could present Einstein to the world as a laudable, untainted German (despite his early renunciation of citizenship): anti-militaristic, opposed to imperialism, and more-or-less leftish like itself. In Ulm, the street of his birthplace was renamed *Einsteinstrasse*.[7] This helps to explain why, during the severest economic emergency and instability, government and industry continued to give official and financial support for the 'pure research' represented by the Tower – despite its extravagance in construction. It was of a piece with the German tradition of conspicuously striking architecture monumentalising abstract ideas (even relativity theory can have a *Denkmal*).

It is in this light, then, that both conception and reception of *der Einsteinturm* should be seen. Yet, apart from its topical association with Einstein's new-found fame, the building might well have created something of an architectural sensation anyway. The popular pictorial magazine *Die Berliner Illustrierte Zeitung* featured it on its cover, and guided tours of Potsdam added it to their lists of scenic attractions. Pure white and highly sculptural, it contrasted radically with the staid red-brick Prussian style of nearby academic buildings. Nothing like it had been built before – not even by Erich Mendelsohn (it was his first building to be executed). It came to be regarded as indicative of Germany's cultural renaissance in the 'twenties, which saw revolutionary developments in all the arts, changed the course of the Western avant-garde, and became legendary all too soon under the official philistinism of a subsequent fascist regime.

On the other hand, the Right of the early 'twenties reacted adversely. Incipient Nazis opposed the free rein given to modern architecture in the Weimar Republic as non-Aryan 'cultural Bolshevism', just as they began organised anti-relativity campaigns as early as 1920. The German half of Findlay Freundlich was Jewish; Einstein had recently become an outspoken Zionist, morally supported the republican government, and knew many modern artists and architects.[8] Thus, the Einstein Tower became a particularly symbolic target for the Nazis. They could hit two birds with, as it were, *ein Stein.*

In this cultural context, defence of the Tower's design may have meant an act of progressive faith. Even so, politically incited hostility should not, conversely, be confused with simple conservatism in the face of a new aesthetic. One baffled German newspaper called it 'a cross between a New York skyscraper and an Egyptian pyramid'; an indignant English critic castigated it as 'a travesty of Einstein's contribution and a monument to complication and bewilderment'.[9] Tastes aside, the building has also confounded scholarly attempts to define its place in modern architectural history. The historian Jürgen Joedicke writes: 'Of the architects who had an appreciable influence in determining the path of modern architecture, Erich Mendelsohn was the most lastingly affected by Expressionism'.[10] Dennis Sharp's admirable *Modern architecture and expressionism* puts it: 'With the tower Mendelsohn reached the climax of his own expressionism'.[11] The authoritative Dr Banham captions the Tower 'the canonical building of Expressionist architecture' but adjudges that Mendelsohn 'himself abandoned this style almost immediately'.[12] The last contradicts Joedicke, but all seem agreed on the stylistic referent.

It is true enough that Expressionism generally dominated German modernism just after the war. Even the Bauhaus, later almost synonymous with 'the machine aesthetic', began under Expressionism's emotive, anti-technological sway – perhaps as a reaction to the war itself – in the crucial years of its Weimar phase (1919–23). Gropius's Foundation Manifesto of 1919 never once mentioned technology. The difficulty in relating the rather flexible styli-

Post-design conceptual sketch of the Tower, by Mendelsohn, 1920

stic term 'Expressionism' to the Einstein Tower, though, is threefold: the Tower is programmatically *about* science and technology; Mendelsohn's ideological links with Expressionism were circumstantial, tenuous, and denied by him; and alternative sources can be adduced.

The prehistory of Mendelsohn's design for the Tower must be sought in a series of visionary architectural sketches dating from 1914 onwards. These remarkable drawings were done during his military service with the German army engineers, which interrupted his professional career immediately it began. Executed in the trenches at the Russian Front and then the Western Front, the drawings boldly delineated imaginary projects for aerodromes, railway terminals, factories and other industrial buildings. Sketches in 1917 of two observatories convinced Freundlich to commission the Einstein Tower from him.[13]

In the spring of 1919 a Berlin gallery exhibited these sketches. Entitled 'Architecture in steel and reinforced concrete', their label hardly accords with the priority which avowed Expressionists gave to the spiritual over the material. Rather, they emphasise structural determinants and a sweeping mechanistic power, reminiscent in form and content of drawings by the Italian Futurist Antonio Sant 'Elia exhibited (in Berlin, among other places) and published in 1912–14.

It is only in 1920 that further sketches by Mendelsohn take on florid Expressionist rhythms and begin to be titled 'Garden or Pleasure Pavilions', 'Agnus Dei or Sacred Buildings', or after musical compositions which inspired him ('Brahms Quintet', 'Bach Cantata', 'Toccata in D Major', and so on).[14] Such an approach was inconceivable for the wartime sketches. His brilliant brush-and-ink sketch of the Einstein Tower, with all the vital freedom and spontaneity of a first back-of-the-envelope form-concept, yet showing the building essentially as erected, was also done in 1920, *after* the detailed design had been completed.

Whether to classify the Einstein Tower as more a Futurist than Expressionist building may well be merely an academic matter; it is an Erich Mendelsohn building in his personal idiom as of 1919. Futurism is apposite in so far as the Futurists, like the Expressionists, celebrated science and technology with compulsive enthusiasm, and were conversant with Einsteinian ideas – however much these may have been misrepresented by their art. Futurist Technical Manifestoes of 1910–12 teem with statements like this:

'. . . universal dynamism must be rendered as dynamic sensation . . . movement and light destroy the substance of objects [which] in motion multiply and distort themselves, just as do vibrations – which indeed they are – in passing through space.'

The painter and sculptor Umberto Boccioni wrote about the dematerialisation of mass, post-Renaissance (or post-Newtonian) space, and 'lines of force'. His 1912 sculpture 'Bottle

evolving in space' incorporates relativistic viewpoints and a visual 'field' concept; in his 1913 'Unique forms of continuity in space', a striding bronze figure is distended by its own velocity. In a sense, therefore, Einstein's theories impinged on Mendelsohn's design indirectly, via Futurist influence upon him; it is perhaps more probable that he was aware of Futurism's 'translation' of Einstein into artistic terms than that he understood the physics directly from Freundlich.[15]

In the 'thirties Einstein was to comment, apropos undistracted freedom for cerebration, that the ideal job for a theoretical physicist would be that of lighthouse keeper.[16] The Einstein Tower resembles nothing so much as a lighthouse, a sort of cosmic beacon; it is certainly a lighthouse in its scientific purpose. Discussing Sant 'Elia's sketches of 1913 and 1914, Banham notes their Futurist inspiration. He singles out '... tall structures titled *Dinamismo Architettonico* and occasionally given the functional justification of lighthouses. Their shapes are bare and smooth, rectangular or semicircular in plan, often battered back in section to give a tapering silhouette ...'. That description fits the Tower too, but the key-word here is 'dynamism', as used by Sant 'Elia and other Futurists, and by Mendelsohn.

Mendelsohn had defined a building's dynamism as a visual effect, like the 'thrust' revealed in the sketches he exhibited in 1919. But in a much quoted letter to his wife shortly thereafter, he extended its meaning to cover the subjective or imaginative, and reconciled the countervailing demands of function, rationalism, and order. 'Function without sensibility remains mere construction.' On the other hand, dynamism must be controlled, must be balanced with its polar opposite: 'Function plus dynamics is the challenge'. His reiterated design philosophy is happily analogous to Einstein's thinking: clear reasoning fortified by intuition and 'joyful participation in the creative processes'.[17] Denis Gabor has said, 'I have never known anybody who enjoyed science so sensuously as Einstein'.[18] Likewise, 'the planning of the *Einsteinturm* is symmetrical, and based on an Academic apparatus of minor and major axes,'[19] yet that static organisation is imbued with dynamic movement (Expressionist *or* Futurist).

Above all it is an image of wholeness, indivisible in its monolithic plasticity. Surface and volume are one. It is indicative of the deliberateness with which Mendelsohn chose exposed structural concrete — quite daring and unprecedented then — that even when it proved economically unfeasible he stuccoed over the brick to give the same desired impression. In a lecture of 1923, 'Function and Dynamics', he explicitly linked architecture to

'the recognition that the two conceptions hitherto kept separate by science — Matter and Energy — are only different conditions of the same basic stuff, that nothing in the Universe is without Relativity to the Cosmos, without connection with the whole.'

Interestingly, it had been the *fragmentation* of objects and interpenetration of plans that Cubists (and the Futurist painters who appropriated their ideas) had seen in relativity. But architecture is necessarily three-dimensional. This is where Sant 'Elia departed from fellow Futurists, only to be followed by Mendelsohn, who moulded the Tower out of the same 'stuff'. This is not to say the Einstein Tower is a paradigm of an Einsteinian universe, as if reducible to some symbol of integrity as elegant as an equation. Einstein himself never admitted the slightest promise of visualising four-dimensional space-time. While the possibility should not be dismissed that Mendelsohn consciously meant to symbolise the wholeness of Einstein's universe in architectural form, his design is less a graphic metaphor than an intuitive interpretation of, as he put it three decades later, 'the mystique around Einstein's universe'.[20] At best it is *appropriate to* its subject.

It is noteworthy, however, that its curvilinear surfaces do tend away from Euclidean shapes. And this was at a time when, apart from 'Expressionist' Germany, the Dutch de Stijl group, French Cubists and Purists in the tradition of Cézanne's cubes, cylinders, cones, and

Einstein in conversation with Dr Ludendorf, brother of the famous general and director
of the Tower

spheres, and the Russian Constructivists all insisted on strict adherence to regular geometry and the right angle as emblematic of Platonic abstraction or Machine Age art.

For example, the same year 1919 saw another extraordinary tower designed (but never built): Vladimir Tatlin's monument to the Third International. Its 300-metre inclined spiral is undeniably dynamic, yet inside the openwork of Tatlin's Tower are suspended a cylinder, a cone, and a cube. Mendelsohn, in later and more orthodox work, reverted to the Modernist vocabulary of rectilinearity, allowing it to be relieved only by single-radius circles or semi-circular arcs. In his Einstein Tower, however, the compound curvatures are extremely complicated; the double-curved planes are so continuous that, at the entrance, for example, they seem to twist inside out — just as, in Einsteinian cosmology, local conditions became more complex as the whole becomes simpler and more complete than the architectonic schemata of Euclid or Newton.[21]

After the Tower had been finished, Einstein was conducted around it by the architect. Einstein examined everything with interest but made no comment about the architecture. Some hours later, during a meeting with the building committee, Einstein suddenly rose, crossed the room, and whispered in Mendelsohn's ear the single word 'organic'.[22] It is a good (and scientific) word for a structure of integrated systems which works together as a whole, with no loose ends: intellectually like music, physically like nature. And, as the form fits the phrase, so does this enduring quality befit the building's history. It survived the dementia of Nazi resentment against it, Allied heavy-bomber raids, and the final destructive assault on Berlin. It has stood three different political regimes and is still in use today.

The Power of Number

In 1941, in America, appeared Siegfried Giedion's influential *Space, time and architecture*, a historical survey and retrospective reading of modern movements in the arts which viewed them as an 'optical revolution' of the early twentieth century. The new ways of seeing, it suggested, were demonstrably related not only to modern science and technology generally, but to the new physics of four-dimensional space-time in particular. To be sure, Giedion rather circumspectly alludes to 'unconscious parallelisms in science and art', calling it a 'temporal coincidence' that Einstein's 1905 *Elektrodynamik bewegter Körper* begins with an explanation of simultaneity just before the Cubists undertook to exploit the phenomenon in painting.[23] None the less, Giedion's implicit assumptions carry the force of a thesis, reinforced by his title (presumably a play on Eddington's *Space, time and gravitation* of 1920). The book has been widely read since 1941, going through five editions and sixteen printings up to 1967, and is still a standard text: it is, indeed, an Apologia for modern architecture. But when it was published, Erich Mendelsohn, by then in America himself, did not think much of it. However, he thought it might be amusing to send a copy, with pertinent pages marked, to Einstein, who was also exiled in America. Einstein promptly responded with one of his droll doggerel verses.

'Dear Mr. Mendelsohn,

The passage you sent me from the book *Space, Time and Architecture* has inspired me to the following reply:

> Some new thought isn't hard to declare
> If any nonsense one will dare.
> But rarely do you find that novel babble
> Is at the same time reason-able.

Cordially yours, Albert Einstein

P.S.: It is simply bull without any rational basis.'[24]

Photo record of Einstein's meeting with Le Corbusier at Princeton, 1946

So much for *Space, time and architecture.* It would seem that Mendelsohn, disarmingly eliciting only the mystique of Einstein's universe, was being more straightforward than Giedion with his *ex post facto* rationalisations. Or, granting speculative prerogatives to the historian on the gounds that he is not himself privy to the inner design act, the objection holds that Giedion failed to penetrate the architectural relevance of Einstein's theories sufficiently, trafficking in their jargon instead. Yet later in the same decade Einstein's reputation, not even ideas, was to be traded upon by a designing architect to promote and enhance his own 'apostolic mission'.

Le Corbusier, deemed by many to have been the pre-eminent architect of this century, met Einstein in 1946. The subject-matter of their interchange was Corbusier's 'Modulor' proportioning system. Under intermittent development since 1938, it was set out in his book *The Modulor* of 1948 and finalised in the second edition of 1951, *Modulor 2.* Briefly, the 'Modulor' purports to dissolve metric and foot-inch units of measurement into a common unit at once more humane and more metaphysical than either, founded on 'human scale', the Golden Section and other classical ratios, the mathematics of musical octaves, the Fibonacci Series of integral increments, and various notions of geometrical and numerical relationships, some of them going back to Pythagoras's 'harmony of the spheres'.

Its keynote visual harmony, the 'Modulor' is an aesthetic rather than a practical proposition, to be used solely for two-dimensional rectilinear dimensioning — even though Corbusier claimed that it was 'universally applicable' to architectural design. As in Renaissance and other academic design disciplines, the appeal has resided in the supposed assurance of a quantifiable beauty. In the 'Modulor's' case additional authority is presumed in the third sentence of Corbusier's Introduction:

> 'Architects everywhere have recognized in it, not a mystique, but a tool which may be put in the hands of creators of form, with the simple aim, as Professor Einstein has put it so well, of "making the bad difficult and the good easy".'

How this unsolicited testimonial came about is told further on in the book. Corbusier recounts that he had gone to New York in connection with the design of the United Nations Building. He had not sought out Einstein, but a friend arranged an introduction and Corbusier made the short side-trip to Princeton. As he tells it:

> 'I was then passing through a period of great uncertainty and stress: I expressed myself badly, I explained the "Modulor" badly. . . . At one point, Einstein took a pencil and began to calculate. Stupidly, I interrupted him, the conversation turned to other things, the calculation remained unfinished. The friend who had brought me was in the depths of despair. In a letter written to me the same evening, Einstein had the kindness to say this of the "Modulor". . .'[25]

and there follows the endorsement already quoted. It may be hard to credit such unqualified approval (as presented by Corbusier) for a system then incompletely formulated, 'explained badly', without a shared native language *or* shared intellectual methodology. Lacking any further clues to what, exactly, they discussed, it is impossible to know just what appealed to Einstein.

What is more certain is that Einsteinian physics can have had virtually nothing to do with Corbusier's aesthetics. The 'Modulor' is exclusively bound to Euclidean geometry, as was Le Corbusier's painting in the style he called Purism (reformed Cubism). Speaking of the Cubists in 1945, he noted:

'They spoke of a fourth dimension. . . . A life devoted to art, and most particularly the quest for harmony, has enabled me . . . to learn something about it in my turn. The fourth dimension is, I believe, the moment of boundless freedom brought about by an exceptionally happy consonance of the plastic means employed in a work of art.'[26]

Though it is scientifically meaningless, this is consistent with Le Corbusier's idiosyncratic 'definition' of mathematics as 'the fabulous fabric of numbers without end'. Seen against pronouncements like 'architecture is not a synchronic phenomenon, but a successive one, made up of pictures adding themselves one to the other, following each other in time and space', suggests that by mathematics and geometry Corbusier really meant arithmetic; that is, additive quantities. As he has confessed, '. . . at school I was very bad at mathematics'.

The 'Modulor' never quite coalesced harmoniously out of its own constituent ideas. It is a patchwork of compromises and, despite Le Corbusier's disclaimer, a mystique verging on the esoteric. So, since magic numerology was never one of Einstein's passions, it must be concluded that Einstein's name was enlisted here in yet another cause. Corbusier invoked Einstein's blessing as a rave review blurb for the 'Modulor', and had his photograph taken standing next to him.

A Fuller view

Einstein's insights have been most effectively taken on their own terms and distilled into design by R. Buckminster Fuller. So sustained and extensive has Einstein's influence been, over the past half-century of Fuller's prolix activities, that only the most meagre outline can be afforded here, nor does limited space permit the requisite biographical grounding: the reader is commended to Fuller's voluminous writings, lectures, and to the designs themselves.

Unlike his other encounters with architects, which occurred with Europeans, Einstein's

Climatron geodesic dome, St Louis, USA

meeting with Fuller involves an American, of outwardly dissimilar background from Einstein — although certain of their experiences offer telling affinities.[27] And, while Fuller was largely a self-taught generalist, he did appreciate relativity as more than the aesthetic cypher exploited by Mendelsohn, Giedion, Corbusier, the Futurists and the Cubists.

Fuller's first publication, *4D* (fourth-dimensional), privately printed in 1927, accompanied a range of schemes for '4D' housing in tower-block and single-family form (patented as the Dymaxion House), a '4D' World Town Plan, and a '4D' transport vehicle, having no connection with architectural or design styles of the day — not even with so-called Functionalism. His first proper book, *Nine chains to the Moon,* was a more comprehensive manifesto, free-wheeling and provocative, written (in Fuller's lively but often unreadably awkward personal language) in 1935 and published in 1938. In between, his publishers demurred at his 'irreverent' arguments based on Einstein's theories, particularly the chapter '$E = mc^2 =$ Mrs Murphy's Horse Power'. Fuller proposed submitting it to Einstein's judgement directly, and the manuscript was posted to Princeton. Three months later Einstein returned it in person to Fuller in New York. He approved the treatment of his energy-mass equation as 'satisfactory' and then is supposed to have said: 'But, young man, regarding myself and Mrs Murphy, you amaze me. I cannot conceive of anything I have ever done (in theoretical physics) as having the slightest practical application'.[28] Fuller is fond of noting that after the uranium atom had been split years later, Einstein was to warn President Roosevelt of just such a 'practical application'.

That Fuller — hitherto taken for an engaging, if probably crackpot, visionary — had himself transposed Einstein's abstract theory into practicality was scarcely recognised until the 'fifties, when more than 1000 of his geodesic domes were built. Their success, in all senses, is well known, not least as a unique structural realisation of non-Euclidean geometry. His first experimental domes of 1948 completed the protracted evolution of what he calls Vector Equilibrium, Tensegrity, and Energetic-Synergetic geometries, in which curvature of four-dimensional space-time is delineated by 'greatest circles' on a sphere: world lines or geodesics.

It should be stressed that, just as Einstein's most famous equation only expressed the behaviour of energy events algebraically, so was Fuller's geodesic dome only a tactic for capitalising upon the same. Fuller's design philosophy is not easy to systematise: his logic is not so much linear as . . . geodesic. It was Einstein's broader conception of matter and energy that informed Fuller's strategy for adapting man to the physical world through design. Fuller's aim is human survival through 'design science'.

Here Fuller is a qualified optimist, seeing $E = mc^2$ as an updated law of the conservation of energy which ensures, in a finite universe, overall negentropy. Within the closed system of Earth, energy must be optimised for maximum efficiency and equity. This amounts to an apolitical social ethic and entails a 'design revolution' in attitudes to the environment. It is incumbent upon everyone to learn the mathematics of science both to apprehend 'the way the world works' and control technology. To this degree Fuller is a populariser of Einstein: 'Really, any child can be taught nuclear physics'.[29]

Notes

1. Ronald W. Clark, *Einstein, the life and times,* Avon, New York, 1971, p. 390.
2. Philipp Frank, *Einstein, his life and times,* Cape, London, 1948.
3. Clark, op. cit., p. 260.
4. Quoted in Clark, op. cit., p. 299.
5. Clark, op. cit., p. 299. At Mount Wilson in 1924, observations made of starlight in the intense field of a superdense white dwarf, Sirius B, did lend much credence to the theory, but conclusive findings have had to await the vastly more precise instrumentation used in recent experiments at Harvard.
6. Banesh Hoffmann, *Albert Einstein, creator and rebel,* New American Library, New York, 1972, p. 148.
7. The name was changed again under the Nazis, and changed back after them.
8. Including, besides Mendelsohn, Peter Behrens. See Donald Egbert, 'The circle of friends of the Bauhaus'. *Social radicalism and the arts,* Knopf, New York, 1970, p. 663.
9. Frank, op. cit.; Manning Robertson, *Laymen and the new architecture,* London 1925, p. 75.
10. J. Joedicke, *A history of modern architecture,* Praeger, New York, 1959, p. 65.
11. D. Sharp, *Modern architecture and expressionism,* Braziller, New York, 1966, p. 111.
12. Reyner Banham, *Theory and design in the first machine age,* Praeger, 1960, p. 173.
13. Arnold Whittick, *Eric Mendelsohn,* Leonard Hill, London, 1940/1956, p. 57. The architect's biographer also mentions that 'Mendelsohn had often visited observatories' with Freundlich. Op. cit., p. 48.
14. Mendelsohn's profound passion for music was extreme even for an architect ('Architecture is frozen music' said Goethe) and comparable to that of Einstein, who believed Mozart 'discovered' music already present in the universe. Mendelsohn did not, as Einstein did, play an instrument, but he did marry a cellist. This parallel serves as a reminder, at least, of their similar cultural backgrounds, including musical families. Both were sons of Jewish businessmen and took their initial schooling in Munich. In the early 'twenties the architect just beginning to practise and the older physicist of world eminence could hardly have been intimate friends, but they remained cordial when their paths crossed again. In Palestine, Mendelsohn designed buildings for the Hebrew University, with which Einstein was long involved, and a house for his friend Chaim Weitzmann, later President of Israel (an office Einstein declined). Both Einstein and Mendelsohn fled from Germany in 1933 and eventually resettled in America for the rest of their lives, which ended within two years of each other.
15. Mendelsohn had often discussed Albert Einstein's theory with Freundlich: see Wolf von Eckhardt, *Eric Mendelsohn,* Braziller, New York 1960. As Banham remarks of Mendelsohn: 'scorn at his views on Relativity should be tempered by the reflection that of all the aesthetic theorists who have mangled Einstein's opinions, Mendelsohn alone knew Einstein well at first hand as a person'. Banham, op. cit., p. 812.
16. Hoffmann, op. cit., p. 170.
17. The words are in fact Mendelsohn's. Banham, op. cit., p. 183.
18. Quoted in Clark, op. cit., p. 395.
19. Banham, op. cit., p. 167.
20. Von Eckhardt, op. cit., p. 9.
21. Clark notes of the building's reception: 'It was even suggested that while the older buildings with their separate bricks epitomized the Euclidean concept of mathematics and atomic structure as understood at the turn of the century, Mendelsohn's long, elegant curves epitomized post-Einsteinian physics'. Clark, op. cit., p. 393.
22. Whittick, op. cit., p. 57.
23. S. Giedion, *Space, time and architecture,* Harvard University, 1967 edn., p. 436.
24. Von Eckhardt, op. cit., p. 14, translation from Einstein's German.
25. Le Corbusier, *The Modulor,* Faber & Faber, London 1951, p. 58.
26. Le Corbusier, op. cit., p. 32.
27. In early childhood both 'suffered' from apparent retardation: Einstein could not speak until the age of three; Fuller had impaired vision till the age of four. Both were indifferent students: Einstein failed his engineering entrance exams in 1895, the year of Fuller's birth, and Fuller was expelled from Harvard – twice. Both had early revelations, and doubts, concerning geometry. Most notably, Einstein worked for seven productive years, including the momentous 1905, in a patent office – 'that secular cloister where I hatched my most beautiful ideas' (quoted in Hoffmann, op. cit., p. 88) – and Fuller is best described as an inventor.
28. Robert Marks and R. B. Fuller, *The dymaxion world of Buckminster Fuller,* Anchor/Doubleday, New York, 1973, p. 7.
29. Fuller, interview in *Domus* magazine, no. 582, May 1978.

Einstein and art
Philip Courtenay

Philip Courtenay was born in London in 1949. He studied painting at Chelsea School of Art and did post-graduate work on the history of art. At present he teaches at Chelsea and at Canterbury College of Art. He is a practising painter.

Introduction

When we consider the work of Einstein it is as if, even now, we look at ourselves and the world in a radically new way. Any scientific revolution reflects a major transformation of vision; as a new world view it profoundly affects the consciousness of those aware of its substance and implications. And the transformation of vision that accompanies a scientific revolution is not limited to the scientific community. Conversely, the character of a new scientific theory is determined from the matrix of possibilities allowed by a culture, the culture that nurtures it. So the interplay of the social forces that shape a culture is vital to our discussion of the parallels between Einstein's theories and the contemporary revolutions in the visual arts.

Both the domain of intellect and the realm of subjective experience are formed by our perception of the world, and perception itself is governed by our sense faculties. However, to bring any semblance of a coherent pattern to our 'bloomin' buzzin' ' confusion of sense impressions 'something like a paradigm is prerequisite to perception'.[1] Whether the conceptual model is the construct of artist or scientist, it is these paradigms that permit us a comprehension of ourselves and our surrounding universe.

Today the word 'relativity' resonates with images of time and space. This is a measure of Einstein's effect upon our thinking. The work of certain artists touches us in a similar way. We speak of physics 'since Einstein' in the same manner as in the visual arts it is common to talk of painting 'since Cézanne'.

In late September 1905, three months after the publication of the special theory of relativity, Einstein concluded that all energy, of whatever sort, has mass. Two years later he realised that the reverse must also hold: that all mass must have energy. Einstein's sense of aesthetic truth may have given birth to this insight: why should he 'make a distinction in kind between the mass that an object already has and the mass it loses in giving off energy? To do so would be to imagine two types of mass for no good reason. The distinction would be inartistic and logically indefensible. Therefore all mass must have energy'.[2] Perhaps it was an intuitive sense of cosmic unity that led to the famous equation $E = mc^2$.

Cézanne once said: 'Things and creatures alike, we are only a little bit of solar heat. The diffuse moral energies of the world may be the effort it is making to become sun again. We are an iridescent chaos'.[3] In their different ways, Einstein and Cézanne show us a profoundly novel, holistic way of seeing and experiencing the world.

The concept of the whole directly contradicts the Cartesian conception of a divided reality, a reality split between such qualities as subject and object, body and mind, and so on. Founding an 'admirable science' which he conceived as an 'ensemble of "concatenated" things',[4] Descartes linked causes with effects, reducing knowledge to the appreciation of a sequence of events. But since Einstein, science has come to see the relation between subject and object, between cause and effect, as a more complex and interactive configuration.

Blake's repudiation of the system of perspective

Against the dominating influence of Descartes lies a more integrated conception. Often we find it situated on the periphery of the cultural stage, the property of an artist or a visionary. Let us look at William Blake, who countered traditional explanations of reality with vigorous attacks against 'Newton's sleep'. Blake's views find favour now that the distinctions between intellect and affectivity, knowledge and feeling, are less and less held useful – except as polarities. Blake speaks of his own age as wrapped in 'single vision':[5] in its various forms, the

'We are only a little bit of solar heat. . . . We are an iridescent chaos': Paul Cézanne,
Mont Sainte-Victoire', 1902–6.

system of perspective used by painters since the Renaissance – until our own artistic era, the
dominant system for the creation of pictorial space.

Perspective was a scheme for securing logical relations within a system of pictorial
symbols. It provided a reciprocal correspondence between the pictorial representations of
shapes of objects and the location of those objects in space. But this rationalisation of vision
gives the observer the illusion of continuous and measurable space. Regarded from a single
'point of view', this homogenous Euclidean space appears to recede continuously to the
horizon, where all parallel lines converge on a single point. An infinity of convincing reproduc-
tions of the world of visual appearances is based upon this 'vanishing point'. In the portrayal
of nature, 'accurate' representation becomes a criterion of truth. But as Gombrich notes,
'the discovery of appearances was not so much due to a careful observation of nature as to
the invention of pictorial effects'.[6] Even before Blake, Bishop Berkeley had denounced
Newtonian visual space as an absurd illusion, arguing that though we 'see' a flat field, we
'construct' a tactile space.

For Blake 'Newton's sleep' was a state of absorption in a 'point of view' that rendered
the observer quite unable to extricate himself from his fixed position. In their search for an
alternative framework, artists such as Blake have come again and again to examine man's
sensory apparatus; to make visible the unseen assumptions that underlie our ways of thinking. As Blake's *Jerusalem* puts it:

'If Perceptive organs vary, Objects of Perception seem to vary: If the Perceptive
Organs close, their Objects seem to close also.'[7]

To the extent that there is equilibrium among them, sense organs are the root of rationality for Blake. The 'ratio' between them Blake calls the imagination, and the ratio between mind and things, made by the shaping imagination, is artistic truth. In Blake's sense, Einstein's theories were the product of an imaginative vision and made manifest an intuitive grasp of artistic truth. Seen, therefore, as an aspect of artistic truth, Einstein's work says as much about the painter's possible view of the universe as the scientist's. Art takes on the challenge to form some understanding of the universe no less seriously than science. In both fields, 'the most precious possession of man is his abiding awareness of the analogy of proper proportionality, the key to all metaphysical insight and perhaps the very condition of consciousness itself'.[8]

Relativity and the new era in art: the role of telegraphy, photography and cinema

As writer, poet, critic and champion of the new movements in the visual arts, Apollinaire was among the first in our century to speculate on the correspondence between developments in the arts and breakthroughs in science. In a lecture in November 1911, he proclaimed: 'Today, scientists no longer limit themselves to the three dimensions of Euclid. The painters have been led quite naturally, one might say by intuition, to preoccupy themselves with the new possibilities of spatial measurement, which, in the language of the modern studios, are designated by the term "The Fourth Dimension" '.[9] Now Apollinaire's use of this term was later partly obscured by his poetic embellishment of it ('the immensity of space eternalising itself'). Nevertheless he was pointing to time as a new factor in the artistic interpretation of human experience. As he put it: 'The Fourth Dimension endows objects with plasticity. It gives the object its right proportions on the whole, whereas in Greek art, for instance, a somewhat mechanical rhythm constantly destroys the proportion'.[10] Apollinaire agreed with Kahnweiler that 'a new epoch was being born in which man was undergoing a transformation more radical than any other known within historical times',[11] and saw in the fourth dimension the means to render tangible the invisible forces that were shaping man's experience: 'for the first time', Berger remarks, 'the world as a totality ceased to be an abstraction and became realizable'.[12] At a moment when the world seemed to be fragmenting into a multiplicity of divergent forms, it became possible to see a pattern in the whole.

Two years before Apollinaire's eulogy, Marinetti, poet and provocateur, declared in the first Futurist manifesto: 'We stand upon the extreme promontory of the centuries. . . . Why should we look behind us, when we have to break in the mysterious portals of the Impossible? . . . Time and space died yesterday. Already we live in the absolute, since we have already created speed, eternal and ever present'.[13] Leaving aside Marinetti's polemical tone, why had so dramatic an alteration in the aesthetic experience of time and space come about?

A succession of advances in science and technology supplied the context for the change. In the middle of the nineteenth century the investigation of electric and magnetic phenomena by Faraday and Maxwell had revealed the inadequacy of Newton's laws of motion, preparing the way for the Einsteinian revolution. At the same time human communications had been transformed through telegraphy. Electricity as a new 'force' had entered into the realm of social reality. This was, as de Chardin agreed, 'a prodigious biological event' in itself. Electricity, McLuhan suggests, had 'originated in the mind an entirely new class of ideas, a new species of consciousness. Never before was anyone conscious that he knew with certainty what events were at that moment passing in a distant city 40–100 or 500 miles off'.[14] The directness of this electric communication thrust people into a radically new contact with events: 'Man was able to extend himself indefinitely beyond the immediate: he took over the territory in space and time where God had been presumed to exist'.[15] This was one aspect of Marinetti's abolition of time and space in favour of speed.

The impact of the telegraph was not confined to simple, one-to-one communication. Nowhere was its effect made more visible than in the mass newspaper, which 'became a daily experience of all the cultures of the globe . . . a space-time landscape of many times, many places given as single experience'.[16] With speed as everything, the newspaper quantised literature in practice, just as Einstein quantised light waves in the realm of theory: the fluid, undulating structure of language was challenged in the economy of the reverberating headline. The energy of sentences was converted into the mass of individual words. In addition, words and their relation to each other regained the magic, powerful and evocative status they had enjoyed in ancient time, not by virtue of poetic metre or rhyme, but spatially – by their mosaic-like juxtaposition against the white field of the page: 'Typography could be a visible metaphor for a new poetic syntax, liberated from the temporal succession of language which had, until then imprisoned poetry in its mechanical, grammatical order'.[17] Aristotle described speech as the arrest of the flowing of thought. By conferring immediacy on the newspaper, the telegraph allowed it to arrest the process of the world. The world became a verb.

With the advent of photography, the quantisation of writing became paralleled by the quantisation of the pictorial, as motion was arrested in the frozen moment of the snapshot – a technique vital to particle physics today. Photography, the process 'by which natural objects may be made to delineate themselves without the aid of the artist's pencil',[18] had a revolutionary impact upon the visual arts. The rationalisation of visual appearances by painter and draughtsman could not compete with this 'automatic process' through which the world of appearances could render itself independently of the visual grammar of drawing. Drawing tended to disappear in the Impressionists' paintings, and in the *pointillisme* of Seurat 'the world suddenly appeared through the painting' instead.[19]

Without photography it would have been impossible to capture organic movement in a single frame. In contrast to Stubbs, whose horses run like foxhounds, Degas was able to grasp the intricacies of rhythm in a single moment of a galloping racehorse. It was left to Muybridge to complete the recovery of organic form from mechanical structure by re-converting the digital into the analogue. His series of thirty cameras, set up at 12-inch intervals, released their shutters automatically as the object passed before the plate. Each picture showed the object arrested in an isolated phase. This was an augury of the cinematic revelation, a visual presentation of the actual movements of the forms of life.

Duchamp was familiar with Muybridge's studies of horses in movement and of fencers in different positions.[20] Examples such as these enabled him to paint his remarkable *Nude descending a staircase* of 1912. Here the cinematic flow of movement is made visible in the way that space is continuously enveloped by the woman's frame as she steps downwards. Space is thus given the form of Plato's 'moulding stuff for everything'; being 'moved and marked by the entering figures', it appears 'different at different times' because of them.[21] Unveiling another new dialectic between the organic and the mechanical, Duchamp gave us an artistic expression of Einstein's space-time continuum which is at once humanistic and scientistic.

In 1913, the Cubist painter Léger proclaimed: 'Visual realism has never been achieved with such intensity in art as it now is in the cinema'.[22] But the realism which many early film-makers achieved was one which was informed by the relativism of the human subject. The pioneer Russian director Vertov shows us this in his vivid account of the movie camera as an extension of man's sensory apparatus, a device which allowed him to explore the dynamism of the universe for the first time and, in so doing, synthesise an entirely new order of feelings: 'I am an ocular. A mechanical ocular. I, the machine show you a world the way

'Chrono-photography was at that time in vogue . . . Muybridge's albums were well
known to me': Marcel Duchamp, 'Nude descending a staircase', No 2, 1912.

'Acoustic space': Georges Braque, 'Mandolin', 1909–10.

only I can see it. I free myself for today and forever from human immobility. I'm in constant movement. I approach and pull away from objects. I creep under them. I move alongside a running horse's mouth. I fall and rise with the falling and rising bodies. This is I, the machine, manoeuvring in the chaotic movements, recording one movement after another in the most complex combinations. Freed from the boundaries of time and space, I co-ordinate any and all the points of the universe, wherever I want them to be. My way leads towards the creation of a fresh perception of the world. Thus I explain in a new way the world unknown to you'.[23]

In 1911, Henri Bergson created a sensation by associating the thought process itself with the cinematic form; it was Bergson's influential philosophy that helped promulgate ideas of the 'fourth dimension' among the Cubist painters. Bergson introduced time as an essential

Copyright Tate Gallery

Cubism attempted to incorporate Einstein's fourth dimension to gain 'realism of conception': Pablo Picasso, 'Seated nude', 1909–10.

ingredient in the artist's understanding of reality. His insistence that reality was a dynamic process, a continuous flow, was widely discussed and reported in journals such as the *Mercure de France*. Those passages of the writings of Cubist painters that deal with time read like paraphrases of Bergson's work.[24] In it originates the notion of simultaneity: a philosophy which insists that the image of a static world is false.

Cubism and Picasso

As we have just seen, the realism of the camera was compatible with subjectivism in cinema itself. It certainly encouraged subjectivist trends in painting. Since the coming of photography, the tendency of artists has been to turn from the world of external appearances to the inner spaces of human activity. The geography of this psychic world of feeling, dreams and fantasy is not susceptible to photography at all, for it comprises a non-visual set of relations. A new set of forms is required to reveal this reality, in much the same way that the physicist has, by means of new mathematical and statistical skills, revealed processes which the concepts inherent in ordinary language can no longer adequately represent. Niels Bohr's statement that 'the great extension of our experience in recent years has brought to light the insufficiency of our simple mechanical conceptions and, as a consequence, has shaken the foundation on which the customary interpretation of observation was based' is as true of modern painting as it is of atomic physics.[25]

'The metaphorical model of Cubism is the diagram', says John Berger, 'the diagram being a visible symbolic representation of invisible processes, forces, structures. A diagram need not eschew certain aspects of appearances; but these too will be treated symbolically as a sign, not as imitations or recreations'.[26] Einstein's famous equation has itself been popularised as a special kind of sign, a visual Gestalt, in its resonant effect similar to a Chinese ideographic character. Indeed Cubism abounds with signs. Letters, labels, numbers and fragments of printed material entered painting from sources far beyond the limits of established subject-matter. As different visual conventions jostle together in abrupt apposition they construct a multi-levelled image of reality. By furthering the integration of totally different styles of representation, Cubism extended the language of art; but more than that, it 'changed the nature of the relationship between the painted image and reality . . . created a system by which they could reveal visually the interlocking of phenomena . . . created the possibility in art of revealing processes instead of static states of being'.[27] The Cubists argued that their relativistic outlook was by nature realistic. 'From now on,' Léger insisted, 'everything can converge towards an intensity of realism obtained by purely dynamic means. Painterly contrasts in the purest sense (the use of complementaries in colours, lines and forms) are the basic structural elements of modern pictures'.[28] In the same remarkable essay of 1913, Léger went even further: 'Visual realism necessarily involves an object, a subject and perspective devices that are now considered negative and anti-realist. Realism of conception, neglecting all this cumbersome baggage, has been achieved in many contemporary paintings'.[29] What was at issue was the desire for realism of conception — that same freedom from established prejudice that informed Einstein's brilliance.

It was exactly this realism of conception that attracted Picasso to the sculpture of tribal Africa. In its exotic objects he found artistic truth. Just as the primitive African 'tends to depict what he knows about his subject rather than what he sees. He tends to express his idea of it',[30] Picasso once remarked that he painted objects as we thought them, not as he saw them. This is reflected in the way Picasso and other Cubists communicate tactile sensations.

It has always been the painter's task to give tactile value to retinal information. But with Picasso textures and surfaces define forms — they do not emphasise purely retinal information in the manner of the perspective system. Light is no longer the principle means by which forms can be revealed. 'Picasso's painting is always exciting because Picasso paints the path of feeling. . . . Did you ever have a teardrop run down your face? . . . Feel it run and you will understand Picasso. Picasso paints a teardrop running down your face. He paints a tragic running down on the face . . . just as you would feel it. Then at the end of the running he paints the teardrop . . . as it feels. He paints the path of a teardrop. . . . He paints a path of feeling . . . he paints the path of every feeling he has at the moment he is feeling. A moment later would be too late'.[32] It has become the prerogative of the modern painter to address our sense of touch as well as our sense of sight.

'Sculpted space': Umberto Boccioni, 'Unique forms of continuity in space', 1913.

Many of the late Romantics suddenly broke through into an 'understanding' of primitive art, embracing not only the curios in anthropologists' collections, but also the paintings of Giotto, and the entirety of pre-Renaissance art. This 'understanding' was dramatically extended in the paintings, collages and constructions of the Cubists, and especially in those of Picasso. Here we rediscover the primitive value of everyday things and objects; we are invited to 'feel' the presence of these objects, as if they themselves create a tangible space. The bas-reliefs of sculpture are echoed in the way forms in Cubist paintings often fill the foreground as volumes set against a flat surface. The particulate nature of light is exploited in order to impress feelings on us forcibly.

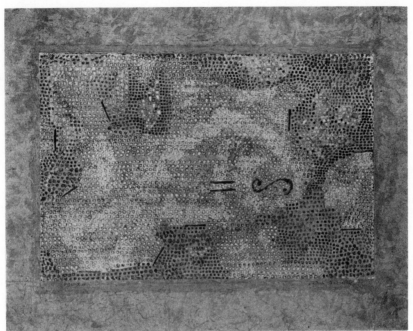

Copyright Museum of Modern Art

Paul Klee, 'Equals infinity', 1932.

The sound of sculpture

Mediated by sculpture, tactile effects give way to auditory ones. Since the beginning of modern art painters have often explicitly employed sculptural effects. Sculpture, the voice of silence, lies on the frontier between the spaces of sight and sound; sculptural ideas have made possible a visual modulation of space – a modulation analogous to the movement of sound waves in space. Again 'Newton's sleep' is disturbed. The anonymous primitive sculptor reveals his non-visual attitude to spatial forms through his indifference to the demands of the eye: 'He lets each piece fill its own space, create its own world, without reference to background or anything external to it'.[33] The multiformity of surfaces, and infinite freedom of direction we find in so much primeval art is evident in the sculpture of Boccioni, Brancusi, Archipenko, Lipchitz and Arp. 'We deny volume as an expression space. Space in a technical age can no more be measured by volume than by linear measure. Depth alone expresses the limited sphere that is space' says Pevsner in the Constructivist Manifesto of 1920. Naum Gabo, a fellow Constructivist, argues: 'Space cannot be seen by the eye, it is all around us like a globe stretching into eternity. Sculpture is to be heard like music'.[34] Abstract art expresses spaces and experiences that are not wholly definable in optical terms, so that the analogy of aural space, of aural relations, can be potently employed in the repertoire of painterly effects. El Lissitzky rails against the use of the word 'abstract' to refer to an art concerned to represent new modes of experience concretely: 'Are radio waves then "abstract" or naturalistic?'[35] For Lissitzky, as for Einstein, energy and mass are interconvertible. Though invisible, radio waves, like all forms of energy, are part of the stuff of reality. And, as mass, sculpture creates its own field; like a sound, it structures the space it inhabits – not only in the viewer's imagination, but also in physical terms.

Conclusion

The development of abstraction in modern painting and sculpture has reflected the artist's traditional concern to represent reality. The post-Perspective tendency to make a complete distinction between time and space has been succeeded by a recovery of the image as a plastic organism. Modern art seeks to include all the relationships in time and space that adequately represent reality. The logic of abstract art is not the mechanical logic of geometrical optics or of perspective, but the connectedness in meaning that is the essential task of representation. Abstraction in painting is a rejection of the inert homogeneity of the three-dimensional model that is Perspective in favour of the dynamic effect of the two-dimensional form. Order and pattern have prominence in a structure that places elements side by side in a relational field. In the correlative universe of abstract art, colour, shape, texture and image interact with one another by a kind of inductance. In art the correspondence of symbols supplies a key to relations that form an organic whole, just as in post-Einsteinian cosmology we encounter one colossal continuum.

In the art of our era there has been a recovery of the proper 'ratio' of senses for which Blake searched. Modern art has played a part in bursting narrow Cartesian dualities wide open. It has turned the soporific system of Perspective inside out: today the 'vanishing point' is no longer situated on the horizon, but in our particular frame of reference. Our protean and pluralistic age offers no certainties; but, in quantising the world and reconstructing it again, we have gained valuable insights into the nature of a universe in flux. Through Cubism and its allies, art has provided a powerful alternative to our trance-like absorption in purely retinal values. How much modern art was aided by Einstein's ideas is an open question; that it was aided is not.

Notes

1. Thomas S. Kuhn, *The structure of scientific revolutions,* The University of Chicago Press, Chicago, 1962, p. 113.
2. Banesh Hoffmann, *Einstein,* Paladin, 1975, p. 81.
3. Joachim Gasquet, *Cézanne,* Les albums d'art Druet, Librairie de France, F Sant'andrea, Paris, 1930.
4. Georges Poulet, *Studies in human time,* E. Coleman, translator, Harper Torch Books, New York, 1959, p. 54.
5. William Blake, in G. Keynes, ed., *The letters of William Blake,* Rupert Hart-Davis, London, 1956, p. 79.
6. E. H. Gombrich, *Art and illusion,* Phaidon Press, London, 1962, p. 279.
7. William Blake, in G. Keynes, ed., *Poetry and prose of William Blake,* The Nonesuch Library, London, 1975, p. 476.
8. Marshall McLuhan and Harley Parker, 'Through the vanishing point', *World Perspectives,* vol. 37, Harper Colophon Books, New York, 1969, p. 240.
9. Guillaume Apollinaire, *Les peintres cubistes,* Paris, 1913, quoted in Edward F. Fry, *Cubism,* Thames & Hudson, London, 1966, p. 116.
10. Ibid.
11. D. H. Kahnweiler, *Cubism,* Editions Braun, Paris, 1950.
12. John Berger, *The moment of cubism,* Wiedenfeld & Nicholson, London, 1969, p. 6.
13. F. T. Marinetti, *First futurist manifesto,* 1909, quoted in Joshua C. Naylor, *Futurism,* New York Museum of Modern Art, New York, p. 124.
14. Marshall McLuhan, *Understanding media,* Sphere Books, London, 1967, p. 263.
15. Marshall McLuhan, *Culture is our business,* Ballantine Books, New York, 1972, p. 198.
16. Marshall McLuhan, *Counterblast,* The Pitman Press, London, 1969, p. 112.
17. Nina S. Hellerstein, 'Paul Claudel and Guillaume Apollinaire as visual poets', *Visible Language,* vol. xi, no. 3, Cleveland, Ohio, 1977, p. 246.
18. In 1839 Fox Talbot read a paper to the Royal Society entitled 'Some account of the art of photogenic drawing, or the process by which natural objects may be made to delineate themselves without the aid of the artist's pencil'.
19. Marshall McLuhan, *Understanding media,* loc. cit., p. 202.
20. Marcel Duchamp, 'Eleven Europeans in America', *Museum of Modern Art Bulletin,* vol. 13, nos. 4–5, New York, 1948.
21. Plato, 'The Receptacle', in *Timaeus.*
22. Fernand Léger, *The origins of painting and its representational value,* 1913, quoted in Fry, *Cubism,* loc. cit., p. 125.
23. Dziga Vertov, *Resolution of the council of three,* 1923.
24. The ideas of Gustav Le Bon and Henri Bergson are discussed in Timothy Mitchell, 'Bergson, Le Bon and Hermetic Cubism', *The Journal of Aesthetics and Art Criticism,* vol. xxxvi, no. 2, 1977.
25. Niels Bohr, *Atomic physics and the description of nature,* Cambridge University Press, London, 1934, p. 2.
26. Berger, op. cit., p. 20.
27. Ibid., pp. 15, 23.
28. Léger, in Fry, op. cit., p. 124.
29. Ibid., p. 123.
30. John Golding, *Cubism,* Faber & Faber, London, 1968, p. 59.
31. Picasso's statement to Gomez de la Serna, in *Revista del Occidente,* Madrid, 1929.
32. Louis Danz, *Personal revolution and Picasso,* quoted in V. J. Papanek, *A bridge in time,* Something Else Press, New York, 1967.
33. E. S. Carpenter, 'Eskimo', *Explorations,* no. 9, University of Toronto Press, Toronto, 1960.
34. Naum Gabo, *Second Constructivist manifesto,* Berlin, 1924.
35. Sophie Lissitzky-Kuppers, *El Lissitzky, life, letters, texts,* Thames & Hudson, London, 1968, p. 325.

Einstein and science fiction

Arthur C. Clarke

Arthur C. Clarke was born at Minehead, Somerset, England in 1917, and is a graduate of King's College, London, where he obtained first-class Honours in physics and mathematics. He is past chairman of the British Interplanetary Society, a member of the Academy of Astronautics, the Royal Astronomical Society, and many other scientific organisations. During the war he was in charge of the first radar talk-down equipment on its experimental trials. His only non-science fiction novel, *Glide path,* is based on this work.

In a technical paper published in 1945 he described in detail the geo-stationary satellite system now used by all commercial communications satellites. His 50 books have been printed in more than 30 languages.

For the past 20 years, his hobby has been underwater exploration along the Great Barrier Reef of Australia and off the coast of Ceylon, where he has resided since 1956.

The impact of relativity on science fiction has been enormous and could be the basis of a major project for one of the many academics now exploring this field. After 1919, of course, every writer who ventured beyond the solar system had to take Einstein into account.

If it is objected that the first classic 'space opera', E. E. Smith's *The Skylark of Space* (1928) did nothing of the sort, it may be pointed out that this famous and still readable story was written between 1915 and 1920, when even a scientist like Dr Smith could send his characters round the universe at as many times the speed of light as he pleased. (This story, incidentally, also contains what must be one of the first anticipations in print of a neutron star, and its effects upon unwary travellers.)

Yet what the theory of relativity took away with one hand, it gave back with the other. Even if the velocity of light is an insuperable barrier (which, of course, no full-blooded science fiction writer will concede[1]), the time dilation effect may still allow voyages of unlimited extent within a human lifetime. There are two trifling problems: to achieve $0.99999c$ might require the total conversion of planet-sized masses into energy; and one would return home (if home still existed) centuries or millenia after setting out. This bizarre possibility has been seized upon by countless writers, possibly beginning with Miles J. Breuer ('The Fitzgerald contraction', *Wonder Stories*, 1930); I have used it myself as a basic plot device in *Childhood's End* (1953).

A philosophical–theological variation on this theme occurred to me in 1965 and I have made it the subject of the following note, 'God and Einstein', later reprinted in *Report on Planet Three*. At the time, I supposed that the problem was a novel one, but I should have known better. After the note's appearance, several readers informed me that the matter had been discussed in various specialised magazines. I regret that I cannot locate the precise references – they are buried several million words back in my correspondence files and must await retrieval by my literary executors, hopefully on the far side of 2001.

God and Einstein

For some years I have been worried by the following astro-theological paradox. It is hard to believe that no one else has ever thought of it, yet I have never seen it discussed anywhere.

One of the most firmly established facts of modern physics, and the basis of Einstein's theory of relativity, is that the velocity of light is the speed limit of the material universe. No object, no signal, no *influence,* can travel any faster than this. Please don't ask why this should be; the universe just happens to be built that way. Or so it seems at the moment.

But light takes not millions, but *billions,* of years to cross even the part of Creation we can observe with our telescopes. So, if God obeys the laws He apparently established, at any given time He can have control over only an infinitesimal fraction of the universe. All hell might (literally?) be breaking loose ten light-years away, a mere stone's throw in interstellar space, and the bad news would take at least ten years to reach Him. And then it would be at least another ten years before He could get there to do anything about it. . . .

You may answer that this is terribly naive – that God is already 'everywhere'. Perhaps so, but that really comes to the same thing as saying that His thoughts, and His influence, can travel at an infinite velocity. In this case, the Einstein speed limit is not absolute; it *can* be broken.

The implications of this are profound. From the human viewpoint, it is no longer absurd – though it may be presumptuous – to hope that we may one day have knowledge of the most distant parts of the universe. The snail's pace of the velocity of light need not be an eternal limitation, the remotest galaxies may one day lie within our reach.

But perhaps, on the other hand, God Himself is limited by the same laws that govern the movements of electrons and protons, stars and spaceships. And that may be the cause of all our troubles.

He's coming just as quickly as He can, but there's nothing that even He can do about that maddening 186,000 miles a second.

It's anybody's guess whether He'll be here in time.

Note

1.   For my arguments with Isaac Asimov on this point, see 'Possible, that's all!', in *Report on Planet Three* (1972).

Einstein and relativity theory in modern literature

Lee Calcraft

Dr Lee Calcraft read physics for his first degree, subsequently undertaking research at the universities of Essex and Lausanne. In 1971, he began a study of the history and philosophy of science at the University of Leeds, and was awarded a PhD in 1976. He is now Senior Lecturer in the history of ideas at Hatfield Polytechnic.

Introduction[1]

On the afternoon of 6 November 1919, Fellows of the Royal Society and the Royal Astronomical Society heard of the dramatic confirmation of predictions made in Einstein's theories of relativity. An expedition to Principe Island on the Gulf of Guinea led by A. S. Eddington and E. T. Cottingham had returned with photographs taken during a total eclipse of the sun which showed, as Einstein had maintained in his general theory of relativity (1916), that light follows a curved path in a gravitational field. From this date, as Eddington reported to Einstein, 'all England has been talking about your theory'. And in a leading article entitled 'The fabric of the universe', *The Times* announced: 'it is confidently believed by the greatest experts that enough has been done to overthrow the certainty of ages and to require a new philosophy of the universe, a philosophy that will sweep away nearly all that has hitherto been accepted as the axiomatic basis of physical thought'.[2] Within a matter of months of these first pronouncements there appeared a great number of publications on the subject, many of which, like Einstein's own *Relativity* (published in August 1920), attempted to explain his theories in terms which the layman could understand. Aided by the press and by such expositions, Einstein's fame spread to a quite remarkable degree. As one account somewhat colourfully puts it: 'In all nooks and corners, social evenings of instruction sprang up, and wondering universities appeared with errant professors that led people out of the three-dimensional misery of daily life into the more hospitable Elysian fields of four-dimensionality. Women lost sight of domestic worries and discussed coordinate systems, the principle of simultaneity and negatively-charged electrons'.[3] Even if not quite to this extent, relativity had become something of a household word.

In view both of the widespread interest expressed in Einstein's work, and of its undeniably iconoclastic nature, it would be surprising if no record of it were to be found in contemporary literature. It is a commonplace that the major developments in science have produced repercussions far beyond the small circle of scientists directly involved, and that on occasion, as in the case of Copernicus, Newton and Darwin for example, a response is evoked in the literary productions of the period.[4] Here we will examine a number of the ways in which writers have responded to the work of Einstein. Yet the interactions between Einstein and literature, taken in the broadest sense, are in practice so diverse that it will be necessary to narrow the field to serious literary works written in prose. Thus for reasons of space we must exclude the rich variety of Einsteinian or relativistic verse, of which the limerick appears to have achieved a certain popularity. The lady called Bright who could travel faster than light,[5] and the fencer named Fisk whose rapier was reduced to a disk,[6] must with reluctance be excluded from this discussion; as must George Gamow's excellent fictionalising of certain aspects of relativity theory,[7] and Stephen Leacock's satirical piece claiming to outline the features of Einstein's work of interest to 'women's culture clubs'.[8] With the scope thus narrowed, we are in a position to identify a number of quite distinct ways in which writers have made use of theories with which Einstein's name is associated. In an attempt to impose some order on the variety of usage encountered, we shall group together the more explicit references to Einstein and relativity, distinguishing them from examples in which his work has had a more subtle if not less pervasive influence.

In what appear to be amongst the earliest explicit references to Einstein's work, examples of which are to be found in the writings of Aldous Huxley and Bernard Shaw, relativity theory or 'the Einsteinian revolution', as one of Huxley's characters calls it, appears as a topic of conversation between non-scientists. In the more interesting cases of this kind which we shall discuss, Huxley and Shaw both stress the adverse effects of the wider philosophical implications of Einstein's work on the morale of their characters. In a second class of examples Einstein's work forms part of the technical backdrop to stories written about scientists of the 'twenties and early 'thirties. Here, as in C. P. Snow's *The search*,[9] and John Abulafia's 'Foolscap',[10] the treatment is in general less anecdotal, and does not specifically bring out the philosophical implications of the scientific theories. In a third class of explicit references we shall consider Aldous Huxley's *Ape and essence*,[11] and Friedrich Dürrenmatt's *The physicists*,[12] in which there is an actual character named Einstein. In both of these works, written after Hiroshima, the Einstein character serves the specific function of focusing on the moral issues involved in scientific research.

The work of Einstein also makes explicit appearance in a fourth and rather different manner: through metaphor and simile. For example, Alexander Solzhenitsyn, a writer trained in science, invokes ideas of relativity of mass and time in *Cancer ward*, to convey the effects which the knowledge of his approaching death has on the young geologist Vadim: 'He became like a moving body approaching the speed of light. His "time" and his "mass" were becoming different from those of other people. His time was increasing in capacity, his mass in penetration. His years were being compressed into weeks, his days into minutes'.[13] This simile, increased in poignancy and relevance by the role played by 'modern' medical physics in the novel, and its failure to cure him, is highly effective. Yet the enrichment of literature with similes drawn from relativity is exceedingly rare. Perhaps marginally less so is the metaphorical use of words made popular or given a new meaning as a result of Einstein's work. In an excellent little book entitled *The language of science and the language of literature, 1700–1740*,[14] Donald Davie describes how such words as 'spirit', 'volatile' and 'acrimony' were carried over from the laboratory of early science into common usage during the eighteenth century. These words were either the products of science, or were ordinary words given a new signification by science, and extended by metaphorical usage back into the common pool of language. This latter process can be seen at work in the context of relativity theory in Lawrence Durrell's *The Alexandria quartet*,[15] where the author consciously applies words from relativity to the human sphere. Words such as 'dimension', 'field', 'continuum', 'curved', and 'gravitational' are all used in somewhat similar metaphorical extensions to those described by Davie. Yet again this is by no means a common occurrence in literature, and these examples are in no sense gratuitous. Durrell's *Quartet* is avowedly based on the 'relativity proposition', and his frequent use of these words forms part of a broader plan, as we shall later argue.

Einstein's theories have also had a less tangible though arguably more profound effect on literature. To complete the breakdown of modes of usage and influence we will indicate three ways in which this may occur. The first concerns the world-view of the writer himself, which, having been influenced by the philosophical features of relativity or quantum theory,[16] may in some sense pervade his fictional writings. Such a case has been argued by F. S. C. Duggan of the works of Samuel Beckett. 'The absurdity and randomness characteristic of Beckett's vision of human existence derive, in large part, from the theories of modern physics',[17] he writes. Beckett 'assumes that his readers are aware of the revolution in modern thought caused by the discoveries of relativity and quantum theory, and how these theories have virtually demolished the common-sense world of classical physical theory'.[18] Yet in spite of Duggan's unequivocal claims, and the lengths to which he has carried his investigation, there is little direct evidence that modern physics lies at the root of these features of Beckett's work; and judgement should perhaps be withheld until further evidence is available. A somewhat less dramatic, although more easily authenticated case may be argued of features of the world-view which pervades Durrell's *The Alexandria quartet*. But the uncertainties of the world of the *Quartet* reduce in most cases to the effects of observer relativities, and we shall treat these, under the rubric of the subject—object relationship, below.

The second class of examples of less tangible or explicit influence of Einstein concerns the notion of space-time.[19] As a result of Einstein's special theory of relativity, the convention of viewing the world as a particular kind of four-dimensional continuum was adopted (so amalgamating space and time); and because of the relativity effect it was also revealed that time could pass relatively more slowly under certain conditions. Again these features were taken up by a number of writers. Duggan, for example, claims that 'a flattening out of time', noticeable in a number of Beckett's works, was a result of the influence of Einstein. A claim of a similar kind has been made of T. S. Eliot. In an article entitled 'Time and reality in Eliot and Einstein', M. N. McMorris argues that Eliot's preoccupation with time derives from a knowledge of Einstein's work.[20] A. M. Bork has been able to argue a far more substantial case of *The Alexandria quartet*,[21] in which Lawrence Durrell avowedly attempts to represent the idea of a space-time continuum, structuring his four-volume work on the basis of the three space and one time dimension, and employing vocabulary which evokes the central features of relativity theory.

The third and final class of examples of the less tangible influence of Einstein which we have identified, features treatments of the subject—object relationship. According to relativity theory, the state or frame of reference of an observer is a determining factor in the outcome of any observations which he may make. Writers such as Hermann Broch and Lawrence Durrell have made use of this feature of the theory, and in the name of relativity have specifically emphasised the subjectivity of *human* observations and conceptions, and the effect of viewing the same people or series of events from different 'frames of reference'. In *The Alexandria quartet* the perpetually reiterated theme of observer relativity underpins the whole novel, and is directly related to its 'four-dimensional' structure, as we shall later argue. In the article 'Hermann Broch and relativity in fiction',[22] Theodore Ziolkowski examines a somewhat similar use of relativity by Broch in his trilogy *The sleepwalkers*.[23] During the course of the book Broch gives a theoretical treatment of aspects of relativity theory which points to his use of it both in the style and structuring of his work. In a manner essentially similar to that of *The Alexandria quartet,* the narratives of the first two volumes of *The sleepwalkers* are revealed in the third to be coloured by what is later learned of the narrator, thus emphasising the importance of the 'frame of reference' adopted by the observer; and as Ziolkowski points out, Broch consciously stresses the intrusion of the subject into any observation, so that all points of view are conditioned by the 'frame' from which they are made.

Anecdotal reference

Having indicated something of the variety of ways in which knowledge of Einstein's work has been turned to use in literature, we shall examine certain examples in greater detail, treating firstly the more explicit references contained in the works of Aldous Huxley, Bernard Shaw, C. P. Snow, John Abulafia and Friedrich Dürrenmatt, and secondly the detailed use of relativity by Lawrence Durrell in *The Alexandria quartet*. The earliest references in fiction to Einstein and relativity theory which I have come across have been, rather as one might expect, of the anecdotal variety; and in a number of cases it is not so much the theory itself which appears to inspire writers of fiction, but its broader and more questionable philosophical implications, and in particular its consequences for determinism and materialism.[24]

Both Aldous Huxley in the two novels *Those barren leaves* (1925) and *Point counter point* (1928), and Bernard Shaw in the play *Too true to be good* (1931), depict materialists whose world-view is undermined by recent developments in relativity theory and quantum mechanics. Cardan of *Those barren leaves* was born 'almost a twin to *The origin of species*', and was 'brought up in the simple faith of nineteenth-century materialism'. 'We were all wonderfully optimistic then,' he claims, 'believed in progress and the ultimate explicability of everything in terms of physics and chemistry'. But times have changed for the worst, and Cardan finds himself confronted by 'that disquieting scientific modernism which is now turning the staunchest mathematical physicists into mystics'.[25] And during the course of the novel, the demise of Victorian materialism finds its parallel in, and in turn serves to accentuate, his own rapidly approaching demise, and the problem of sickness and death with which Huxley was particularly concerned throughout his life. In this example the 'scientific modernism' which was one source of Cardan's philosophical malaise is not explicitly attributed to Einstein. In the later *Point counter point,* however, Huxley mounts a similar assault on the communist Illidge, specifically naming the villains of the piece. Illidge felt that he could not be a true communist without a faith in the nineteenth-century materialism upon which principles his communism was based. But as a scientist he had to acknowledge the latest work in science which was undermining these very principles: 'Poor Illidge,' notes Spandrell with glee, 'He's sadly worried by Einstein and Eddington. And how he hates Henri Poincaré! How furious he gets with old Mach! They're undermining his simple faith.... He's a scientist, but his principles make him fight against any theory that's less than fifty years old. It's exquisitely comic'.[26] Huxley, who was unsympathetic to the cause of Marxism, delights in Illidge's plight, and relativity becomes a source of amusement, in contrast to his earlier and more serious treatment of Cardan's predicament in *Those barren leaves.*

The philosophical implications of modern physics again provide the source of some light humour in Shaw's play *Too true to be good.* But here, ideas from relativity are specifically combined with those from quantum theory to provide a technically more appropriate bulwark against philosophical determinism.[27] For Aubrey's father, a confirmed atheist, determinism had been the mainstay of his life. But now, as he complains, 'All is caprice: the calculable world has become incalculable'. The new physics had shown that nature did not obey simple rules after all: 'The orbit of the electron obeys no law ... it is as capricious as the planet Mercury',[28] he observes. And here Shaw has juxtaposed anomalies from the two fields of physics: the quantum mechanical work on electron orbits, and the anomalous motion of the planet Mercury which could be explained on the basis of relativity theory. Yet having hinted at quantum mechanics and indeterminacy, Shaw, like a number of other writers and lay commentators, sees Einstein in the vanguard of the assault on determinism, although one might more properly associate this with the names of Planck or Heisenberg for their contributions to quantum theory. Newton's universe, which was 'the stronghold of rational determinism', 'has crumbled like the walls of Jericho before the criticism of Einstein'.[29] And with it, crumbled Aubrey's father's faith in atheism, whose loss he laments with the bitterness of one willfully deceived: 'Determinism is gone, shattered, buried with a thousand dead religions, evaporated with the clouds of a million forgotten winters. The science I pinned my faith to is bankrupt: its tales were more foolish than all the miracles of the priests, its cruelties more horrible than all the atrocities of the Inquisition.... And now look at me and behold the supreme tragedy of the atheist who has lost his faith – his faith in atheism'.[30] Shaw does not fail to see the humorous nature of the situation, but nevertheless the parallel with Cardan in *Those barren leaves* is quite striking, for as well as his similar lament at the loss of determinism, Aubrey's father's private life, like Cardan's, begins to collapse about him. His wife died cursing him, and his son whom he had brought up to be a 'God-fearing atheist' has become a thief and a scoundrel, a villainy only compounded in his father's eyes by his taking of the cloth. But now that determinism has been defeated, his father can put up no objections: 'Go, boy: perish in your villainy; for neither your father nor anyone else can now give you good reason for being a man of honour'.[31]

Able no longer to base his system of values on a deterministic philosophy, he reluctantly bids his son do as he will. But for Huxley at least, modern science could also point the way out of the dilemma. Cardan had commented that the staunchest mathematical physicists were turning into mystics, and by the end of *Those barren leaves* Calamy, inspired in part by the questions raised by modern physics, has set out on the road to mysticism.

Huxley's interest in modern physics was probably aroused by J. W. N. Sullivan when he stayed with the Huxleys in Florence early in 1924. Huxley suffered few qualms over the repetition of ideas in his novels, and the relativity theme appears in three of the six novels which he wrote between 1924 and 1944. In the last of these, *Time must have a stop* (1944), it is no longer used to undermine determinism or materialism, but appears largely as a conversation piece which is employed in the re-creation of the intellectual atmosphere of the 'twenties. In this case, however, Huxley parodies the cause of relativity by overplaying his protagonist's enthusiasm in a manner which will be familiar to readers of his earlier works. Paul De Vries, who is in 'cereals', is nevertheless passionately interested in the 'scope and significance of the Einsteinian revolution'. 'And what a revolution, he went on with mounting enthusiasm. Incomparably more important than anything that had happened in Russia or Italy. For this was the revolution that had changed the whole course of scientific thinking'.[32] Eustace Barnack, to whom De Vries's mealtime monologue is addressed, is far more interested in his food, and perpetually interjects to this effect. 'Could any subject ['Einstein'] be more exciting?' asks De Vries. 'None,' comes the rejoinder, 'unless it's the subject of lunch when the clock says half-past one'.[33] And once at table, the theme is reiterated: 'Everyone ought to know something about Einstein', De Vries begins. 'One moment,' retorts Eustace, 'Let's start by deciding what we're going to eat'.[34] As the meal progresses, Eustace's deflating tactics continue, and there is even a hint during the conversation that De Vries intends to use the results of Einstein's work to support a relativity of morals. 'Everyone ought to know something of Einstein,' he says again. 'It's only the mathematical techniques that are difficult. The principle is simple – and after all, it's the understanding of the principle that affects values and conduct'.[35] This view is reinforced by De Vries's somewhat unusual intentions with regard to the young Veronica Thwale, whom he later marries. Yet *Time must have a stop* marks the last light-hearted treatment of modern physics in the Huxleyan *opus*. Profoundly affected by the use of atomic weapons, Huxley wrote the novel *Ape and essence* (1948) depicting the horrors of a third world war; and when he did return to the subject of modern physics in his novella *The genius and the goddess* (1955), set largely in the 'twenties, he stressed that the days of innocence were now long passed. 'Those were the days,' remarks his stoical protagonist, 'when you could be a physicist without feeling guilty . . . in 1921 infernal machines were safely in the future'.[36]

Scientific furniture

In the works of Huxley and Shaw discussed above, ideas from modern physics are propounded and reflected upon by non-scientists who are largely concerned with their philosophical implications. By contrast, C. P. Snow's *The search*, Aldous Huxley's *The genius and the goddess* and John Abulafia's 'Foolscap' all deal with scientists engaged upon research during the 'twenties or early 'thirties, and relativity or quantum theory forms part of the scientific furniture of each piece. In general in such cases, the treatment of science is, as one might expect, somewhat less anecdotal than in those works so far considered; a fact which tends to impose greater demands on the scientific expertise of the writer. In this respect Snow, who was involved in research at Cambridge before turning his hand to writing, is at a considerable advantage over Huxley and Abulafia, both of whom graduated in the arts rather than the sciences.

The search tells of the rise and fall of the rather boring and immodest semi-autobiographical character Arthur Miles, a research worker in X-ray crystallography. Modern physics, in the guise of quantum theory, forms part of the scientific background to Miles's work at Cambridge during the mid 'twenties, where he brushed shoulders with Rutherford, Bohr and Eddington. In a chapter entitled 'Effects of a revolution', Miles describes the new quantum theory which was causing great excitement amongst the more eminent of his colleagues, but of which, as an X-ray crystallographer, he was barely aware until its later stages. He soon managed, however, to 'get the general drift of Dirac and Heisenberg', and after working through 'most of the quantum mechanical papers', maintains with typical immodesty, 'I think I understood it better than many physicists at that time'; a claim which his rather vague descriptions of the theory does little to support. In practice Miles is much more at home with classical physics, and decides that although quantum theory would be an enormous aid in his field of research, he does not have the time to master the mathematical techniques involved, and returns to his work in classical X-ray crystallography with redoubled intensity, spurred on by the fear that his lack of competence in the new field might cost him the directorship of the research institute to which he aspires with pathological intensity. It is only in his treatment of classical physics that Snow goes into technicalities that suggest a personal acquaintance with research. This occurs in Miles's account of the testing of models: 'I had brought back to mind some calculations of the scattering curves, assuming various models. None of the values had been anything like the truth. I saw at once that the new structure ought to give something nearer. . . . I was startled when I got the answer: the new model did not give perfect agreement, but it was far closer than any of the others. So far as I remember, the real value at one point was 1.32, my previous three models gave 1.1, 1.65 and 1.7, and the new one just under 1.4'.[37] The passage conveys something of the way in which a theoretical model of an organic structure might be tested against experimental data, and the dénouement of the novel suggests how easily it is to be led into error in such procedures. In general, however, Snow keeps technical detail to a minimum in *The search;* his book about scientists successfully avoids being overburdened with science.

This is also true of Aldous Huxley's novella *The genius and the goddess,* which depicts a mathematical physicist at work on quantum theory in the early 'twenties. But although Huxley came from a family which achieved a certain reputation in science, and he read a good deal of popular science himself, he was not, unlike Snow, trained in science, and he does not attempt to treat the working life of the physicist Henry Maartens in any detail. Snow on the other hand is concerned both with the personal and the professional life of Miles. More strikingly, the style and manner of description of science in the two works is quite different, and again this may be traced to the backgrounds of the authors. As we have suggested, Snow is able to give a moderately technical account of Miles's attempts to fit theory to fact in his crystallographic researches. It is stylistically rather plain, and contains certain technical details, although written in the first person. Huxley's account on the other hand, which he puts into the mouth of Maartens's research assistant, could hardly be more different. Dr Rivers's moments at the laboratory with Henry Maartens were, as he claims, some of the most memorable of his life: 'The whole thing was pure idyllic poetry, like something out of Theocritus or Virgil. Four young PhDs in the role of goatherd's apprentices, with Henry as the patriarch, teaching the youngsters the tricks of his trade, dropping pearls of wisdom, spinning interminable yarns about the new pantheon of theoretical physics. He struck the lyre and rhapsodised about the metamorphosis of earthbound Mass into celestial Energy. He sang the hopeless loves of Electron for her Nucleus. He piped of Quanta and hinted darkly at the mysteries of Indeterminacy. It was idyllic'.[38] That the lyrical quality of this passage should cause us to question very seriously the scientific credentials of Dr Rivers is perhaps more of a reflection on the dullness of ordinary scientific prose than on Huxley's failure to sound like a theoretical physicist; and indeed suggests that there are features of the 'two cultures' divide which Snow, with his rather lifeless prose style somewhat reminiscent of the science textbook, was himself unable to bridge.

The third piece, John Abulafia's 'Foolscap', is considerably more ambitious from a scientific point of view than Huxley's novella, although like Huxley, Abulafia received no formal training in science. From a succession of letters, diary jottings and other miscellaneous extracts, 'Foolscap' builds up an unusual picture of a scientific hoax. It tells of how the mysterious John Gray of the Cavendish convinces three Edinburgh University academics, physicist Richard Barnes, mathematician George Medlicott, and philosopher Ian Prescott, that he has evolved a unified field theory; an enterprise in which Einstein himself did not succeed. All three academics persuade themselves of the validity of Gray's theory, and each in turn attempts to monopolise Gray and his work for his own ends. Before long Medlicott's wife Elizabeth becomes infatuated with the mysterious Gray, whose name is by now upon everyone's lips. But as arrangements are made for a meeting of the Physical Society at which he will give his paper to an audience including Hermann Weyl and Ernst [sic] Schrödinger, he mysteriously disappears. On the day of the meeting, 1 April 1932, Gray is nowhere to be found, and at the meeting itself Medlicott, Prescott and Barnes are each discredited in turn; at which point a sheet of foolscap which Gray has left for the press is read to the assembled company. It says simply: '1st April 1932. Unified Field Theory by John Gray. A hoax?'

It is a nicely composed piece, and the tensions between the four predatory characters Barnes, Prescott, Medlicott and his wife Elizabeth increase steadily and inexorably until the final showdown on All Fools Day 1932. Here Abulafia uses the device of a parallel time sequence provided by Elizabeth Medlicott's diary and H. Talbot-Murray's *A history of medical and natural sciences at Edinburgh* dramatically to reveal the full consequences of Gray's activities. By the end of the piece, however, one is left in some doubt as to how the three academics should so easily be fooled by a scientific paper of only three pages in length. We are given the impression that Gray was particularly gifted, but must also conclude that Barnes, Prescott and Medlicott were particularly gullible, and that personal ambition made them incautious; made them *want* to believe in Gray. It is also conceivable that Abulafia is making a point about truth and subjectivity, and so broadly using the theme of relativity at a second level. The format of the piece is probably intended to emphasise this. 'Foolscap' does not use a narrator, and consists simply of a succession of documents which the reader must evaluate in his own way. Unresolved questions such as how the academics were deceived, whether Gray really intended a hoax, and whether he existed at all, each call for interpretation on the reader's part, and suggest the intrusion of a similar kind of subjectivity to that encountered by Barnes, Prescott, Medlicott and Elizabeth in their impressions of Gray and his work.

One of the primary sources from which 'Foolscap' is built is Gray's scientific paper. This is reproduced in its entirety, and one wonders here if Abulafia does not fall between two stools. For at first sight it appears to be a somewhat imposing document, with a series of equations which might deter the non-specialist from reading the piece at all. A scientist on the other hand might be attracted by the equations, but would soon realise that they were quite meaningless and inconsistent.[39] The sections dealing with Medlicott and Barnes's defence of Gray's theory at the public meeting also fail to ring completely true from a scientific point of view. But these minor technical deficiencies do not detract from the excellent dramatic effect which Abulafia creates in this piece.

By what at first sight appears to be something of a coincidence, each of the three works which we have considered in this group, *The search, The genius and the goddess* and

'Foolscap', features scientists who are discredited in some way. In *The search* Miles 'drops a brick' in his research, and eventually leaves the scientific world for good; in *The genius and the goddess* Maartens is quite out of touch with everyday reality and mishandles his personal relationships; while in 'Foolscap' Medlicott and Barnes are publicly disgraced. Yet in practice the discrediting or satirising of the activities of the scientist is a relatively common theme in treatments of science in literature, and one by no means associated only with scientists engaged on research in relativity or quantum theory. Its pedigree extends back almost as far as modern science itself; through Aldous Huxley's *Antic hay* (1923) and Thomas Love Peacock's *Nightmare abbey* (1818) to Jonathan Swift's *Gulliver's travels* (1726) and Thomas Shadwell's *The Virtuoso* (1676) — and indeed beyond the emergence of modern science to Chaucer's treatment of the alchemist in 'The Canon's Yeoman's Tale'. The characterisation of Medlicott, Barnes and Maartens in 'Foolscap' and *The genius and the goddess* falls squarely within this tradition. Furthermore these two works were written, as it appears were the majority of treatments of this kind, by non-scientists. In *The search,* by contrast, Miles 'drops a brick' but retains mastery over the situation, and begins a promising career as a writer.[40] Unlike Barnes, Medlicott or Maartens, he is neither an object of pity nor derision. In this sense Snow falls clearly within a second tradition of treatments of science in literature — written typically by science-trained authors such as H. G. Wells and Alexander Solzhenitsyn — in which scientists are generally portrayed (though not without exception) as relatively sane and complete individuals, and are not the butt of satire.

Einstein as a fictional character

In the grouping to which we now turn, science becomes the object of a more serious and profound scrutiny. Both in Aldous Huxley's lesser-known novel *Ape and essence,* and Friedrich Dürrenmatt's play *The physicists,* Albert Einstein himself, or at least a character of that name, plays a part. And in each the Einstein character is used to focus on questions of responsibility in science, alluding to the actual role played by Einstein both in furnishing the theoretical basis for atomic power, and in drawing the attention of the American government to its wartime potential. *Ape and essence,* written shortly after Hiroshima, reveals in stark detail the horrors of post-atomic war America. In the year 2108, about a century after a war involving both atomic and biological weapons, human mutants still scour the sterile earth of California, mining libraries for fuel and cemeteries for clothing. And in theatrically staged flashbacks, Huxley shows the role which science played in bringing about this state of affairs. After giving a graphic account of the way in which a specially modified strain of glanders kills its unfortunate victims, he provides a plain indictment of the scientists who produced the deadly disease; and, to underline the role of science, each of the teams which releases the biological weapons has as mascot Louis Pasteur on a chain. Once the biological weapons have been unleashed, it is the turn of the nuclear missiles. Again each of the opposing armies has a mascot on a lead. This time it is Einstein. Each Einstein is kicked and beaten until he is forced to activate the missiles, for which he is symbolically fed carrots and a few cubes of sugar. After the weapons have struck, the two Einsteins confront each other. Through the narrator Huxley clarifies their role in the playlet:

FIRST EINSTEIN. It's unjust, it isn't right . . .
SECOND EINSTEIN. We, who never did any harm to anybody;
FIRST EINSTEIN. We, who lived only for truth.
NARRATOR. And that precisely is why you are dying in the murderous service of

baboons. Pascal explained it all more than three hundred years ago. 'We make an idol of truth; for truth without charity is not God, but his image and idol, which we must neither love nor worship.'[41]

Yet although one can clearly see the logic of Huxley's indictment of scientists working on biological weapons, the rationale of his attack on pure science is less clear. From their role in the novel he would appear to hold Einstein, Pasteur and Faraday responsible in some way for the unforeseeable consequences of their researches. That this was indeed Huxley's intention is further suggested by his castigation of the Einstein characters for what he calls the idolatry of truth. In spite of the vehemence with which his allegations are expressed, however, Huxley does not offer a practical critique of the ethics of pure science in support of his viewpoint; although his claim is naturally reinforced by the rhetoric of the novel, with its overwhelming statement of disgust at the possible outcome of such research.

In the considerably later and less emotive piece *The physicists,* which examines the fate of a scientist who attempts to behave responsibly, Dürrenmatt makes the point about the idolatry of truth which Huxley failed to do in *Ape and essence.* The entire play takes place — perhaps not inappropriately in this treatment of the Faustian theme — in a sanatorium for the insane and dispossessed, housing three physicists who call themselves Newton, Einstein and Möbius. As the play evolves it emerges that Möbius, an eminent physicist who has been in the home for the past fifteen years, has solved 'the problem of gravitation' and the 'unitary theory of elementary particles', both of great political importance. He has also deduced the 'Principle of Universal Discovery' with which he is able to calculate the disastrous effects which his scientific theories would have if they became widely known. In order to save mankind from the consequences of his discoveries, Möbius successfully feigns insanity, continuing his work in the relative privacy afforded by the sanatorium. Two agents of rival powers, however, infiltrate the home, and, under the assumed names of Newton and Einstein, attempt to wrest his secrets from him. But when Möbius explains the position to these two well-meaning fellow physicists, they agree to guard his secret with him. Their noble resolve, however, is quite in vain, for the forces of evil in the guise of Dr von Zahnd have already won the day. Von Zahnd has made copies of Möbius's jottings during the 15 years of his stay at the sanatorium, and, with the scientist's discoveries, prepares to lay siege on an unsuspecting world.

Dürrenmatt uses Einstein in his play to focus on the situation which Möbius tries to avoid by his voluntary incarceration. Möbius has taken this option because he remembers the use to which weapons have been put in the past. 'There are certain risks which one may not take,' he tells Newton and Einstein, 'the destruction of humanity is one. We know what the world has done with the weapons it already possesses; we can imagine what it would do with those which my researches make possible. And it is these considerations that have governed my conduct'.[42] That Dürrenmatt specifically has in mind Einstein's work and the atomic bomb is suggested in the closing lines of the play when, after von Zahnd has roundly defeated the three physicists, each in turn introduces himself to the audience. After a brief biography from Newton, the spotlight comes up on Einstein: 'I am Einstein. Professor Albert Einstein. Born the fourteenth of March, eighteen-seventy-nine, at Ulm. . . . It was I who evolved the formula "E equals MC squared", the key to the transformation of matter and energy. I love my fellow-men and I love my violin, but it was on my recommendation they built the atomic bomb'.[43] The play deals with Möbius's attempt to find a way out of Einstein's dilemma.

Even with such political insight as he possesses, however, Möbius fails; and the inference which he draws from this, and indeed the note on which the play ends, is that 'What was once thought can never be unthought'.[44] Yet the actual events leading up to the discovery of Möbius's work appear in reality to suggest a somewhat less fatalistic view of things than Möbius adopts. He was already aware of the probable consequences of his work when he first entered the sanatorium, and had he resisted the temptation to pursue it at this stage, he would obviously have prevented any possibility of its discovery by von Zahnd. Thus, perhaps unwittingly, Dürrenmatt makes Huxley's point about the idolatry of truth in a much more convincing manner than he himself had done in *Ape and essence*. Had Möbius desisted from his search for the truth — which he knew might have terrible consequences — he might truly have averted, or at least postponed, the disaster which now faced mankind.

Relativity in *The Alexandria quartet*

One of the most sustained applications of relativity theory is found in Lawrence Durrell's *The Alexandria quartet*. In this work, consisting of the four novels *Justine, Balthazar, Mountolive* and *Clea*, the theory underlies not only the conceived relationships between the characters, but the entire structure of the piece. Neither can there be any doubt as to Durrell's intentions in the matter. As he openly declared in the Note to *Balthazar:* 'Modern literature offers us no Unities, so I have turned to science and am trying to complete a four-decker novel whose form is based on the relativity proposition'.[45] In his *Key to modern poetry*, published in 1952, Durrell had expressed considerable interest in the ways in which modern science could be of use to the writer, discussing at some length the theory of relativity. As far as the writer was concerned, he claimed, 'only two aspects of it interest us: its attitude to time, and its attitude to the subject—object relationship'.[46] It is principally these two features of relativity which he makes use of in *The Alexandria quartet*, completed a decade later.

The actual structure of the *Quartet* with its four component parts is based on a unity of the kind for which Durrell was avowedly searching: that of the space-time continuum. As he explains, 'The three first parts [*Justine, Balthazar* and *Mountolive*] are to be deployed spatially . . . and are not linked in a serial form. They interlap, interweave, in a purely spatial relation. Time is stayed. The fourth part alone [*Clea*] will represent time and be a true sequel'.[47] To a large degree Durrell achieves this rather difficult effect. The first three 'siblings' as he calls them, do indeed interweave temporally, although in practice *Mountolive* comes dangerously close to giving a linearly progressing time span. Each of the three provides an account of selected facets of essentially the same series of events, written, as it were, from a different 'frame of reference'. The fourth novel, *Clea*, deals with a time sequence which begins after the end of that treated in the three spatial variants, being, as Durrell maintains, the only true sequel.

A precise representation of the four dimensions would, as Bork points out, require time to stand still for the first three volumes;[48] a quite impossible demand to impose on a work of fiction. But even if he cannot freeze time, Durrell does indicate his awareness of the changed nature of time in relativity theory. In his *Key to modern poetry* he had written that 'Einstein's time was not a past—present—future object. . . . It was a sort of time which contained all time in every moment of time',[49] and as authority for this idea he quoted from James Jeans's *The mysterious universe* a passage which ends with the following lines from Plato: 'The past and future are created species of time which we unconsciously but wrongly transfer to the eternal essence. We say *was, is, will be,* but the truth is that *is* alone can properly be used'.[50] On very rare occasions in *Justine* Durrell actually applies this dictum, referring to past events in the present tense, as he does for example in Darley's reminiscences of Pombal.[51] Durrell further stresses the new role of time in a scene in *Balthazar* in which all the clocks are stopped in order to 'escape from the despotism of time altogether'. Yet apart from the device of using a four-dimensional structure for his novel, Durrell's representation of time in *The Alexandria quartet* does not suggest any very radical debt to relativity theory. The suggestion of time's despotism, which appears in the clock-stopping incident in *Balthazar* and on a number of other occasions during the *Quartet*, is by no means new, and indeed arguably suggests a pre-relativistic conception of time. There is also evidence at a number of instances in the novel of the two conflicting suggestions that the future is in some way predetermined, and that it is also, in other respects, quite undetermined and unknowable. James Jeans, one of Durrell's sources on relativity, conveys a very similar viewpoint.[52] Time, he says, either drags us through a temporal landscape already painted, in which we have no power to affect the future; or alternatively we do actually participate in the process and can alter the future by our present actions. At the time of writing, Jeans tells us, science is not able to decide between the two versions; and this would explain why Durrell appears consciously to convey first one, and then the other interpretation. But ambiguity of this kind does not worry Durrell unduly. It is quite clear that his intention in writing *The Alexandria quartet* was not to provide an accurate representation of the theories of modern physics, but to achieve a broad translation of them within the context of the novel. And it is with this intent, though in a much more thorough fashion, that he merges a second feature of relativity theory with the idea of four-dimensionality. For as well as representing the four space-time coordinates, the four volumes also represent four complete 'frames of reference' from which the same series of events is differently observed. And in practice the theme of observer subjectivity and the 'subject—object relationship' which Durrell discussed in the *Key to modern poetry* is fundamental to *The Alexandria quartet*, finding repeated and varied expression throughout its length.

This feature is most noticeable in Durrell's first three volumes where it proves to be remarkably effective. In the first we are presented with a series of memories of the time spent in Alexandria by the British writer Darley. *Balthazar*, the second volume, is again from the pen of Darley, but includes additional information supplied by Balthazar on reading Darley's first account. This reveals many facets of the story of which Darley was completely ignorant, and which paint a very different picture from that of the first account. For example, one of the dominating events of the first volume is Darley's affair with Justine Hosnani. But in the second, Balthazar reveals to Darley that Justine was not in love with him at all, but was merely using him as a decoy to draw her husband's suspicions away from her true lover Pursewarden. The account from Darley's original frame of reference is thus quite different from that suggested by Balthazar's corrections, so that the reader is confronted with a *relativity* of observation and interpretation between the two 'frames of reference'. In order to make this quite plain, Durrell has Darley quote from the writings of Pursewarden, who claims to have made a study of relativity theory in order to improve his understanding of art and literature. ' "We live" writes Pursewarden somewhere "lives based upon selected fictions. Our view of reality is conditioned by our position in space and time[53] — not by our personalities as we like to think. Thus every interpretation of reality is based upon a unique position. Two paces east or west and the whole picture is changed." '[54]

With Balthazar's account the whole picture is indeed changed, and yet we are left somewhat closer to the truth than after Darley's original account; and with the objective, if not absolutely complete, account provided in *Mountolive*, it becomes clear that in working through *The Alexandria quartet* one builds a progressively more truthful picture of events, shedding layer after layer of 'selected fictions'. One might judge a completely objective account to be out of place in a novel of relativities, but Durrell explains its inclusion in his Note to *Balthazar*. 'The subject—object relation is so important to relativity that I have tried to turn the novel through both subjective and objective modes', he writes; and for this reason he has made *Mountolive* 'a straight naturalistic novel'.[55] The account presented in

Mountolive complements those given in the first two volumes very effectively, providing a fuller and again rather different interpretation of the events treated earlier. It is now revealed, for example, that Justine and her husband Nessim are involved in smuggling arms into Palestine, and that Justine had encouraged Darley's affections for purely tactical reasons associated with this enterprise. And not only Justine, but each of the major characters changes as he is viewed from successively different 'frames of reference'.

These observer relativities are skilfully manoeuvred by Durrell, and even though in one sense he treads the same ground three and sometimes four times over, the different perspectives provide such a changing view, and the pieces of information dovetail so neatly, that repetition is almost completely avoided. But the objective and naturalistic account presented in *Mountolive* seems to indicate that we are dealing with a slightly different notion of observer relativity than in the strictest interpretation of Einstein's theory, in which all relativistic accounts are attributed with equal truth content.[56] For while the first two volumes of the *Quartet* present selected fictions, untruths, the third conveys the objective, though incomplete, truth. And at a number of points in the novel, it would appear that it is by this interpretation which Durrell stands. 'We are after all totally ignorant of one another, presenting selected fictions to each other', says Justine. But this provokes Darley to quote a line from Pursewarden: 'However hard the road, one is forced to come to terms with the truth at last'.[57] And by this stage in the *Quartet* (that is to say, early in *Clea*) this is exactly what has happened to Darley. The selected fictions have been slowly and progressively shed until he confronts the major features of reality. Yet Durrell nevertheless goes some considerable way to redressing this balance, to suggesting that even when we arrive at the final page of *Clea*, we have only glimpsed at certain facets of reality. This is achieved by the inclusion of a number of 'workpoints' at the end of the book which suggest further, and as yet unexplored, facets of the story. Durrell specifically explains their function in the Author's Note to *Clea*: 'Among the workpoints at the end of this volume I have sketched a number of possible ways of continuing to deploy these characters and situations in further instalments – but this is only to suggest that even if the series were extended indefinitely the result would never become a *roman fleuve*[58] (an expansion of the matter in serial form) but would remain strictly part of the present word-continuum [*sic*]'.[59]

The four volumes of *The Alexandria quartet* together suggest the theme of the relativity of observation from the three different spatial and one temporal frame of reference. But throughout each of the four books one is repeatedly reminded of the relativities of observation and interpretation as they apply to its many characters, so that the novel reveals not four but a multitude of 'frames of reference'. As Darley wonders of Pursewarden, 'How much of him can I claim to know? I realise that each person can only claim one aspect of our character as part of his knowledge. To every one we turn a different face of the prism'.[60] In order to illustrate this point, Darley gives the example of Pombal. To Justine he was 'one of the great primates of sex', whereas to Darley himself, Pombal had only seemed self-indulgent and inherently ridiculous, but never predatory. Often when these relativities occur Durrell indicates the reason for them, and frequently this is presented as being a result of the state of the observer, an idea consistent with popular conceptions of relativity theory. As Justine declares to Darley in the final volume of the *Quartet*, 'You see a different me . . . but once again the difference lies in you, in what you imagine you see!'.[61] One of the more commonly invoked causes of observer relativity is the emotional state of the observer – perhaps not inappropriately since, as Durrell avowed, 'The central topic of [*The Alexandria quartet*] is an investigation of modern love'.[62] The point is made specifically on a number of occasions. As Darley reflects, 'Once again, as always when the drama of external events altered the emotional pattern of things, I began to see the city through new eyes'.[63] And at an earlier point Darley had recognised that his envy of Pursewarden, his passion for Justine and his pity for Melissa all acted as 'distorting mirrors' and that as a writer it was his duty to try to strip away the 'opaque membrane' which stands between him and the reality of their actions. Or in Justine's words, 'We are all in the grip of an emotional field which we throw down about one another'.[64] Yet this is not invariably the cause of observer relativities, and while it is clear that Darley's love for Justine colours his account of the events in *Justine,* his interpretation is also considerably affected by the deceit of Nessim and Justine. As Darley comes to realise by the beginning of *Clea,* changes in his 'frame of reference' as he calls it, are frequently caused by the intrusion of new knowledge. He had failed in his task of storing and codifying the past because, as he says, 'no sooner had I embalmed one aspect of it in words than the intrusion of new knowledge disrupted the frame of reference, everything flew asunder, only to reassemble again in unforeseen, unpredictable patterns'.[65]

This imagery of unpredictable patterns is suggestive more of quantum theory than relativity. There is also a hint of quantum indeterminacy in Pursewarden's claim that the actual act of taking notes about a person's behaviour alters his perception of that person.[66] And in practice Durrell has blended, and perhaps even confused, the notions of observer relativity and quantum indeterminacy. We find support for this idea in a passage from his *Key to modern poetry* in which the two theories are spoken of as one: 'Another aspect of the Relativity theory is the manner in which it sidetracks causality. . . . The Principle of Indeterminacy, as it is called, is founded upon the theory that we cannot observe the course of nature without disturbing it'.[67,68] That it was indeed Durrell's intention to employ features of both theories in his novel is further suggested by the revealing outline for a novel sketched in *The Alexandria quartet* by the writer Pursewarden; an outline which closely resembles the *Quartet* itself. The book, as Pursewarden describes it to Darley, would be a 'four-card trick in the form of a novel; passing a common axis through four stories. . . . A continuum, forsooth, embodying not a *temps retrouvé*[69] but a *temps délivré*. The curvature of space itself would give you a stereoscopic narrative, while human personality seen across a continuum would perhaps become prismatic? Who can say? I throw the idea out. I can imagine a form which, if satisfied, might raise in human terms the problems of causality or indeterminacy. . . . And nothing very *recherché* either. Just an ordinary Girl Meets Boy Story'.[70]

From the examples it is clear that Durrell was not concerned with a precise representation of relativity or quantum theory in his novel; rather, he sought a fairly loose translation of aspects of these scientific theories into the human idiom. Indeed one of the chief functions of relativity theory in *The Alexandria quartet* is as a source of literary metaphors for the treatment of interpersonal relationships and human perception. The terms 'field' and 'frame of reference' are used in precisely this way in two quotations given earlier: 'We are all in the grip of an emotional field',[71] and 'the intrusion of new knowledge disrupted the frame of reference'.[72] The expressions 'field' and 'frame of reference' both come from the vocabulary of relativity theory, and are used in the context of *human* experience in the novel. At frequent intervals during *The Alexandria quartet* Durrell makes similar use of a number of such words, each of which have been given a new significance by, or are associated in some way with, relativity. The terms 'observed object', 'curved surface', 'field', 'gravitational field', 'continuum', 'dimension', 'space', 'time' and 'frame of reference', all perform the dual function of bringing to mind the 'relativity proposition' on which the novel is based, while at the same time describing the thoughts and activities of the novel's characters. Durrell's use of these metaphors from relativity theory is similar to that described by Donald Davie,[73] who shows how the vocabulary of the new science of the seventeenth century was consciously employed by Dr Johnson and others for literary purposes. In some cases words used in this way were not new to the language, but had been given a changed meaning or a heightened significance as a result of their scientific usage. This is the case of the words which Durrell takes over from relativity theory.

An allied function is served in *The Alexandria quartet* by the recurrent use of a number of visual symbols, either directly or in metaphorical constructions. Masks and cases of visual handicap act as reminders of the partial concealment which can result when a person from one 'frame of reference' attempts to observe or interpret the actions of someone from another. A multitude of mirrors, reflections and prisms, on the other hand, symbolise the different facets of a personality or situation comprehended by different observers: the 'selected fictions' by which all of Durrell's characters live. This interpretation is suggested by Justine's reaction to the multiple mirrors at her dressmaker's. 'Look! five different pictures of the same subject', she declares to Darley. 'Now if I wrote I would try for a four-dimensional effect in character, a sort of prism-sightedness. Why should not people show more than one profile at a time?'[74] The mirror motif, carrying with it the suggestion of a relativity of observation, occurs at frequent intervals throughout the novel,[75] and is particularly invoked when any event of importance takes place. Just before Pursewarden commits suicide, for example, he scribbles a message to Nessim across his bedroom mirror, which he says is 'an appropriate place'. After Nessim has told Capodistria that he is to be married to Justine he stares at the reflection in his polished desk. As Mountolive and Leila begin their love affair we are told that 'their muttering images met now like reflections on a surface of lake-water'. After Nessim has made love to Melissa we read that 'he questioned his reflection' in the mirror of a lift; and even the blind Liza turns towards a mirror when she is faced with an important decision. The whole *Quartet* is a hall of mirrors and masks used as symbols to represent notions based on relativity theory, which itself functions as a reservoir of metaphors for the treatment of specifically human questions. Durrell's intention is not to elucidate Einsteinian relativity, but to translate features of it from the arena of high velocity physics into the context of human relationships; and this he does with mastery.

Notes

1. I am most grateful to John Abulafia for answering questions about his work, and to Dr Dorothy Koenigsberger and Dr Geoffrey Cantor for their particularly helpful comments during the preparation of this paper.
2. *The Times,* 7 Nov. 1919, p. 13.
3. A. Moszkowski, *Einstein the searcher* (1921), extract reproduced in R. Clark, *Einstein: the life and times,* London, 1973, p. 240.
4. See, for example, M. Nicolson, *The breaking of the circle* (1960) for the influence of the Copernican revolution; M. Nicolson, *Newton demands the Muse* (1966) for the influence of Newton's *Opticks* on eighteenth-century poetry; and Leo Henkin, *Darwinism in the English novel* (1963) for Darwin's influence on literature.
5. J. A. Coleman, *Relativity for the layman,* 1959, p. 62.
6. Ibid., p. 56.
7. G. Gamow, *Mr Tompkins in paperback,* 1965.
8. S. Leacock, *Winnowed wisdom,* 1926, pp. 23–4.
9. London, 1958 (first published 1934).
10. In John Abulafia *et al., Introduction 6,* London, 1977.
11. London, 1966 (first published 1948).
12. London, 1963.
13. *Cancer ward,* Harmondsworth, 1971, p. 271.
14. London, 1963.
15. London, 1968 (first published 1957–60).
16. Whilst more widely known for his work on relativity, Einstein also made important contributions to quantum theory, and although we are not principally concerned here with this field, we shall have cause to discuss it both with reference to C. P. Snow, and to writers who have blended, or even confused, ideas from both fields.
17. F. S. C. Duggan, *Relativity, quantum theory and the novels of Samuel Beckett,* PhD thesis, University of Chicago, 1971, pp. 4–5.
18. Ibid., p. 1.
19. We exclude from these discussions representations of time of the kind to be found in the so-called stream of consciousness novel such as Virginia Woolf's *To the lighthouse* and James Joyce's *Ulysses* which are generally considered to represent a Bergsonian psychological time rather than an Einsteinian relativistic one; although as Tyndall points out in *Forces in modern British literature,* Joyce's use of such expressions as 'Eins within a space' in *Finnegans wake* point to Einstein's influence in this much later work.
20. *Main currents in modern thought,* vol. 29, 1973, pp. 91–9.
21. A. M. Bork, 'Durrell and relativity', *Centennial Review,* vol. 7, Spring 1963, pp. 191–203.
22. *Wisconsin studies in contemporary literature,* vol. 8, Summer 1969, pp. 365–76.
23. London, 1932.
24. That relativity theory might be used to support the anti-materialist lobby was soon realised. See, for example, H. Wildon Carr, 'Metaphysics and materialism', *Nature,* vol. 108, 20 Oct. 1921, pp. 247–8.
25. Aldous Huxley, *Those barren leaves,* Harmondsworth, 1951, p. 34.
26. Aldous Huxley, *Point counter point,* Harmondsworth, 1955, p. 158.
27. More appropriate, since quantum theory maintains that there is an upper limit to the accuracy of all observations in science, and consequently to predictions based on them.
28. G. B. Shaw, *The complete plays,* London, 1937, p. 1157.
29. Ibid.
30. Ibid., p. 1159.
31. Ibid., p. 1157.
32. Aldous Huxley, *Time must have a stop,* London, 1945, p. 86.
33. Ibid., p. 85.
34. Ibid.
35. Ibid.
36. Aldous Huxley, *The genius and the goddess,* London, 1955, pp. 37–8.
37. Snow, op. cit., p. 92.
38. Huxley, *The genius and the goddess,* loc. cit., p. 37.
39. Abulafia, op. cit., p. 21. E^x cannot equal both $E^n + E^e + E^g$ and $E^n + E^e + E^g/M$.
40. In an interesting article entitled 'Autobiography and "The two cultures" in the Novels of C. P. Snow', *Annals of science,* vol. 32, 1975, pp. 555–71, Nail Bezel reveals that Snow himself left scientific

research after a piece of work 'went wrong' through oversight, and suggests that his preoccupation with errors and fraud in science in such novels as *The search* and *The affair* probably stems from this incident.

41. Aldous Huxley, *Ape and essence*, loc. cit., p. 38.
42. Dürrenmatt, op. cit., p. 44.
43. Ibid., pp. 52–3.
44. Ibid., p. 52.
45. L. Durrell, *Balthazar*, London, 1958, p. 7.
46. L. Durrell, *Key to modern poetry*, London and New York, 1952, p. 28.
47. *Balthazar*, loc. cit., p. 7.
48. A. M. Bork, op. cit., p. 196.
49. Durrell, *Key to modern poetry*, loc. cit., pp. 28–9.
50. Ibid., p. 29.
51. See *The Alexandria quartet*, loc. cit., p. 23.
52. See James Jeans, *The mysterious universe*, Cambridge, 1931, p. 105.
53. In Einstein's special relativity it is relative *motion* rather than relative *position* in space which would condition one's view of reality.
54. *The Alexandria quartet*, loc. cit., p. 210.
55. *Balthazar*, loc. cit., p. 7.
56. In fact Einstein was not concerned with 'truth' or 'untruth' in relativity theory. These are concepts which come from Durrell's extrapolation of relativity into the human sphere.
57. *The Alexandria quartet*, loc. cit., p. 693.
58. Durrell was particularly anxious to distinguish his relativistic conception of time from the Bergsonian 'stream of consciousness' variety to be found in Proust and Joyce.
59. L. Durrell, *Clea*, London, 1960, p. 5.
60. *The Alexandria quartet*, loc. cit., p. 100.
61. Ibid., p. 692.
62. *Balthazar*, loc. cit., p. 7.
63. *The Alexandria quartet*, loc. cit., p. 366.
64. Ibid., p. 698.
65. Ibid., p. 657.
66. See *The Alexandria quartet*, loc. cit., p. 520.
67. Durrell, *Key to modern poetry*, loc. cit., p. 29.
68. This statement bears out Bork's view (op. cit., p. 193) that on occasion Durrell uses the term 'relativity' to refer to all of modern physics.
69. Again emphasising the difference between Proust's Bergsonian time, and his own use of a conception of time based on relativity theory.
70. *The Alexandria quartet*, loc. cit., pp. 757–8.
71. Ibid., p. 698.
72. Ibid., p. 657.
73. Davie, op. cit.
74. *The Alexandria quartet*, loc. cit., p. 28.
75. In reply to criticisms that mirrors and masks obtrude excessively in the *Quartet*, John Unterecker has pointed out that together with other devices these serve the important function of alerting the reader to the otherwise bewildering structure of the world encountered in the book. See J. Unterecker, *Lawrence Durrell*, USA, 1964, p. 37.

Afterword

Einstein and other seekers of the larger view

John Archibald Wheeler

John Archibald Wheeler, PhD, ScD, LLD, MNAS, is Ashbel Smith Professor and director of the Center for Theoretical Physics of the University of Texas at Austin, and Joseph Henry Professor of Physics Emeritus at Princeton, where for seventeen years he worked with Einstein as a colleague. He is past president of the American Physical Society, author or co-author of seven books, and recipient of the Einstein and Fermi awards and the National Medal of Science. He is best known for his discovery of the scattering matrix, his paper with Niels Bohr on nuclear fission, his contribution to developing the first nuclear reactors and thermonuclear devices, and his elucidation of fundamental concepts in nuclear and gravitation physics, including the concept of the 'black hole'.

Adapted from *Science and Public Policy,* vol. 6, no. 6, December 1979, and from the fifteenth annual Science Policy Foundation Lecture, London, 1979, with the aid of the Center for Theoretical Physics, University of Texas at Austin, and of National Science Foundation Grant PHY7826592.

Bern, the capital of Switzerland, remembers those creatures from which it gets its name by having an open-air bear pit. There one can watch the bears go round and round on all fours with head to the ground. A young patent office clerk named Albert Einstein liked to take his visitors there. Only very rarely, he pointed out, does one of the animals rear up on its hind legs and look around for the wider view. To Einstein that bear represented the thinker. To us, let it symbolise, by extension, one who rises to the larger view — and from that vantage point recognises what is missing, and fills the gap.

Hutton, Darwin, Mendeléev, Bohr and Einstein: 'discover unity'

In 1795 James Hutton opened out a great new perspective on geology, as a process going on everywhere and all the time. This view highlighted the consideration missing from all previous thinking, the enormous time scale of the history of the earth.

Charles Darwin, through his observations on the voyage of the *Beagle* (1831—1836) and subsequently at home, won his way to a comprehensive picture of variations in plants and animals, and of the favour granted to some of these variations by nature. This bird's eye view showed to him, in October 1838, the missing element: 'The result of this [enough such variation] would be the formation of a new species'.

Dmitri Ivanovitch Mendeléev developed the periodic system of the elements to try to display chemistry to his students as a harmonious panorama. By 1871 his system was so well developed that it forced him to recognise the existence of three gaps in his tables. It also gave him clear predictions of the properties of the three as yet unknown elements and their compounds. These predictions were verified with the discovery of gallium in the same year, of scandium in 1879, and of germanium in 1886.

In 1905 electricity and magnetism presented physics with a clutter of facts and a legion of little laws. The action of a magnet on a coil of wire fell under different systems of book-keeping according to whether the magnet moved toward the coil or the coil moved toward the magnet. In contrast, mechanics had a single conceptual system which served as well when the ball hit the racquet as when the racquet hit the ball. The systems of mechanics and of electricity and magnetism were incompatible.

Struggling to get a view of the unity that had to be there, the patent clerk discovered the missing idea, one that reached far beyond electricity and magnetism to the nature of space and time themselves. As Einstein's former teacher, Hermann Minkowski, was later to phrase the young man's finding, 'space by itself, and time by itself, are . . . mere shadows, and only [spacetime] a kind of union of the two . . . preserve[s] an independent reality'.

In 1908 the Swiss civil servant, striving for a still larger view (one that included gravity), came to recognise the missing concept: gravitation is not something foreign and physical acting *through* space but a manifestation of the curvature *of* space. In November 1915 Einstein, by now professor at the Kaiser Wilhelm Institute in Berlin, discovered the law governing the response of space-time geometry to matter. Today we know how to state the content of Einstein's 'general relativity' in a single simple sentence: space tells matter how to move and matter tells space how to curve.

In the last 30 years of his life Einstein sought a unified geometrical theory of all the forces of nature. The endeavour came to nothing. However, physics today, adopting a new and wider concept of what geometry is, in the sense of a 'gauge theory' or 'phase theory', is making marvellous progress toward this dream of unification.

I first saw and heard Einstein in Princeton in the fall of 1933, some days after he had taken up his long-term residence there. Our last time together came 21 years later when he kindly accepted an invitation to speak at my relativity seminar, the last talk he ever gave, 14 April 1954, almost exactly a year before his death.

The most extraordinary feature of the man I glimpsed the first day, and came to see ever more clearly each time I visited his house and climbed the stairs to his study. Over and above his warmth and considerateness, I came to see, he had a unique sense of the world of man and nature as one harmonious and someday understandable whole, with all of us feeling our way forward through the darkness together towards that harmony, that larger view, that sense of the unity of all things, great and small.

Not only to his visitor but in his writings Einstein expressed this lifelong yearning for the larger view. 'Out yonder', he exclaimed, lies 'this huge world, which exists independently of us human beings and which stands before us like a great eternal riddle.' No one has ever affirmed more vividly than he the faith that the mystery will someday be unravelled: 'The most incomprehensible thing about the world is that it is comprehensible'; and again, 'All of these endeavours are based on the belief that existence should have a completely harmonious structure. Today we have less ground than ever before for allowing ourselves to be forced away from that wonderful belief'.

What did Einstein mean by 'harmony'? Anyone will know who has seen his words of admiration for Niels Bohr and for Bohr's ability to see amid a maze of distracting evidence the quantum nature of the atom — 'He has the highest form of musicality in the sphere of science'.

What did Einstein mean by harmonious structure? He meant what his mentor, model and hero, Benedict de Spinoza meant: a universe that is beautiful, simple and understandable — even if not yet understood. As Josiah Royce puts it, speaking of Spinoza, but for us speaking of Einstein, he is one who

'sees everywhere an all-pervading law, an all-conquering truth, a supreme and irresistible perfection'

and, even if he himself does not yet have, nevertheless envisages us all as someday having

'a clear vision of the supreme and necessary laws of the eternal world.'

Discover new unity! That is how Hutton, Darwin, Mendeléev, Einstein and Bohr made their contributions. That is not the only way to mount that trilogy of actions, to rise to the larger view — and from that vantage point recognise what is missing, and fill the gap.

The bear of Bern knows only one way to get and use his wider view, but man, working as he does with other men and ideas, knows more ways — more than seven; but seven will suffice for our survey. For examples we might, but shall not, turn to the finest lawyers and leaders of finance and industry of past and present days, perceptive policy makers and statesmen — those men of the larger view who by their imagination and judgement raise the level of life and hope of all the rest of us. Already among those who deal with science and technology there is enough human variety, enough downright individuality of thought and action, to more than occupy us here.

What are these seven versions of our trilogy of action: to seek the larger view — and from that vantage point recognise what is missing, and fill the gap?

- Discover unity.
- Draw together pieces of science and technology to *create a system,* whether that system is xerography, telegraphy, or steam navigation.
- Find the *economic feasibility* for a new technology by virtue of a wide grasp of the worlds of man and matter.
- *Reach harmony through intuition,* by meditating on the base of a wide and deep knowledge of the field so as to arrive at a new result.

- *Build a model,* a simplified representation of the problem at issue, subject to experimental or calculational analysis.
- *Serve as a science-technology generalist* who, not once or twice in his life, but many times in a year, and generally in the service of others, extracts the single, simple missing point out of a complicated situation.
- *Make decisions,* or help others make decisions, *by imaginative interaction with alternative scenarios* calculated as consequent on those decisions.

Under what one name shall we summarise such apparently different activities? The patient may not complain if he receives no cure from his physician, but he is unhappy indeed if he does not at least receive a name for his disease. Yet who can find one word to stand for the trilogy of climbing to the higher view, recognising from that view what is missing, and filling the gap?

The classical scholar may propose the Greek-based 'deictic' for the nature of this activity, meaning 'showing, pointing out or proving directly'. However, no one who believes in the importance of this kind of enterprise in the world of today will want to shackle it with such a word. Will it not be better for us to use the first phrase in our trilogy, 'larger view', and in that way imply also the other two parts of the trilogy? Shall this then be our understanding when we speak of 'seekers of the larger view'?

Fitch, Fulton, Morse and Carlson: 'create a system'

Achieve the larger view. Capture the full panorama. Paint a picture. Are these totally different intellectual activities?

Eugene S. Ferguson points out that 'the designer and the inventor, who bring elements together in new combinations, are each able to assemble and manipulate in their minds devices that as yet do not exist'.

Is it any accident then that the steamboat designer, Robert Fulton, had earlier been a painter of portraits and landscapes; or that the perfecter of the telegraph, Samuel Finley Breese Morse, had earlier been a painter and first president of the National Academy of Design; or that John Fitch, a pioneer in steamboat navigation, had earlier been in turn a clockmaker, brass founder, silversmith and surveyor?

As Brooke Hindle, the historian of science and technology, points out, who better than a surveyor, a designer or an artist to picture in his mind's eye the trial placements and adjustments of critical parts. Who could better envisage the resulting device as a system in daily use?

It was not necessary for Chester Carlson to have had a painter's background to initiate xerox, one of the greatest enterprises of our times. He had the equivalent experience – as an inventor – when he conceived xerography. In his mind's eye he rose to the larger view, of users and use, of what a simple method of copying would do for a civilisation dependent as never before on the easy flow of information. From that vantage point he could see what was missing in the way of system and parts. He could start his long struggle to fill the gap by the marriage of unfamiliar physics and yet-to-be-developed engineering.

What followed is well known. Carlson, now in the grip of his greatest conception, went from company to company trying to get one that would back his idea. All said no. How could any already existing industry possibly put together the necessary constellation of talent?

Whoever was tempted to say yes to the idea today knew that tomorrow he would be confronted by an impossible combination of challenges. Illuminate the master text with brilliance and reliability; build an unusual lens inexpensively and accurately; image the master on a selenium cylinder; guarantee photoelectric charge-up of that selenium surface; discover a powder that would seek out unerringly this electric charge; transfer this powder to the copy paper; make it stick; build a mechanism to bring about all the necessary motions with the right timing; and guarantee that the mechanism will work over and over again, not hundreds of times, not thousands of times, but hundreds of thousands of times. No one in his senses would touch such a hydra-headed enterprise with a ten-foot pole.

Defeated in selling his undeveloped idea to any company, Carlson took it to the Battelle Memorial Institute, headquartered in Columbus, Ohio, the largest non-profit research organisation in the world. It offered the wide range of expertise and the interim financial backing that he needed.

This is not the place to tell about all the technical problems that had to be overcome or the years of work required. Neither is this the occasion to describe all the judgement required, when a baby is at last alive and well, to find the right foster parent to take it over. The company must not be too large. Otherwise the new development does not receive the urgent attention of the top people. Neither must it be too small. Otherwise the capital and the sales force are lacking.

The Haloid Company of Rochester, New York, had the right size and the right management. Moreover, it had the most powerful of all incentives to go into a new enterprise; Haloid's traditional photographic market was shrinking and it would go out of business unless it could find a promising new field of endeavour. It is no wonder that Haloid looked with the greatest interest at the invention of Carlson and the impressive development of that invention by Battelle.

Joseph Wilson: 'find economic feasibility'

Why at this stage did not everyone leap at the opportunity to pioneer one of the greatest industries of our times? In a private conversation some months ago the vice-president of one of the world's largest companies revealed that he and a committee working with him had evaluated xerography for his company at the time when Haloid was considering it. 'No, no, no,' the committee had advised the management. 'No one could possibly be interested in buying such an expensive machine. Battelle probably can make the device operate but we certainly can never find a way to make it economically feasible'. This problem of price the smaller firm, Haloid, could foresee as clearly as the larger company.

Joseph Wilson, the leader of Haloid, had the two advantages that Einstein also had: first, unsurpassed motivation; and second, the larger view. In this case 'the larger view' meant an appreciation of the worldwide interplay of technology, business, and tax laws, and the potential economic impact of fast and inexpensive copying. From this vantage point the missing element became clear, a proper pricing policy. Joseph Wilson filled the gap. He came up with the winning idea: Don't sell, lease; and add to the lease charge a use charge of so much a page. That second, commercial, invention brought economic feasibility. It was indispensible for the success of Chester Carlson's first technological invention.

The well-driller and the chemist: 'reach harmony through intuition'

Most fields of pioneering endeavour are not well enough surveyed to be entirely accessible to logical analysis. In such fields, as Charles Kettering, early director of General Motors Research, once put it, 'Beware of logic. Logic is an organized way to go wrong — with confidence'. One would do better to call on another human faculty, judgement, defined by Du Pont's George Graves as 'an awareness of all the factors in the situation and an apprecia-tion of their relative importance'.

For the beginning of that 'appreciation', judgement generally has to call intuition to its help, intuition defined as 'the power of knowing or the knowledge obtained without re-course to inference or reasoning; insight; familiarity; a quick or ready apprehension'.

Let us turn for illustration to the humblest 'seeker of the wider view' of them all, a most improbable person: the countryside driller of wells.

He is no geologist, but he knows something of geology, the folds and strata of the local rock, which are porous and which are not. He is no historian, but he knows enough of the history of wells drilled in his county to know which were dry and which gave water; what their depths were, and what their yields. He is no reader of Einstein, but what Einstein told us of his search for the laws of nature the well driller knows from his own seeking for the right places for his wells: 'There is no logical path leading to [them]. They can only be reached by intuition based upon something like an intellectual love of the objects of experience'.

The provider of wells is no psychologist, but as he surveys the land around the farm he realises that his intuition is blanketed out by the worried questions of the farmer about the cost, the refrain of worry from the farmer's wife and children, and the gratuitous but conflicting advice of the neighbours. Einstein sought and found quiet for his meditations. The driller cannot find quiet. He has to create it.

For that purpose he uses the invention of a wise man of long ago. He holds up a willow wand, utters some abracadabra, and finds that silence reigns. He can listen undistracted to the inner voice and seek the wider view: 'Over there on firmer ground I got a good well. Down that way is a brook. Halfway up that hillside another man once drilled a dry well'.

He feeds all the facts and indications into his mental computer, picks the spot, lowers the willow wand, finds everyone nodding approval and starts to drill. In this homely example one sees what Einstein called, 'intuition based upon . . . an intellectual love for the objects of experience'.

An able chemist once asked me to suggest a good new material for a fuel cell. I had seen enough of him, and knew enough of his work, to realise that nobody in the world knew more about fuel cells than he. On the physics I knew I couldn't possibly help; but I think I did on the psychology. I told him to get himself the paraphernalia of a seer, an oracle, a fortune teller; to sit before the table, draw the red velvet curtain shut, and stare into the great glass ball. Whatever the means chosen to promote intuition, it lets the mind peacefully make its way through the pasture of memory to the larger view — and from that vantage point lets it recognise what is missing.

Norbert Winter and the insurance company: 'build a model'

The seeker of the wider view has to depend on intuition on some occasions, but on others he does better to develop and exploit a mathematical model. No such model is better known than that given for economy in the famous book of John von Neumann and Oskar Morgenstern, *Theory of Games and Economic Behavior*.

Today there is a big business in the making of mathematical models for individual firms, industries, or commodities. What else is 'microeconomics' and 'macroeconomics'?

Historically, physics has been one of the great developers of models and purveyors of models to other areas of endeavour. The pendulum, the best known example, is also one of the oldest. Who has not learned from it to speak of equilibrium, natural period of vibration, damping, excitation, and resonance?

And who has not used these terms, if not the beautiful and far-reaching mathematical analysis that goes with them, in understanding phenomena where no pendulum is seen, phenomena as diverse as the shaking of a bridge, the rise and fall of tides, the flutter of an airplane wing and the power of an earthquake?

Today no field of physics is more imaginative than elementary particle physics in conceiving and analysing models for the interactions going on in multicomponent systems.

Five years ago a Munich student of elementary particle physics, especially gifted in the analysis of such mathematical models, having received his degree, decided to move to new territory. His professor, director of a Max Planck Institute, thereupon recommended the young man to one of Germany's great insurance companies.

Today Norbert Winter has a senior position in the company. He put his talent for building simple models and thus capturing central features of elementary particle transformations to use on arrival in the firm. He won a wider view by constructing, with a colleague, a 'dynamic balance model' of a smaller company in the field. From that vantage point — and after a year of selling experience — he recognised a missing element in the industry. Important tax consequences of a new German pension law were going unappreciated and unexploited by anyone.

He saw how to fill the gap. His company offered gap-filling insurance contracts and sold them. Today they make up one of the major segments of its business.

His model gave a harmonious view of the whole field that had proved difficult to come by for people accustomed to work with bits and pieces. A good model displays the simple central point of what has seemed a complex situation.

Helmholtz, Kelvin and Tukey: 'serve as science-technology generalist'

You can't count on one man to do it all; let someone come into the picture who is good at inspiring and guiding others in this work. He is the scientific generalist[1] or, more appropriately, science-technology generalist.

It is difficult to say where a generalist cannot contribute. It is easy to say where he can and does: in innovative industry; in an institutional group located in government, a university or a foundation; in the guidance of work or policy wherever the problems are broad enough to require a group instead of a few isolated researchers; and in fields as widely varied as economics, medicine and biology, engineering, and social, military and political policy.

No investigators were better known in their day as scientific generalists than Hermann von Helmholtz and William Thomson (Lord Kelvin). Inspiring and guiding others, one contributed importantly to fields ranging from physiology to mechanics, and from ophthalmology to electromagnetism; the other, to subjects from thermodynamics to the compass, and from the tides to the Atlantic cable.

What would these two men think of the combination of talents and the training recommended for one who would serve as a science-technology generalist in our day? Or think of the injunctions in Table 1?

An impossible course of training for an impossible profession? Perhaps this is the moment to apply to the science-technology generalist what Einstein said about the work of a scientist, 'Don't listen to what he says, look at what he does'.

No one is better known in our day as a science-technology generalist than John Wilder Tukey, for many years a colleague of Einstein in Princeton. He has become famous for his role of generalist, pushing experts by his questions to think as they would not otherwise think and act as they would not otherwise act. Statistics is his magic weapon in seeking the larger view.

The generalist so armed may not have a single new fact to supply. Like the statistician R. A. Fisher of an older time coming fresh to genetics, the statistician of today may have to start as a child in the new field, convinced, however, through long experience that out of the clutter of facts that confront him some larger harmony can be seen.

Of all generalists none spans a greater range than the statistician. Tukey, as the chairman of a committee on impacts of stratospheric change, has exerted a decisive influence on policy on chlorofluoromethane release. Similarly, acting as a generalist, he has strongly affected the policies of more than one country on chemicals and health, on governmental statistics, on environmental pollution, on educational testing, on detecting underground nuclear explosions, and on regulating stream pollution-by-use charges. He has altered the direction of work of many experts, inspiring early applications of spectral analysis to oceanography and geophysics and pioneering the concept of the fast Fourier analysis that is so central to much of the instrumentation in use today in medicine and industry, as well as in academic and government research. His unique book, *Exploratory data analysis,* is the bible of the new breed of statisticians to whom the whole world beckons as a field of endeavour, happy hunting ground for him who 'seeks the wider view'.

Table 1[2]

Recapture the universalist spirit of the early natural philosophers

Learn *science* and not *sciences*

Know in capsule form the dozen central concepts of each of the major sciences

Learn the habits of mind of the chemist, psychologist and geologist

Use in each science some of the intellectual equipment of the other sciences

Be exceptional in breadth of appreciation

Be able in biological and medical science to suggest physical explanations or mathematical models for known or conjectured facts

Be familiar with forging and milling, the functions of a turret lathe, the kinds of heat treating used and their effects, what an industrial still looks like, and how it operates and with industrial processes generally

Deal enough with systems problems to know how to make parts into a balanced whole, whether this means weights that are balanced, or sizes or complexities of component pieces of mechanism, or expense or efforts or research time applied to different phases of the problem

Be experienced in design of experiments

Be well practised in judging, guessing, estimating and predicting

Be practised in data analysis and in mathematical methods and techniques

Be practised in the scientific methods of description and model construction as in many ways the most efficient techniques yet devised for covering a broad field quickly

Do not become baffled and uncomfortable – like so many specialists – when confronted with unfamiliar and ill-defined issues

Know how to isolate critical elements, establish the essentials of the logical framework, reduce the problem to a few critical issues

Know how to say what you mean, orally and in writing

Czech choose-as-you-go film and Bruno Ante's group: 'make decisions by interaction'

How is one to seek for the wider view in making the right decisions about the future? The future is out of reach. It is at the mercy of the unpredictable decisions of others. Yet the future, as Charles Kettering once put it, is 'where I expect to spend the rest of my life'. Where is tomorrow made if not by the decisions of many a today?

Of the world's 21 greatest needs as recently identified and studied by Battelle, one was singled out as 'of almost overriding importance: Improve the presently inadequate methods for decision-making in complex situations'.

The 20 other problems ranged from hunger to war, overpopulation to nationalism, and from energy to the malfunction of institutions. Every one of these difficulties 'would be far less pressing', the report went on, 'if proper decisions had been made before the problem reached crisis proportions'.

But how? How is one to scrutinise a future that is inscrutable? How is one to interact with a future that is out of reach? Is there any other solution except imaginatively to bring it within reach — and interact with it? In a world that is often lacking in imagination and foresight, that calls for magic. Perhaps then a few Czech film makers, or a few German Wirtschaftsprognostikers, might know the beginnings of a little magic.

Thirteen years ago, as we took our seats in a little theatre in Montreal, we congratulated ourselves that in spite of a long wait in line we had finally got into this Czechoslovak fantasy, one of the most popular of all the attractions at the 1967 International Exposition.[3] As the lights were going out we noticed the green button and the red button installed inside each seat arm for voting 'yes' or 'no'. The film began, unfolding a charming animation in the spirit of *Little Red Riding Hood.* The bad and the good began to reveal themselves, and also the character, apparently good but really bad. The drama rose, and with it came a revelation and a chase. The pursuer had almost caught the pursued when the film stopped, the lights went on, and the announcer stepped forward. 'What happens next is for you to decide', he explained. 'Vote yes if you want him to escape; otherwise, no. Each of you has one green bulb and one red bulb showing at the front of the theatre around the border of the proscenium. Push the button of your choice to make your vote light up'. The border did not take long to come alive with red and green lights. We could all see that the vote favoured escape. The lights went out and projection resumed. There was an exciting escape, and eventually another point of crisis and another vote.

When the film ended, we were offered the possibility to go back to the original point of choice and change our decision from 'escape' to 'capture'. We accepted. A revised programme began. It started with the capture. The *dramatis personae* were unchanged. Their character traits were unaltered. The course of the drama itself, however, had been transformed completely in clear consequence of the one decisive audience-voted change.

'See vividly, or let others see vividly, the future consequences of present decision'. Is any point more central to what decision-making ought to be and someday will be?

If 'imaginative interaction with alternative scenarios' is the key requirement, and has been explored in one way by the Czech creators of the choose-as-you-go film, it has been reconnoitred in another way through the Abteilung Wirtschaftsprognostik of Battelle-Institut e.V. of Frankfurt, by Bruno Ante and his colleagues.

They have helped a North German community to make up its mind whether and by what route it wanted its new rapid transit line to snake through. Two alternative but evolving scenarios for the route and for its economic and social consequences provided the backbone of evening study sessions. The drawings and prices together with the demographic studies and traffic estimates associated with each alternative led to questions, objections and proposals, further projections, and further proposals. One of the townspeople suddenly conceived a new route that combined most of the best features of the other two. It eventually won approval, and is now going ahead.

Part of this projection of alternative futures is familiar to every architect on a major project. The new feature is the early involvement of those affected. To guide this large-scale interactive development of scenarios, special skills were essential:

- practice in guiding meetings,
- impartiality,
- prevention of confrontations,
- eliciting the best thinking of those present; and (between conferences) digging out facts and figures quickly, as well as getting others to do the same,
- testing in advance that information is bias-free and battle-proof, and
- imparting maximum impact to the two alternative scenarios for each new meeting.

Such a jump into the future requires vivid and truthful scenarios, ones that will prod the imagination and guide action. Today's audiovisual technology promises great prospects for assembling vivid and accurate thinking on whatever topic. Its use is inevitable; what other way is there for a community or a nation to cope with crisis?

Different aptitudes surely characterise the one who finds, or helps others to find, the larger view of the future; the science-technology generalist; the one who provides a wider view by building a model; the user of intuition; the finder of economic feasibility; the creator of an engineering system; and the discoverer of new unity in science.

More interesting for us here than these differences, however, is the faith that drives all these seekers: the faith that the larger view exists. In brief, each believes in 'harmony'. He may not know the word, or how Einstein and Spinoza used it; but he lays his course with the conviction that the world is understandable.

How did Einstein, or how does anyone, acquire a faith in this larger view so powerful as to take control of his life?

The traditions of the family and the community are important, education counts, but is there anything more central than a role-model? Do not Thomas Mann and Erik Erikson and other analysts of achievement tell us that each one of us models his or her life consciously or unconsciously on someone who has gone before? If they are right, then surely the role-creator for Einstein was Spinoza.

The young Einstein had a few close student colleagues, and those still closer colleagues he met in books, from Leibniz and Newton to Maxwell and Boltzmann; but closest of all was Spinoza. No one did Einstein admire more; and no one expressed more strongly a belief in the harmony, the beauty and — most of all — the comprehensibility of nature. In a letter to his close friend, Maurice Solovine, Einstein wrote, 'I can understand your aversion to the use of the term "religion" to describe an emotional and psychological attitude which shows itself most clearly in Spinoza. (But) I have not found a better expression than "religious" for the trust in the rational nature of reality that is, at least to a certain extent, accessible to human reason'. Where else better than from a great man animated by a great faith can one acquire a great vision?

What more than anything else do I want to say about the life and work of the 'seekers of the wider view', including Einstein? He had and they have a *happy,* and useful, outlook because they feel that the world, or the part of it that they have to deal with, is in some way *beautiful and understandable.*

Notes

1. Hendrik Bode, Frederick Mosteller, John Tukey, and Charles Winsor, 'The education of a scientific generalist', *Science*, 1949, *109*, pp. 553–558.
2. Adapted from Bode *et al*., op. cit.
3. *Time*, 5 May 1967, pp. 48–9.

Name Index

Subject Index